# ANOTHER LAND, ANOTHER SEA

ANOTHER LAND, ANOTHER SEA

Walking round Lake Rudolph

by

STEPHEN PERN

*With a Foreword by
John Hillaby*

LONDON
VICTOR GOLLANCZ LTD
1979

© Stephen Pern 1979
Foreword © John Hillaby 1979

ISBN 0 575 02676 6

The quotation opposite is taken from "The City" in *Collected Poems of Cavafy* translated by Rae Dalvern and reprinted by permission of the publishers, The Hogarth Press.

PRINTED IN GREAT BRITAIN
BY EBENEZER BAYLIS AND SON LTD
THE TRINITY PRESS, WORCESTER, AND LONDON

"... I will go to another land, I will go to another sea..."
"The City" Constantine Cavafy

For Gregory and Laroi

THANKS

I HOPE THIS book will express the debt I owe to Gregory and Laroi and to Esenyon, Erdund, Elizabeth, Helen and others who helped and taught me on the journey. To my mother I owe the necessary support and encouragement firstly to have attempted the journey and then to have written about it.

Many people gave me advice and help before I began and in particular I would like to thank Mrs Pat Lane who taught me Swahili, Henry Lawrence whose brave attempt to teach me fishing deserves more than the poor results I achieved, Lau and Sue Larsen who put me up in Nairobi, and Mr and Mrs Richard Muir who saw me off so splendidly.

John Hillaby who has kindly offered to write a foreword was instrumental in my attempting to write the book and very generous with advice and help. My brother and sister-in-law read the first and indigestible draft and lived to smile me on, and suggestions from Henry Cass, Anne and Margaret Moss and others have been most helpful. I would also like to thank the staff of the Royal Botanic Gardens, Kew, in particular Dr G. Wickens, and the librarians at the Royal Geographical Society and the School of Oriental and African Studies, for their help; and Mrs R. M. Harris and Jane Adams for their endurance and intelligent work in typing an at times indecipherable manuscript.

The final appearance of this book owes more to the faith of the publisher and editor than to the efforts of the author. I am more than grateful to Peter Day for the tactful surgery he performed on the "spaghetti" of a manuscript that I dished up, and for the patience of Livia Gollancz in her dealings with a raw and rather ignorant young bushman.

S.P.

NOTE

LAKE TURKANA

Named after the Archduke Rudolf in the days when Kenya was British East Africa, the Lake has been spelled variously Rudolf and Rudolph by different authorities. Since the founding of the State of Kenya, it has been renamed Lake Turkana. The British author of this book has chosen to refer to it as Lake Rudolph.

LIST OF ILLUSTRATIONS

Following page 64

Laroi
Day 1. Loading up
"The Luos had long since dragged the lagoon . . ."
Esenyon plodding towards Ileret in his hat
Orip stirring blood
The women in Loolim's Manyatta
Goodbyes in Ileret
Natiant—the Moran with TB
A good day's catch, two snout fish carried off the Omo river bank by a Shangalla youth
Shangalla herdboy and his charges
A dugout on the Omo below Geleb
Dandel, one of the police guards at Geleb
An old Shangalla walking through Geleb Post

Following page 160

Yergulem
Walkari
Greg and Edekoi—our kitchen at Geleb
The great escape
Kaset fires an arrow into the cow's neck
Atol hangs on while blood pours into a bowl
Atol, Kaset and their father ferrying Komote and Lobrolei
Atol getting Komote out of the mud
Christmas dinner, Lowarangak
Esenyon's cousin, Nakutha
Karim, our guide in the Loriu
Laroi crossing the Kerio river
A typical Turkana with blanket and stool in the Lapurr Hills
"A hundred silent camels"
Me and the donkeys skirting the lava fields

All photographs by the author

A section of maps follows this page.
A glossary will be found at the back of the book.

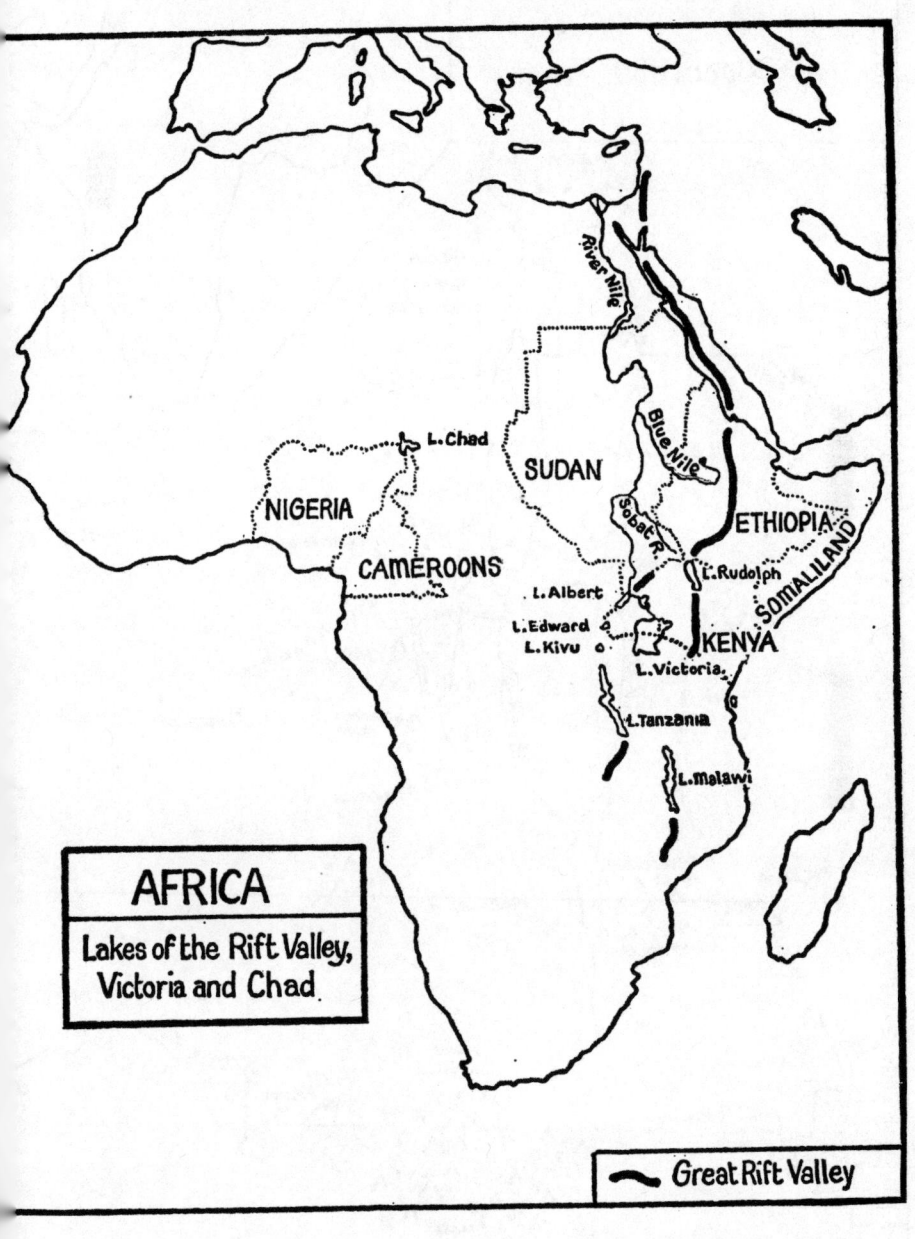

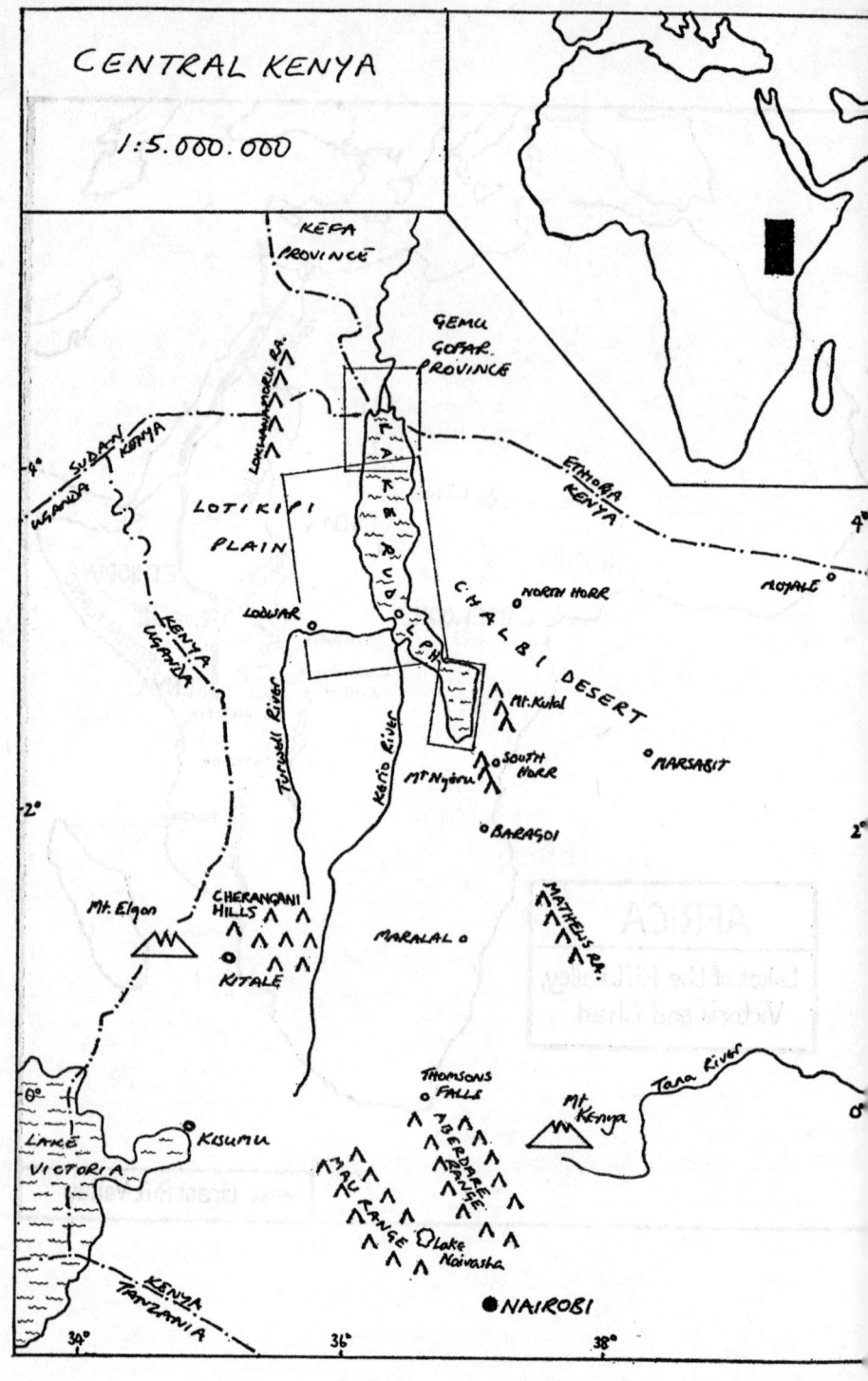

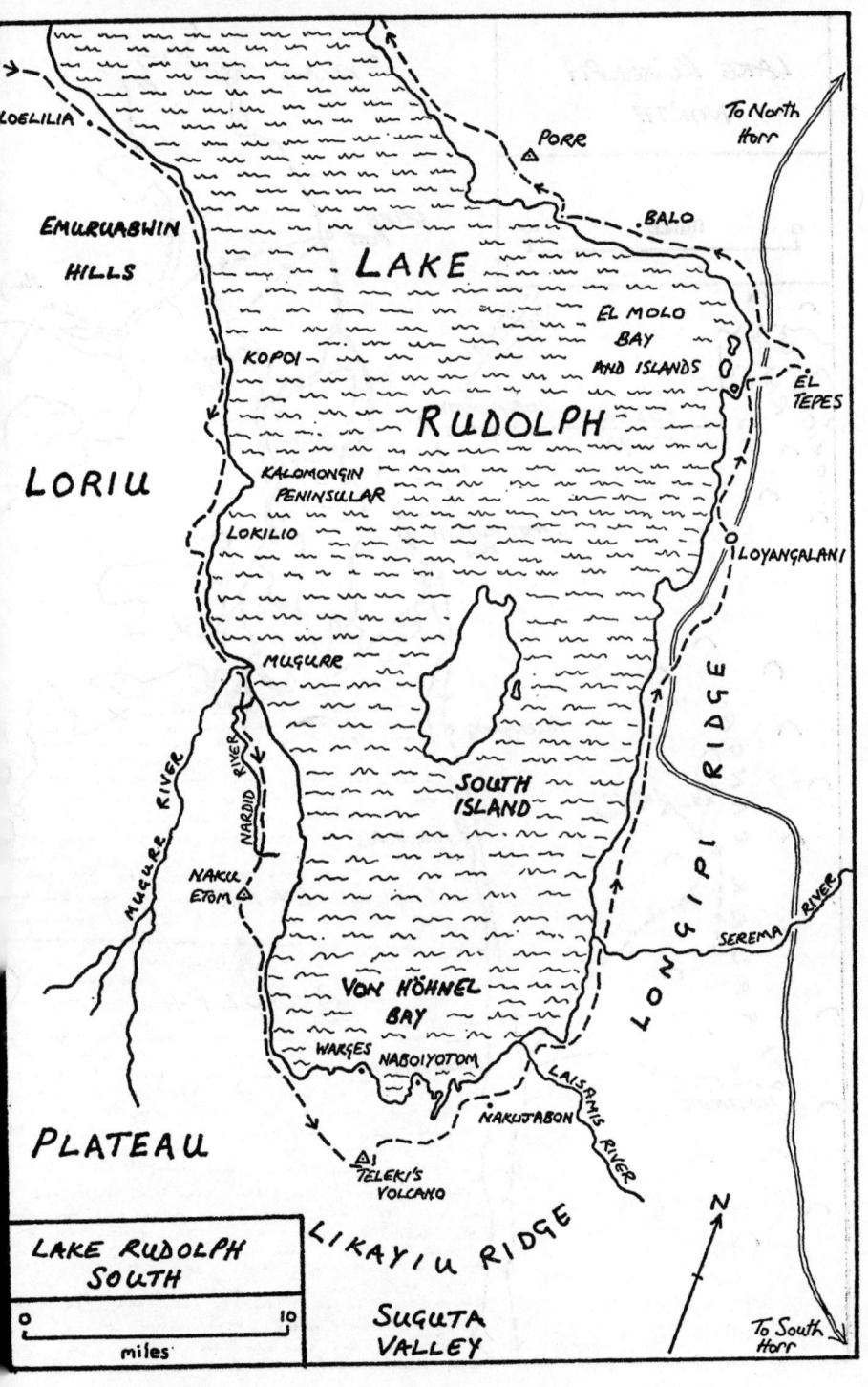

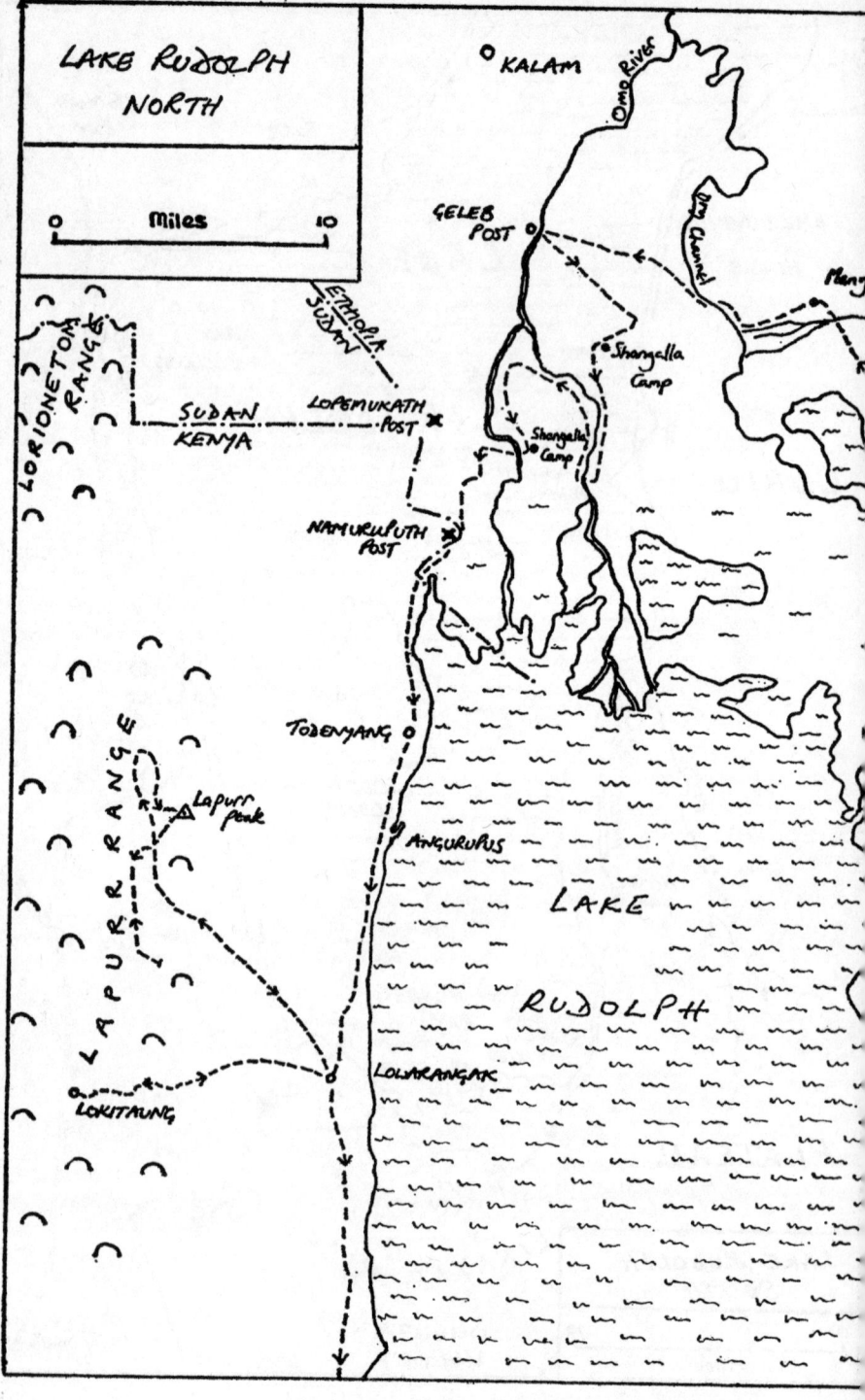

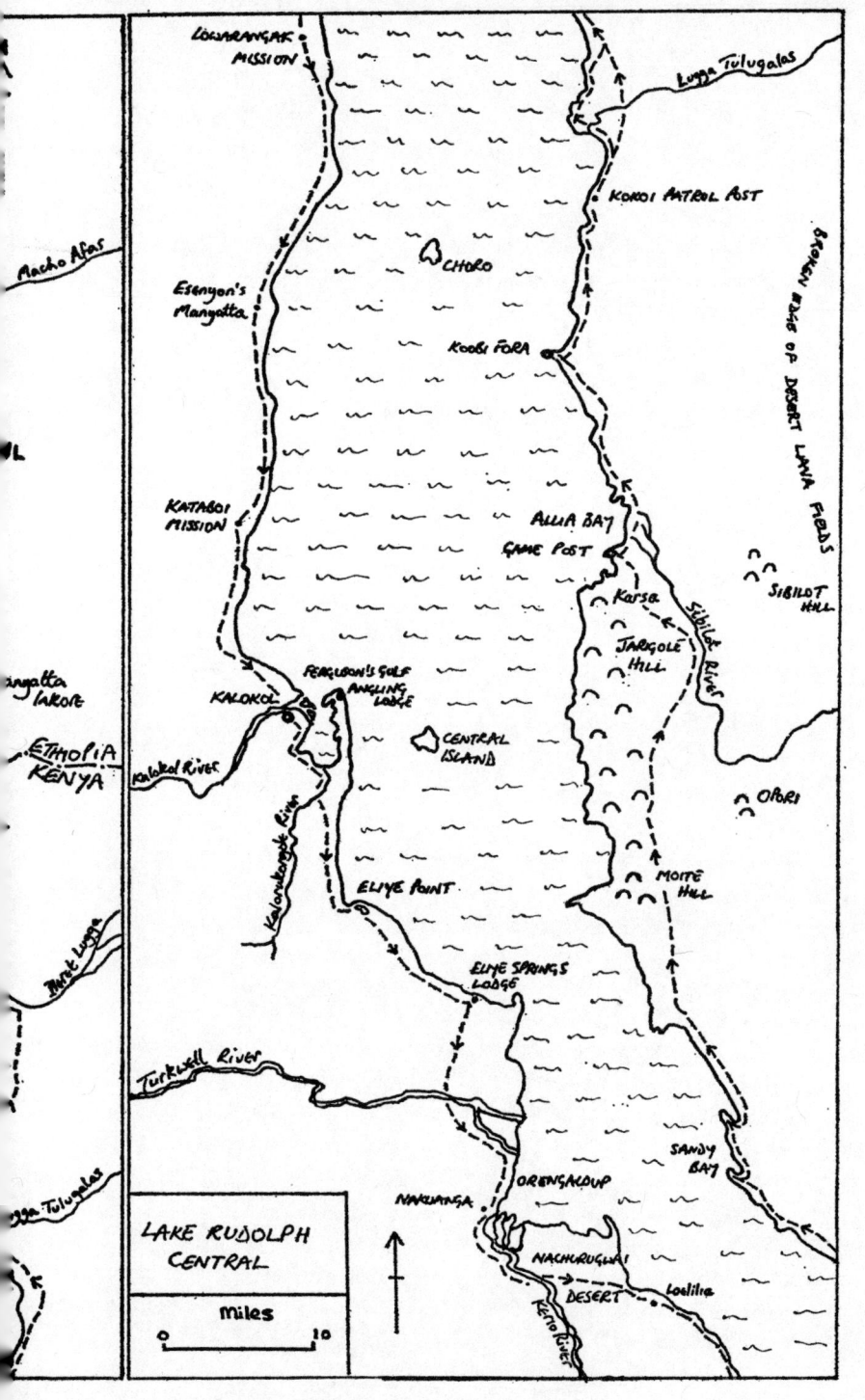

FOREWORD
by John Hillaby

LIFE MUST BE lived forwards but understood backwards. It follows, therefore, that memories of accomplishment are a source of much solace. When the barbarians were at her gates, thoughtful men began to leave the political ruins of Rome. They were the *fratres peregrinos*, those monks who scourged their flesh in the deserts of Egypt and North Africa. With their intelligence vastly quickened, they returned, many of them, to teach, to pray and to comfort down-at-soul fellows. In a more secular setting, there is a parallel in this for those of us who feel that cities take a man out of the truth of himself. I know for sure that often in my imagination I travel back to one of the most remarkable lakes in Africa, that wind-thrashed waterway which, in a matter of minutes, might change from an enormous sun-flashing sapphire to an opaque piece of jade. The volcanic rocks around that crack in a continent are apocalyptic in appearance: coal-black, pumice-grey or of the colour of dried blood. They put you in mind of the Inferno. The land around Lake Rudolf in North-west Kenya is one of the driest and one of the hottest places in the world. Stephen Pern walked around that lake with two good companions and three donkeys.

He is a man of considerable resolution. Had he heeded my advice and not made the journey, he would have missed something which, I'm pretty sure, has changed his attitude towards life, and you and I could not have shared his experience from the comfort of an armchair. I have no diffidence about saying I don't know how he did it because, although I was once fortunate enough to spend three months alongside that lake, by comparison with the author's modest *entourage*, I travelled like a prince, that is, with scouts, an armed guard and a string of fifteen camels. He did it with far less trappings and went all the way around which, as far as I know, has never been done before.

When I heard that he had arrived back safely I wondered, first, what he had got out of the trip and, second, how he would handle his account of it which, he will be the first to admit, is as difficult as the physical exertion. What stands out like the isolated mountains of the Northern Frontier District is his honesty. He presents travelling on foot under extremely difficult conditions for what it is, not making the bad worse for effect or the good better for romance. There is none of the bogus expertise, or the suggestion of more than ordinary courage or skill or resourcefulness that one so often gets in tales of adventure. He is much the same with his presentation of himself and those around him. With the exception of that man who, like myself, was not encouraging at the start, he speaks highly of the old administration. Those good people, the up-country Africans trusted and respected the British and the pity is that more people do not know how we handled our responsibilities there. For a variety of reasons I warmly commend this work.

J.H.

INTRODUCTION

Tarzan and the greasy Limpopo notwithstanding, Africa is a dry continent. A country like Kenya with its extensive uplands where wheat and barley grow is atypical, but even Kenya, away from the teeming game parks high on the plateau, is half a desert. The dry half is called the Northern Frontier District and in general the further inland you go the drier it becomes. Beyond Marsabit, which is about 350 miles from the Indian Ocean, lies the Chalbi desert and on the horizon, far across the barren lava, a mountain wobbles in the haze. The mountain is called Kulal and it forces the last of the moisture-bearing winds from the sea up over its 7,000-foot spine until they condense and rain on to the backs of the elephants which live on the jungle-clad slopes below. If one evening you were to climb the green mountain, its surprising abundance, at odds with the surrounding desert, might leave you unprepared for the spectacular oddity hidden beyond the summit. Lying beneath you in the darkening wastes would be a shimmering finger of gold crooked west then beckoning north for as far as you could see. You would be looking at Lake Rudolph, the last of the great lakes of East Africa to be discovered.

Arab slave traders from the coast had long known of other lakes lying in the southern reaches of the rift valley, but hostile Masai and scorching bush made trading expeditions so unprofitable and hazardous that the discovery of the lake in the desert was left to two Austrians who first set eyes on it on 6 March 1888. The account of their trip, kept with Germanic efficiency ("We were off at six minutes past four") by Lt Ludwig von Höhnel, begins with their reasons for going.

> Imbued with a passion for research, Count Samuel Teleki von Szek, a nobleman with an estate in Transylvania, undertook to lead [an] expedition into the interior of Africa. With ample means of his own and inured to hardship in many a sporting trip, Count Teleki was admirably fitted to carry out

to a successful issue an undertaking of this kind; and early in 1886 when he was beginning his preparations he received an invitation to Lacroma from Crown Prince Archduke Rudolph, who took the greatest interest in the proposed expedition.

Teleki and von Höhnel were away exploring in Africa for two years, during which time the Crown Prince had shot his mistress and committed suicide. Transylvanian noblemen and deranged princes are wholly in keeping with the harsh and enigmatic nature of this brackish sea which, like the Caspian, has no outlet. Nine-tenths of the lake water comes from one river, the Omo, whose headwaters drain the mountains of Abyssinia in the far north. For the rest, short-lived streams rush down in flood after the rains and two larger rivers flow erratically from the hills of upland Kenya. However, the inflow does not keep pace with evaporation and the lake is very slowly drying up.

I had my first experience of Africa after leaving university, when I spent nearly two years in northern Nigeria as a game-preservation officer. Most of the work required common sense rather than a detailed knowledge of the bush, which I did not have. I enjoyed the time there and when people asked me if I liked Africa I answered Yes; but it was difficult to define what exactly it was I liked about it. Partly it was the freedom bestowed by unlimited sunshine, especially when combined with unlimited time and space. Africa is boundless, I say, in comparison with Europe. But many expatriate Europeans have told me of the claustrophobia and loneliness they experience in their quarters of Nairobi or Lagos or Calabar. Africa is boundless, but the freedom of the sun and the bush will not penetrate a car windscreen nor a mosquito-proof bungalow. That freedom cannot be tasted on forks of tinned vegetables nor in the boiled water and bottled beer so dear to the tropical hygienist. It comes like stone and thorn through the soles of bare feet on the earth, and slowly pervades a body in the sun, the smoke of fires and the starlight. I like being in the bush, close to nature one might say, where normal conditions of domesticity do not apply. The distance between people of different cultures tends to diminish when they eat from a common pot, or lie under the same leaking mosquito net, and, for myself, part of the pleasure of being in the bush is that "apartness" almost disappears. Language always remains a barrier, but even that wall gently cracks in the days of shared experience.

I spent almost a year in South America and three back in Europe before I returned to Africa. One April day in the army, with the daffodils up to their necks in snow, I read John Hillaby's book, *Journey to the Jade Sea*, and from then on I ceased to worry about my future, although I often doubted my wisdom. Hillaby's long journey took him through the mountains and deserts of the Northern Frontier District to the eastern shore of the lake, which he followed until he was turned back by the administration. The problem of knowing what to do after the army had stopped worrying me thanks to Hillaby—I was going to Lake Rudolph. Two years later I was free and I had the money. I had learned a little Swahili and made a desultory stab at reading up the available literature, especially the accounts by early explorers, to which I will refer.

They were a mixed bunch—soldiers like Austin and Bright of the Royal Engineers, the indefatigable elephant hunter Arthur Neumann, and independently wealthy men like Teleki and the American Dr Donaldson Smith. Von Höhnel's diaries elicit easy laughter and even incredulity, especially the section on the complex logistics of nineteenth-century expeditions, as Count Teleki and his lieutenant struggle with their red-felt spine pads and double-barrelled elephant guns to recruit the hundreds of porters they need to carry their tons of beads and cloth and copper wire, their scientific instruments and folding boats, and their boxes of ammunition and pre-packed rations, all in the heat and chaos of old Zanzibar; but they were courageous, enduring men and for the most part honourable. Common to all their journeys was a challenging omission—none of them had, nor, as far as I have been able to ascertain, has anyone else, ever actually walked right round Lake Rudolph. To do that became the object of my journey.

Preparation in England was minimal. I decided not to take guns as they are an encumbrance and trying to obtain a licence is laborious and brings one to the attention of the authorities. Guns are also attractive to thieves and often stimulate the violence they are intended to prevent. I had read that the lake was teeming with fish and so I went to see my uncle who is a keen angler and lives in Torquay. He gave me a lesson one November night in a howling gale on the pavement of Livermead Road. He was showing me how to cast a spinner.

"The main thing," he said, casually arching the line up the road, "is to get a good, fluent flick to the rod, then reel in slowly." The spinner came jumping back along the gutter, glistening in the streaming rain. "Here," said Henry, handing me the rod, "have a go." I gingerly cast out over the road and the hook vanished into the gloom of the opposite garden. We retrieved it before any poor motor cyclist lost his head. I tried again but nothing happened. Henry is much taller than I and so he unhooked the line from the bush where it had snagged behind me. "Yes," he said patiently, "always check behind you and give a good confident heave." He demonstrated the heave a few times more, oblivious in his duffle coat as a lighthouse keeper in the gale. I felt wet and cold, but Henry had gone beyond simple casting and was doing clever things with his wrists and the spinner was flying all over the place. I was about to suggest that we call it a night when an especially vigorous flick sent the spinner looping high into the darkness and over the neighbour's telephone lines. It took half an hour's cursing to get it back. We went home for a tutorial over a bottle of good Scotch, and Henry read bits from the *Compleat Angler*. The following day we went down to Woolworths and bought some basic equipment which served me well throughout the trip.

Fitness was no problem. I like running, and walking too, although I draw the line at carrying stuff around in rucksacks. I solved that problem later with pack animals. I put together a simple first-aid kit: blue Aspirins for colds, red ones for fevers, a snake-bite kit for dramas, and other potions for stomach, bowels and head. A morning on the telephone got me a cheap ticket to Nairobi via Moscow. What I really lacked was first-hand advice. John Hillaby had written a very full but uncouraging letter two years before and most other people had been doubtful of my chances. But warnings to the foolhardy are usually useless and I saw the trip as a challenge, especially with letters like the one below to spur me on. The writer has got the Sudanese border wrong but it sounds thrilling stuff.

British High Commission
Nairobi

498951 Lt S. A. N. Pern
A Coy 2 Para
BFPO 801

14 Feb 1977

Dear Lt Pern,

PROPOSED WALK ROUND LAKE RUDOLF

Thank you for your letter of 7 February to the High Commissioner about your proposed walk round Lake Rudolf later this year.

I should perhaps say at the outset that I would be inclined to discourage such an enterprise: there are numerous reasons why such an expedition would present both administrative and practical difficulties which, when I have explained them to you, may cause you to reconsider.

(a) As you will see from a map, the shores of Lake Rudolf run through three different countries, that is to say Kenya, the Sudan and Ethiopia. It would be impossible to make a circumnavigation [sic] of the lake without crossing into all three of these countries.

(b) The security situation for a lone walker is likely to be hazardous: although the Kenyans and the Ethiopians do what they can to mount a police presence in the area, it is by its nature a wild and remote place in which it is difficult to maintain a tight control of the various tribes. There has for many years been extensive cattle raiding across the various borders and it would not be unlikely that you would encounter tribesmen whose attitude towards a lone traveller could not be guaranteed to be friendly.

(c) The security situation in Ethiopia continues to be somewhat uncertain, and even if you obtained permission from the Ethiopians to wander in the area, which in any case I believe might be difficult, your personal safety would be in question.

(d) We have recently noticed an increase in the amount of poaching by Somali "shiftas" in the area to the east of Lake Rudolf: these poachers are organized in quite large bands and they sometimes carry heavy and sophisticated weaponry. Last year a French tourist was killed by such raiders some way to the east of Lake Rudolf, while there are several reports of travellers in the area encountering the "shifta".

As you will doubtless know the shores of Lake Rudolf are arid and extremely hot, and a circumnavigation [*sic*] would, to say the least, be an arduous endeavour. You mention that your friends might teach you some Swahili to enable you to communicate with the tribesmen—it is worth noting that it is most unlikely that any of the tribesmen whom you might encounter would be able to speak Swahili, since they have little or no contact with the officials who use the language more frequently.

I am afraid that all this sounds rather discouraging, but in the present circumstances I would advise strongly against making such an expedition, no matter how experienced you are in the ways of Africa. I do not for a moment doubt your ability to undertake such an expedition but there are serious doubts about your being able to complete it without putting yourself at considerable personal risk.

If, in spite of this letter, you remain determined to make the journey, I should be grateful if you could let me know in due course.

Yours sincerely,
[The letter is signed]

ANOTHER LAND, ANOTHER SEA

PRELUDE

"Forget it, boy," said the voice on the telephone. The South African accent was assured. "East Rudolph is swarming with Somalis, you'll never get through. There're a lot of nice parks round Nairobi, you could visit them instead." A few days before I was due to leave England a full-scale war had broken out between Ethiopia and Somalia, and the Somalis were on the offensive. The man on the phone was an adviser to the Kenyan Wildlife Department, home on leave. At last I had some first-hand advice and it hit me right in the guts. "Well, thanks very much anyway," I said lamely, "have a good leave. Goodbye."

I felt completely wrung out as I went upstairs to finish my packing. I was still going but decided to throw in some climbing gear: I could always do Mount Kenya as a consolation prize. The last two days were full of "hard lucks" and "never minds" and "it's a lovely country anyway". My family was silent. I had embarked on lost causes before but this one might be expensive.

My woolly vests and climbing socks were useful during the flight to Nairobi as there was a three-day stopover in Moscow; but eventually, as things turned out, I did not need to go climbing at all. In fact at the end, when I had become very tired, I went down to the coast instead.

"Forget it, boy." Forget it? Well, I don't think I ever will.

I

"Tea or coffee?" An Aeroflot lovely, bursting from her autumn blue flannel and boots, looked down at me balefully. "Tea, please," I said. Her eyes were the colour of old ice and it was only November. We were five passengers in the sky, halfway between Khartoum and Entebbe, with the Nile below and empty seats all around. You could have all the tea you could drink. We landed at Entebbe and in the new air terminal I saw a group of thin and faded mammals waiting, unnaturally juxtaposed. There was a leopard and a klipspringer, several kinds of antelope and an overstuffed hippo with a wide pink yawn, like a bewhiskered pudding. Some of the animals stared with dusty eyes at the whisky and the cameras in the duty-free shop. The rest gazed apathetically through the picture windows overlooking Lake Victoria, watching the Mig 21s whizzing up and down the runway.

Delegates from a conference of African ministers in Kampala filled the plane and with them a sprinkling of white reporters. They fastened their seat belts. The humid air condensed as it was sucked into the cabin's cooling system—it looked like smoke and the ministers were alarmed. Some of them removed their sunglasses and one shouted, "Stan' by me!" His friend's face appeared over an armful of goodies. "De fire brigade out?" it enquired. We flew on over the high plains to Kenya.

It was evening when I caught the bus from the airport down to Nairobi town, and dark when I arrived. I felt rather alone, as one does in a strange town, and the people I was to stay with were out. I went to the YMCA for the first night but I found my friends the following day and having secured a base I set out my plan of action. I solicited advice from all and sundry, moving from one contact to another and another, a travelling salesman in reverse. I went to the museum and the university, spoke to ex-white hunters and safari people and to missionaries and officials from the game department, but I soon concluded that hanging around Nairobi was useless and decided to go up to the lake on a reconnaissance. I reckoned that two-to-three weeks would be enough time to visit a few stations on the lake and to decide from where to start and in which direction to go. I would then return to Nairobi with first-hand knowledge and plan accordingly.

During those first four days in Nairobi I bought a few necessaries, mostly in the market areas beyond the tall city blocks of the centre. The town is just small enough to walk round, with a pleasantly warm climate and plenty of cool bars. The old frontier image is gone, but the safari industry flourishes. Camera shops and travel agencies have replaced the gunsmiths and taxidermists, and now even the knick-knack shops are closing because of the strict laws prohibiting the sale of animal products like skins, ivory and horns. My friends drove me out to the Ngong Hills one evening to see the moon-blue jacaranda blossom, a mist of violet cones on leafless trees. The dull sound of wooden cow bells clonked up from a manyatta in the valley below, where gazelle and zebra were grazing alongside the cattle. A boy and his goats appeared over the wind-swept crest where we sat, he following the animals as they nibbled their way between the legs of the radio mast on the hilltop and down to the drifting woodsmoke below. That morning I had seen a poem about the jacaranda in the window of a shop, quite close to the Nairobi Hilton. It began with disarming simplicity:

> It has transformed itself
> Into the sky
> Bringing the colour of heaven
> Down to earth.

In the next shop, a chemist's, was another poem written in blunt crayon. It was called "Cosmetic Shop", and should be read with a strong Kenyan accent to get the full flavour:

> We can really
> Make you look chic
> With our wide selection
> Of lipstick

And you can
Safely assume
That we have
Your choice of perfume

And if you want
Your face to beam
And your skin to
Shine and gleam
Then you must try
Some beauty cream

We'll make it a pleasure
For you to sit
Before a mirror with
Your make-up kit
Fixing yourself up
To look trim and fit

And of yourself you'll
Feel even prouder
After trying some
Of our facial powder

For we know a woman
Can only feel aloft
When her face skin and hands
Are smooth and soft

The wet season was prolonged and heavy that year and although I knew that the Northern Frontier District was pretty dry I bought a six-foot square of tarpaulin as a makeshift tent. I eventually used it as a groundsheet and saddle blanket, and it is one of the few souvenirs that I kept and brought back to England, bloodstained, faded and torn. There were rumours that the lake was twice its normal size, vast areas were said to be flooded, but there was little talk of renegade Somalis.

My preparations continued. Against the sun I had a sheet, with a hole for my head which was to be wrapped in the four yards of cheesecloth I had bought to make a turban. I had some canvas food bags made up and bought a kilo or two of dates, sugar, rice and tea, dried milk, salt and porridge and a bag of boiled sweets. To find out where I was going I went to the Public Map Office for an improvement on my historically informative but undetailed sheet which covered the Indian Ocean out to the hundred-fathom mark and a good part of the eastern Sahara as well. The largest scale available was 1:250,000 and to cover the whole lake I needed five sheets.

A licence to fish in Lake Rudolph costs 150/- Kenyan which struck me as rather a lot and so I bought one for Lake Naivasha instead. It cost 40/- and I hoped that it looked similar to the more expensive one. I added what I thought was a rather professional touch to my gear in the form of a special little fish-hook sharpener, a useless piece of kit in retrospect for in the following two months I lost most of my hooks, landed only two fish and tripped over natural grinding stones daily.

Thus equipped I set off on my three-week recce. I missed the bus to Naivasha, but my host's company driver gave spirited chase and we caught it with much blaring of horns in the western suburbs of Nairobi. The bus was very crowded.

"Dis compresshun too bad, man," the conductor gasped, "bad for womens. De bus here for gents only." We dropped 2,000 feet to the bottom of the great rift valley in which Naivasha lies. The gents' bus put me down on the yellow plain and sped off ignored by the giraffe browsing nearby. Those giraffe, nibbling away like rabbits in a hedge, nudged me from my European consciousness and began the sudden adjustment to another lifestyle. The exhaust fumes soon dispersed and I was free. It was a strange feeling. The bustle of preparation was over and I was suddenly by myself without the usual barrage of stimuli to my brain. I was at something of a loss and slightly scared. I could see the Mau escarpment far over on the valley side with rain coming towards me in swooping columns like squalls on a dark-grey sea and I tucked myself in under a thorn tree to sit it out. The feeling of being a city boy on a farm passed with the rain.

Right, I thought. Get started. Considerable self-doubt. What the hell do I do? Just pick up your loads and walk, I told myself. It was only five miles down the sideroad to the YMCA campsite at Lake Naivasha which I had seen advertised on my first night. I was breaking myself in. I wanted to try out my fishing gear and blacken the new pots. In West Africa everyone uses cheap, brightly coloured enamel ware but I had looked in vain for it in Nairobi. Everything was too sophisticated and non-stick and I eventually asked a shop assistant what his mother used.

"Oh, you need this localpots," he informed me. He tore off the brown paper wrapping on a stack of simple aluminium pots with flat rims and no handles and I bought two. Knowing about the pots made me feel a bit more at home.

The warden of the campsite was called Mike. He had been there eight years which rather depressed him. I hope the fact that I left my prize stainless-steel mirror hanging in the ablution shed cheered him up. I set up the rod and tied on a spinner and walked half a mile to the edge of the lake which was overgrown with weeds and grass. This was my first physical contact with Kenya. Two children watched me from a marshy rice garden, urging me into the water with encouraging smiles and waves. The undergrowth thinned out slowly and I had no choice but to start casting when the water reached my chest although the hook became continually entangled on submerged plants. My tiptoeing foot sank into the mud but the tepid water remained clear. I suddenly remembered about crocodiles and twirled rapidly to face the children.

"Mambas?" I yelled, remembering that much Swahili. "Are there any mambas around here?" They assured me that the whole place was mamba free and I cast on. Two cool-looking Americans sputtered up in a boat. They both caught a fish on their first throw and I felt insanely jealous. My struggle with the aquatic growth continued, and eventually I hauled in a fair-sized lump of weed. A silver tilapia hung in the dripping garland. My excitement was great and praising the name of the Lord I unhooked it carefully. It weighed about a pound and a half and made quite a decent plop as it slipped from my fervent grasp. I made a mental note to equip myself with a large blunt instrument forthwith and the Americans advised me to get a "stringer". This is something that people like Huckleberry Finn use to hang their catfish on. The Americans' success was boring. Their keep nets were full but they refused to sell me any fish, and so I waded back to camp.

On the way I passed the largest carnation farm in the world. It was early evening and many of the 4,000 employees were leaving. They were nearly all carrying fish.

From Naivasha I hitched up to Thomson's Falls on the equator. It was raining and quite chilly, as the town lies high up on the Laikipi Plateau at an altitude of nearly 8,000 feet. Early-morning hoar frost is common on the plateau and must have been a pleasant surprise for the mercurial explorer Joseph Thomson who arrived there in October 1883. He and his second-in-command, James Martin, were the first whites to penetrate the interior and it says much for Thomson's tact and ingenuity that, despite sore trials, he did not once fire a shot in anger. He fooled the hostile Masai into thinking that he was a great laibon or medicine man by removing his false teeth, and persuaded them that he could do the same with noses and eyes. The potion he prepared from Eno's fizzy liver salts and attendant mumbo-jumbo "caused the natives to shrink with intense dismay". His medicine was held to be an infallible cure for the rinderpest which was decimating the Masai herds.

Thomson had been hunting in the area and, startled by a leopard, he had been unable to shoot it before it bounded away. Rushing to the top of a ridge to sight it again he "was suddenly arrested by an object which fairly took my breath away". He could see the black Aberdare Mountains which he had named after the President of the Royal Geographical Society.

> These features, however, were not what fascinated me. It was something more distant. Through a rugged and picturesque depression in the range rose a gleaming snow-white peak with sparkling facets which scintillated with the superb beauty of a colossal diamond. From the base of this beautiful peak at a very slight angle shaded away a long glittering white line, seen above the dark mass of the Aberdare range like the silver lining of a dark storm cloud. This peak and the silvery line formed the central culminating point of Mount Kenia. As I stood entranced at this fulfilment of my dearest hopes I drew a great sigh of satisfaction . . . I am not very sure but there was something like a tear in my eye.

Ninety-four years and one month later I sat under a eucalyptus tree within a few miles of Thomson's vantage point, waiting for the afternoon bus to Maralal. Zebra-striped tourist cars drove past in the light rain down to the Falls Hotel. How utterly appropriate it was that someone of Thomson's appreciative nature had been the first to see that diamond now hidden by the clouds. Exactly four years after him the Austrians crossed the Aberdares on their way to climb Mount Kenya. They were in Kikuyu country and their experience was rather less conducive of compromise than was Thomson's with the Masai. One of their men had fallen behind and as they were hunting for him they saw a number of warriors gathered together about 400 paces off, one of whom was mockingly holding up a blood-stained shirt. No false teeth or fizzing magic for them, but a fairly positive response. "A shot from us avenged his death," wrote von Höhnel, tersely.

Pulling my rucksack in under the tree I fell into conversation with a chap who worked as a barman at Treetops, the famous game-viewing hotel. He gave an interesting account of the Queen's visit there as princess in 1952.

"Yes," he said in happy recollection, "when she come to Kenya she just little toto playing with new husband, but when she leave her father die and she Mzee. Then you have the war and she tell other Wazungus to come to Kenya. That why all German and French and Italian mans doing tourist in Kenya at this time." The barman had studied neither history nor economics and as it turned out had been born in 1953.

Things change between Thomson's Falls and Maralal. The bush remains more or less dense but open cultivations become rarer as farming land gives way to unhindered cattle ranges and tribal grazing areas. There are no hard-surfaced roads beyond the Falls, no spivs in sunglasses nor power lines along the way. Tall thin men stand motionless by the roadside as the bus slithers past in the rain. They are Samburu, ochre-smeared pastoralists, God's own children with razor-sharp spears to prove it. The Samburu and the Masai are famous for their aristocratic independence of Western ways, and for their haughty carriage, toughness and bravery epitomised in the hunting of lion with shield and spear. Less well known are the tribesmen of the far north and paramount among them are the Turkana. Turkana are fairly basic folk and do not strike

elegant poses nor spend hours each day on their appearance
like their cousins to the south, but for straightforward savagery
the Turks are hard to beat. They are, or were, to Kenya what
the Mongols were to Europe. The Northern Frontier District is
quieter now and full-scale clashes are rare but the Turkana are
still spreading south, gradually encroaching on territory of
their neighbours, the Samburu and the Pokot.

There were eight Turkanas occupying the rear section of the
bus. The one next to me was a wrinkled old crone of at least
279. She wore a leather goat skin round her waist and had a
threadbare blanket tied across her shoulders. Her head was
shaved but for a narrow crest running from front to rear. The
hair was long and plaited and dangled down like a horrible wig,
complementing her grossly extended ear lobes from which five
or six brass earrings hung one above the other climbing the
outer rim of each ear. Her lower lip protruded slightly and from
it hung a brass lip plug about two inches long. Every few
moments she wiped the spittle leaking on to her chin, leant over
me and squirted a long stream of tobacco juice on to the floor.
Everything about her was floppy and wrinkled and loose except
for her fearsome scowl. Like the other two women in the party
she had a long-stemmed pear-shaped gourd on her lap. We
communicated in an elementary way and I asked her what was
inside it. She took off the cap and pulled out a selection of rags
containing beads, tobacco, flour, some snuff and a few safety
pins. Usually her handbag held milk.

Behind us were two young men in sandals of cowhide and
blankets. They were tall and skinny and annoyed people by
insisting on holding their sticks and spears across their laps.
One of them was further armed with a wrist knife: a plate of
iron with a sharp rim and a hole for one's hand, a nifty weapon
for slashing backs in close-quarter fighting. They both had
ivory lip plugs and heavy silver earrings with balls of half-
chewed tobacco stored behind their ears. Their hair was drawn
up in a mud-caked bun at the rear from which hung little
ornaments—small chains, pegs of wood and ostrich feathers.

I was fascinated by these creatures who smelt of milk and
leather and gabbled ceaselessly between powerful emissions of
saliva. They stood out from the other passengers (all warmly
dressed at a mile and a half above sea level in the usual

European-style clothes) like ethnographic exhibits in a museum of modern art. The bus took quite a beating through the mud and slush and eventually a spring broke. While the crew replaced it the Turks and I exchanged pleasantries in the mud and drizzle. They ate most of my cigarettes and taught me to say "Ejok!" which I took to mean hallo. A young Kikuyu policeman, drunk and full of himself, kept interrupting. He spelt most of his proper nouns phonetically. His opening gambit was, "Give me a Sierra Mike Oscar Kilo Echo. You Alpha Mike Echo Romeo India Charlie Alpha November? I'm Papa Oscar Lima India Charlie Echo. Maralal Post."

It was well past midnight when the bus drew up outside the Jamuhuru Inn. Maralal has a generator and the neon strip light on the sidewalk illuminated the garish yellow-and-blue exterior of the single storey inn. The bus driver's brother was both proprietor and barman, and when the bus was empty the brother opened the courtyard gates at the back and drove it inside for the night. Four or five rooms gave on to the courtyard which boasted a shower and standpipe, a chicken run and a very deep lavatory. The empty bar had been enthusiastically decorated by someone who signed himself Joe Kim, Young Artist. The style was primitive but vivid: murals covered the walls from floor to ceiling depicting the mountains and wildlife of Kenya, a familiar theme in many Boardings and Lodgings as such establishments are called. Zany lions leapt after hunters wreathed in smoke while red-and-green snakes chased birds up to the ceiling. One wall had a bar-room scene showing a snappily dressed operator in patent leather shoes leaning over a table where a chunky but experienced-looking woman was knocking back half bottles of Guinness. His opening gambit in fat letters a foot high was, "How's the world treating you, dear?"

Boardings and Lodgings are usually very good value for money and are not to be confused with hotels which range from Intercontinentals to shacks where even a mug of tea requires considerable effort to produce. I suppose that they are the Kenyan equivalent of a pub with rooms and the ones I stayed in were all maintained with an air of independent pride, summed up in this notice to guests hanging in the Hydro Hotel, Mombasa:

Let merit be the criterion. The hotel has opened its doors since the year 1959 and is serving delicious food at cheapest rates and welcomes everybody without any discrimination of caste colour creed or nationality. The Management requests the guests and visitors to observe the rule of discipline, laws, customs, manners and etiquette of citizenship.

Cash dealing is the fashion of the day. Save Exigencies.

Satisfaction is our Motto.

I had a chat to the barman over a mug of tea and a doughnut. He wore a spotless white apron and had two pencils stuck in his hair. I withdrew one to sign the visitors' book before I went to bed, replaced it in the inclined mop and bade him goodnight. I slept until five-thirty when the bus left the courtyard with a shattering roar on its way back to Thomson's Falls. I woke up again at nine and wandered into the bar where Charles, the proprietor, was having breakfast, his pencils already in place. Bread, tea and eggs came shooting off the oven kept stoked all night by the old Samburu watchman. While we ate I told Charles that I was making for South Horr, a mission station some 60 miles south of the lake, to reconnoitre the possibilities of starting my walk from there. He was incredulous but extremely kind and he sent the kitchen boy off to ask about transport. Many tourists drive through Maralal on their way to the lake and lorries regularly go north to supply Baragoi, Barsaloi and other smaller settlements nearer the lake. Because of the appallingly prolonged rains the road was bad and Charles was quite surprised when the boy came back to report that the mission Land-Rover from Loyangalani was in town and would be leaving for home that afternoon. Loyangalani is on the lake, at the end of the road for north-bound traffic following the shore. I meandered up Main Street and found the driver who was also called Charles. He was happy to take me to South Horr, and we arranged to meet at four. In the meantime it occurred to me that since things were going so well I might as well acquire a few more supplies. Nothing had crystallised as yet and I was rather playing things by ear.

Like country towns in south-western Ireland, Maralal did not really open until about ten o'clock. The main street slowly filled with umbrella-toting women, Samburu in bright beads and body cloths of cotton and Turkana in sombre leather cloaks. Towards mid-day beautiful shoals of Samburu moran appeared parading their willowy bodies wrapped tight in spotless white cloth beneath immaculate arrangements of hair and bead. It was still raining gently when I entered the largest general store, which was run by a Somali family, with my biggest food bags. I had a vague idea that I might need more food if I was to trek around for ten days, and with a Land-Rover to carry it all in I might as well stock up. I got a twenty-kilo sack of maize meal and held the bags open for ten kilos of rice and three of sugar. I bought a few handfuls of snuff from a vendor in the street and went across to a hardware store where I bought six strong sacks, a large cooking pot and some sisal rope, and two five-gallon white plastic jerry cans. Finally I got a sordid little mirror with a plastic handle to replace the one I had left behind.

I dumped all my kit in the Land-Rover and went off to look at the secondary school, about two miles out of town. I had read about it that autumn in a book called *Dirtroads* by Mary Cole. It lay in a bowl of hills amongst tangled woods and was quite as beautiful as she had described it. I sat on the thick wet turf with two of the masters who remembered her and felt that my journey was beginning to come together.

We left Maralal at four in the afternoon and found the Somalis from the general store badly stuck in their lorry about five miles down the road. The passengers sat in the mud but the Somalis' wives, draped in fine cloth, were dry in the cab. Had they been Samburu or of another tribe they would have been in the mud with the rest. Islam gives women a certain status and privacy of their own. I have noticed that Moslem women, even perched on the back of a jolting lorry, manage to retain some territorial integrity, just like Englishmen on a train. We stood around and watched daring things being done with jacks and spades. We could do little to help but lent moral support, for, as Charles the mission driver explained, we had to wait, even if we were not helping because the same thing could happen to us.

Slipsliding on we descended from level to level off the plateau through broken hills, wet and wooded, a confusion of junipers and hanging beard moss, then out over the wide grassy plains. Just before midnight we were flagged down by people standing in the teeming rain and furiously waving torches. An emaciated old Samburu supported by two young men was shivering in the headlights. He had been bitten on the ankle by a snake and he looked pretty sick. Charles opened the back flap of the Land-Rover to let him in, but there was hardly enough room to crawl between the canvas roof and the jumbled mass of boxes and crates. The sick man did not have the strength to brace himself against the jolting and so I tunnelled into the back while he sat in front, wedged between Charles and Ilo the turnboy. I opened the cabin window and pushed a hand through to hold the lolling head silhouetted against the dashboard lights. Charles and Ilo completely ignored the man who seemed to me to be fading rapidly—sickness receives scant sympathy in Africa. We arrived in Baragoi at two o'clock in the morning and took him up to the mission hospital. We thought that he would die, but I heard later that he survived and returned to his family and herds.

A couple of women were still awake on Main Street, squatting in the orange glow of a hurricane lantern with their scratchy radio on full blast. They had a small booth selling mirar, a thin, succulent shoot chewed as a mild stimulant by the desert tribesmen. Ilo tried to chat the younger one up but he didn't have any money and you don't get nothing for nothing from ladies who sell mirar in the small hours. I talked to the older woman about donkeys. I had at first thought to buy camels but they were roughly five times the price although they do carry more stuff and can operate in harsher conditions. I felt that I could handle a donkey but camels were a more complicated proposition, and getting camels over flooded rivers was as nightmarish a thought as dragging seals through a desert. The woman advised me to get males. Good ones she told me would carry about a hundredweight and do 50 miles between drinks. I had made no conscious decision to buy for this was only the recce, but on her advice I did get four good lengths of woven sisal rope, unavailable further north and just right for donkeys.

The night was warm as we were lower now and the clouds had at last dispersed. Lying on the canopy of the Land-Rover with Charles snoring on the sidewalk below and Ilo's furtive whisperings with the mirar woman from across the street in my ears I was beginning to feel that I belonged. It was as if I were a man in a boat, trying to reach the seabed. I had taken the first step and left the boat, and now I was slowly immersing myself.

We left Baragoi at first light and out on the open plains we could see the blue mass of the Ndoto Mountains hiding the rising sun. The grassland turned to scrubby bush as we dropped from the plateau into more broken country under the towering massif of Nyiru ahead. South Horr lies under the 9,000-foot peak, completely dominated by sheer green ramparts now hidden in swirling cloud. There is a mission station there, a dispensary and a school and several small shops but very little for sale. The place was full of wet Samburu and I joined a group huddled under the mission veranda out of the rain. I wanted to speak with the priest and he eventually asked me in. The interview was brief. He advised me to move on to Loyangalani. Heavy rain, a resurgence of cattle raiding in the area and, I sensed, an understandable reluctance on his part to harbour itinerant travellers were the reasons he suggested I go on. While Charles and Ilo unloaded goods for the mission I went in search of tea.

I crossed a damp stream bed and entered a small, steaming hut roofed with flattened kerosene cans. Four Samburu boys were brewing tea on a charcoal brazier, their long spears stuck in the mud floor. I think they were quite surprised to see me, but took my 50 cents and produced a mug of sweet, creamy tea. The drizzle turned to rain and with a shattering crash of thunder the clouds burst, beating off the tin roof in a fine spray and drowning out all conversation. A rush of scum and branches swept down the stream bed in a swirling torrent that was waist high before I had finished my tea. Charles and Ilo sat in the Land-Rover on the far bank, resigned to the deluge. They had to wait for three hours until the rain stopped and the water had subsided enough to allow me to rejoin them.

From South Horr the track ran north between Ol Doinyo Nyiru to the west and the Ol Doinyo Mara hills to the east. The Horr valley is a gateway to the barren deserts and the volcanic seas of northern Kenya and beyond it stretch the broken plains of lava which like ancient scabs mark the colossal trench of the great rift valley, in which Lake Rudolph lies. We soon came across a lorry stuck to the axles in a stream bed, hopelessly overloaded with bales of dried fish from Loyangalani. It was returning to Kisumu, in Nyanza province on the shores of Lake Victoria, from where a group of Luo people had moved north to fish Lake Rudolph.

We dug and pushed for several hours until a party of six Americans with lots of cameras came driving through the rain. One of them earned his daily crust by organizing white water canoeing trips on the Sobat river in Ethiopia. The situation in Ethiopia was delicate, especially for Americans, and he had decided to take this latest group on safari to Kenya instead. He had plans to start the canoeing business again in New Guinea. He did not know the Omo river delta, the area which I was interested in, but made some prophetic remarks about the sluggishness of the Ethiopian bureaucratic process. His party took lunch and a few photographs while we hitched up their Toyota to our Land-Rover and the lorry and arranged ourselves at the rear. The lorry driver did a terrific job of whipping up local support from the nonchalant Samburu who had gathered to watch. The engines roared and he urged us on with cries of encouragement. "Push!" he yelled. "Push! Push for Kenya!" We did, and the lorry came shuddering out of the stream.

We drove on slowly through torrential rain and reached the Serema river at about four o'clock. The rain ceased but layers of thick grey sky hung over the rocky foreland, a chilly, humid threat. The river was in full spate and having marked the water level we sat down to wait. As I was climbing into the back of the Land-Rover to sleep, I noticed a wild hunting dog walking slowly down the track towards us. It stopped at 50 yards to observe. I got out my binoculars and told the others. Ilo stuck his head out of the window and looked back.

"Oh God!" he gasped, "lions!" and slammed the door.

Charles threw stones and the dog loped off, followed silently by the rest of the pack which emerged from cover in a single disciplined stride. I ran up a little hill and watched them rippling away over the lava. Every so often they all stopped and looked around, the snow-white tips of their tails and their big round ears showing up plainly against the rusty coloured stones. They are dangerous animals.

While I had been watching the dogs we were joined by a Range-Rover containing a party of British people on a camping trip with their relatives who worked in Nairobi. They quite naturally asked me what I was doing and I told them with some embarrassment, for my evident lack of kit or companions labelled my expedition a forlorn hope—the dream of an English nitwit. They took me seriously though and said all the right things, for which I was most grateful. By an extraordinary coincidence I had known the brother of the party's host quite well when I worked in West Africa. We perambulated gently in the direction that the dogs had taken and caught a glimpse of water ahead in the grey evening light. The lake looked less exciting than the Serpentine on a wet winter's day and we returned to the vehicles for a tea of fruit cake and whisky.

We were unable to cross the river until after dark and found the plain beyond flooded to a depth of two to three feet. Ilo and I walked ahead of the vehicles, feeling for the track with our toes in the squelching mud. By mutual towing over the worst bits we reached firm ground after about a mile and a half. Without the extra power of the Range-Rover, the Mission Land-Rover would not have got through that night. We washed off the worst of the mud, had a smoke, and drove over the Longipi ridge. The clouds had dispersed and below us lay the lake, still, black, and silver in the moonlight.

Wow! That's really it, I thought, but didn't ask to stop. My morale shot up to record levels. It was like being in a queue for ice cream and finally reaching the counter. Despite the excitement and the bouncing cab I kept nodding off to sleep, but came to when we stopped again, about six miles short of Loyangalani. Another river was in spate across the track, but Ilo waded across to the far bank where a light showed from the rear of another Land-Rover. As Charles eased his vehicle into the water I looked downstream and saw a black mass lying on the rocks. A group of Germans watched us coming up the bank towards them and as we drew up they explained in dejected fatigue that the black thing on the rocks was their other vehicle. The driver had tried to cross that afternoon and had been hit by a surge of water which swept the vehicle aside and rolled it down onto the rocky outcrop. Luckily no one had been hurt but all the possessions had been scoured out of the cabin and were by now well out into the lake. We helped to turn the stricken Land-Rover back on its wheels and could see that it was badly crushed although the lights were still working. The Germans followed us on to Loyangalani in their good vehicle. We arrived at three o'clock in the morning and fell asleep in the mission garage.

2

"Wek up! hey, Mr Stevon, wek up."

"Oh, hallo Charles," I croaked. He was shaking me gently and I uncurled myself from the front seat of the Land-Rover. Ilo's shredded mirar fell out of my hair. "Church begins at nine o'clock," he informed me.

"Er, right, fine," I said, feeling less than penitent. "Can I have a wash?"

The garage was opensided although I could not see much through the surrounding palm trees, but as I lurched over to a standpipe the ridge of Kulal rose up to the east, obscured by moving clouds. A fresh breeze rustled the palms and I thought what a marvellous Sunday morning it was. Charles led me back across the compound to the church before going off to retrieve the Germans' Land-Rover.

The building itself was cleverly made of wood and local stone to give maximum shade and draught. The service had started and I slipped in at the back. The priest's body was hidden behind the altar as he knelt to face the people. I had an odd feeling that the congregation was actually worshipping a severed head. The holy father conducted the service in Swahili which the Luo and Kikuyu understood very well. These people from the south were dressed for Sunday-morning church but the majority of the congregation were hardly dressed at all—greased and beaded women who sang energetically enough and a few grizzled old men who laid down their sticks and sat on the pews chatting and squirting amber jets of tobacco juice on to the concrete floor. Occasionally a sucked-out ball of tobacco would be rolled hard between long fingers and lodged behind an ear. Four old nuns clucked up and down the aisle like hens keeping order amongst the younger brethren, ejecting from time to time a small boy or a goat.

Divine inspiration came to me during the service and I formed a definite plan. With the help of the father (who was

Italian) I would recruit men and buy some donkeys and with all my gear we would set off on a practice walk, probably southwards, for a couple of weeks.

After the service I went round to the priest's house. I knocked on the open door by custom, although I could see him sitting in the front room. He ignored me, and so I knocked again and called out a cheery good morning in Spanish, as I do not speak Italian. This further overture elicited an unexpected response.

"Go away," he said, "I doanna wanna talk wiz you."

Rebuffed! The great trek would obviously not be starting from the sanctuary of the mission. The next line should have been, "But, father, I've come to rescue you. The ship is waiting," but anger displaced humour in my thoughts.

All I wanted was some friendly advice, and ignoring his instructions I walked in and asked for it. He mellowed fractionally when I had explained myself, and managed a handshake at the end of the interview. He said that he would ask about the donkeys and men that I wanted and told me to "reply" to his house at nine the following morning. That did not fool either of us. Charles thought that his dislike of the British stemmed from the Second World War in which he had been wounded, but I reckoned that he was probably fed up with people asking him for things. He had the only garage and petrol supply in town and the nuns ran the hospital.

I needed a base and some friends, and a spot of breakfast. It has often been my experience in Africa that when all seems lost a small boy will appear, all eyes and grin, and in a husky little voice and magnetic English simply solve one's problems. So it was in Loyangalani and before long a group of midget guides were leading me down the only street, staggering under my considerable loads. We must have looked like Snow White and the Seven Dwarfs. We stopped outside a crumbling edifice of wattle-and-mud bricks advertised in rude script as the Amani Hotel. It was run, but not owned, by a mild Luo called Peter and his bandy factotum, Joseph Banyango. Joseph made chappatis and brewed the tea and Peter dealt with the customers.

I introduced myself and unfolded the grand design over a cup of tea. Peter was a sympathetic listener and immediately offered to help me with spontaneity and openhandedness wholly

African. He would put the word around town about the donkeys and men, and he cleared a place in the backyard for me to sleep. The guides and I collected the remaining kit from the mission and, on the way back to Peter's, it struck me once again how enormous is the difference between European and African in matters of social intercourse and how blinkered I had been in a strange and fairly isolated town to have thought first of asking an Italian holy man for advice when all around me were knowledgeable and friendly countrymen.

The small boys and I went fishing in the afternoon. They gave me a thorough tour of the village on our way to the lake and explained in fragile English that Loyangalani took its name from the green trees growing around the perennial warm spring which flowed down towards the lake. Herdsmen of the region and their flocks tend to concentrate near it. Barnabas, the little boy carrying my rod, ran up to one of a group of 30 huts on the outskirts of the village, skipping over the fish-bones and calling to his mother. She was a small woman in a red gown with a plate of bright beads about her neck in the Samburu fashion, but she was actually an El Molo. They are a curious group, first reported by von Höhnel from El Molo Bay, just north of Loyangalani, where he found two or three hundred of them living on an island. ". . . El Molo is a name from the Galla dialect meaning 'poor devil'," he wrote. "They support themselves by fishing which must be very fruitful of results, for though they neither cultivate cereals nor obtain them by barter, they did not look as if they suffered from scanty diet. They were ignorant of the use of tobacco."

Nowadays most of the El Molo live in Loyangalani where they subsist on fish and goats much as they always have done. They are probably the descendants of an isolated group of Samburu, but they are losing their old language and are merging back into the mainstream of the tribe again. They are small people and I thought that many of them had signs of malnutrition including bad teeth and twisted limbs. The women are accepted as wives by other tribes, but the men do not marry strangers as they are considered unworthy by the Samburu, Turkana and other pastoralists, partly because they are small in number and powerless, but mostly because they have no cattle and eat fish.

Barnabas rejoined us with a fishing spear. The other boys had pointed out the police post above the village and the Oasis Safari Lodge among the Doum Palms. Visitors fly or drive there to fish for giant Nile perch, and at night they can watch local dancing if they order it in advance. Because of the high running costs lodges are expensive, but the admirable system of nationally fixed prices for essential foodstuffs keeps the beer very reasonably priced, and it is cold. Most of the lodge employees are Kikuyus from the south, but a few locals are employed as well.

We walked on past the corrugated-iron fish store and along the stone jetty. There was a fair acreage of split fish drying in the sun, and several huge bundles had been made up ready for transport. Four big canoes with outboards were pulled up on the beach and the lodge boats were anchored in the lee of the jetty. Due to the peculiar configuration of Mount Kulal, Loyangalani is a very windy place and the lake can be dangerously rough. One or two canoes are lost every year, but I was lucky enough not to experience much wind at all.

I sat on the warm boulders at the end of the jetty looking across the grey-green waters to the far shore. The lake is only fifteen miles wide here and I could clearly see a mountain range dipping straight down into the water without, as far as I could make out, much of a beach. However, a more immediate problem confronted me, something which I had ignored up to then but which could well wreck the whole trip. Was the lake water drinkable? I dived in.

"Yuk!" It tasted of dirty old inner tubes, but was just about palatable. Because the lake has no outlet and is slowly drying up, salts in the water are becoming increasingly concentrated. I had been told that the alkalinity of the water gives it laxative properties and I had taken the precaution of buying plenty of soft paper in Maralal.

Fishing space on the jetty was limited as dozens of boys and not a few girls swung enormous hooks and grotty bits of fish on nylon handlines, dexterously flinging them out into the water. A nubile young Samburu on the rock next to me gave a shriek and started pulling in her line against some dancing creature hooked below. A tiger fish with teeth to grace the meanest shark emerged and with a heave the girl flicked it on to the stones behind her. A vulturine mob surrounded it and quickly stoned it to death, then scraped off its scales with sharp pieces of iron. The blood and guts festooning the rock indicated a successful afternoon and I felt honour bound to catch something with my grand rod and reel. Two small tiger fish threw themselves on to my lure in quick succession and, honour satisfied, I handed the rod over to the boys.

On our way back to Loyangalani I stopped at Ilo's hut to give him the fish.

"Hodi!" I cried, flexing my Swahili from a fair distance. Hodi is a sort of warning that one is approaching a house or camp.

"Karibu!" replied Ilo. That means "come in" or "draw near". The hut was similar to others in Loyangalani, a dome-shaped structure of sticks, reeds, cardboard and skins tied down over a circular mud wall with ropes of twisted grass. Inside it was dark. There was just enough room for a bed and a table and a cooking area, where Ilo's wife was preparing tea. Studio photos of Ilo's family hung on the wall. His few possessions were stowed in a battered suitcase under the bed. Ilo is a Rendille, a pastoral tribe of the eastern Northern Frontier District and closely related to the Somalis. Fish are unclean food by their custom and so the boys kept them. I gently refused the bow and quiver of arrows Ilo offered to lend me for the journey, but was touched by his generosity for they were obviously prized possessions.

Mount Kulal was coming blue and massive through the descending haze as I went over to the Amani for chappatis. A young man stopped me and asked if it was right that I wanted men for a safari.

"Yes," I said, "I need two people."

"Hokay, I am Gregory," he said. "You need another man. I will bring it back to you later." He strode away. Peter had obviously passed the word as he had promised to do. He was showing my kit off to an older man as I entered the courtyard, also a Luo. His name was Martin, and he owned both the hotel and the lorry which we had pushed for Kenya the day before. We talked and he invited me round to his mother's house to eat.

The staple of both townsmen and agriculturists in East Africa is maize flour or posho, boiled up in water until it thickens to a dough called ugali. This is eaten with a soup or relish of meat, fish or vegetables. Martin ushered me into a substantial mud-brick house and we joined two other men squatting on the floor. A bowl of water was passed for rinsing hands before Martin's mother set down a tray with ugali and a dish of tilapia cooked with spices and oil. It was quite delicious and fell sweetly off the bone. I ate far more than the others and Martin's mother was evidently delighted with the appreciative noises I made throughout the meal. I sensed an air of surprise amongst the others that I had not demanded a chair, a table or cutlery, and when I thanked Martin for the meal he told me that I was the first European he had seen eating African food with his hands.

"When in Rome," I intoned, and he laughed. He said that he wished more visitors thought that way, which I took as a great compliment. I said goodnight.

Two figures moved through the dusk towards me. The younger man was about five feet ten inches tall and looked intelligent and fit. I recognized him to be Gregory.

"This my huncle," he said. "We will come with you. My huncle name Laroi." Laroi was a little shorter than Gregory and about 40 years old. His sad eyes stared evenly from a face which had felt its share of pain. The stubble on his chin was white and his short hair was grey, and a small blue earring hung from each distended ear lobe brushing his shoulders as he cocked his head and spat into the cool dust.

"Ver' naice," he said, "me Rendille. Ver' naice." He lifted his shirt and jabbed urgently at the scars on his stomach. "Dis Rendille OK?" he asked, pointing to a line of short marks running across his waist like a belt. "Dis good, di Turkana, ver' naice," he continued, and traced a cicatrisation encircling his navel. His lineage established and proven, he sucked in his cheeks and spat again as I settled against a fence post to conduct the interview. He and his nephew sat beside me with a good supply of snuff and cigarettes which diminished steadily as we talked in the fading light. Gregory had completed his secondary education at Marsabit and so he spoke reasonable English and fluent Kiswahili as well as Samburu and his native Turkana. Laroi's own language was Samburu, but he spoke fluent Rendille from his father's side and other languages of the eastern deserts including Borana and a little Somali. His Turkana was very good but not fluent, and his Kiswahili was of the rough-and-ready variety. I had already heard all his English. He had been a police storeman at various posts in the Northern Frontier District, but had given up regular employment when Kenya became an independent country in 1963. He and Gregory had acted as guides to mineral prospectors in the area, and he made a little money by selling attractive stones and crystals to the tourists. His wife made a lot more working as a cleaner in the mission hospital. I asked him if he knew how to rope camels.

"Ver' naice. Dis kazi OK," he replied.

"How about donkeys?" I asked.

"Plenty of donkeys," said Gregory, "this man she knows all donkey workings."

The Swahili language has only one word for he and she and it is a common mistake to muddle pronouns in translation. Laroi said that he knew most of the eastern shore of the lake, and Gregory had recently walked from Lodwar on the western side.

"It was 1975 I bring the goats from Lodwar with my brother John," he said. "We just continue forward eating our food walking with the goats for two weeks and half before we reach to Loyangalani and greet our parents. This man, hivyo, my huncle he know all the Chalbi and Kulal very well the water and the grazings."

We talked on through the darkness and I became fairly sure of Laroi, but vacillated over Gregory because of his education. I have found it generally true that the more educated a man is the cleaner he likes to keep his hands and nothing spoils a trip more than having a prima donna along. With no references nor any local knowledge I was at a disadvantage and whoever I employed could turn out to be a bad one. I just had to judge by intuition. At least I had here a good interpreter and an experienced older man and having worked together before they presumably got on with each other. They did not seem very concerned about my hazy plans, but suggested that we strike north, rather than south, following the lake in an anticlockwise direction.

"Hmm," I mused, "left hand down. OK chaps, you're on."

We agreed a wage of five shillings a day plus rations and a bonus to be decided by me. They were to start immediately and our first job was to assemble our baggage train. We arranged to meet just before dawn to begin our search for donkeys. Relaxing on my groundsheet with a cigarette I wondered how my recruits would be: it had certainly been no problem hiring them.

A gentle rain began to fall, pleasantly cooling the night air. Joseph scuttled into the courtyard and blew up the embers of the fire. He washed three glasses while the tea was brewing, one for himself, one for me and one for Martin who had come in for a chat. He asked me how my arrangements were going and whether he could have a cigarette. We gradually fell into a long conversation which ranged from Watergate to Uganda and settled most of the world's problems on the way. He was a very easy man to talk to and had a much better grasp of world affairs than I. He also had a good understanding of the ecology of the lake and told me something about the booming fishing industry. From him I got some idea of how much of a stranger the Luo is in this arid northern region. He left me well after midnight with a good impression of the enterprise and hospitality of his people and an empty cigarette packet.

3

IN THE TROPICS the sun always rises at six-thirty but dawn, African time, is not necessarily that early. An event to take place "at dawn" can reasonably occur at any time between the small hours and elevenses, and so it was that Laroi and Gregory turned up as promised at the crack, which happened to be at ten o'clock that morning. 'This isn't the Trooping of the Colour,' I reminded myself, 'time doesn't always happen on watches.'

Our leisurely approach to the day's task had given the sun a head start on us and it was disturbingly warm as we left the last of the village's shady palms. The plan was to call at the outlying encampments, one by one, until we struck a bargain. I tried to explain to Gregory how I valued this chance to acclimatize myself slowly.

"I expect that it'll take a few days to get the animals together," I suggested tentatively, screwing up my eyes against the glare, "we can afford to wait for the best donkeys—no rush at all." Gregory saw straight through that phony little speech. The sooner we get these mokes the better, he could see me thinking. It's too bloody hot to be wandering around the desert like tinkers at a horse fair.

I wanted three beasts, two for the loads and one to spare. After three miles over the rocks I would have bought two-headed calves, but I knew that it was unrealistic to expect to get the donkeys in one day. I was still suspicious of my luck in finding Gregory and Laroi so quickly.

The brown red lava had a delicate fluff of new grass belying the normal harshness of the landscape dominated to the east by the forested slopes of Kulal, a vast green whale in an empty sea. The lake was hidden by folds in the lava which in places became mere rubble reducing us to a refugee crawl as we picked our way over it like earthquake victims leaving town.

We walked north for about an hour, crossing gully after gully until we stood at the broken edge of a small cliff. Below us in a natural amphitheatre were seven huts and four or five thorn enclosures. Nothing moved in the heat but oblivious livestock. About 30 camels were browsing in slow motion on scattered acacia trees down in the ravine and a few goats nibbled among the rocks watched by a thin naked boy of about twelve. We moved down over the sizzling boulders to where a dozen men lay sleeping in the sun. A fire blazed beyond them, its heat lost in the furnace of the day. We sat in silence beside the first man. To describe them as naked savages would be unjust and crude, but they were naked and they did look utterly savage crashed out all over the rocks.

Ten minutes passed before one of the Turkanas stood up slowly and came over to sit with Laroi. He carried a spear, a blanket and a wooden stool and from where I sat he seemed to go on forever. He draped himself down beside Laroi and they exchanged an amiable greeting before dozing off into easy silence.

This is like the caveman scene from *A Million Years BC*, I thought to myself. Those guys look prehistoric. I half expected a clockwork monster to appear on the cliffs. The sun cranked up the sky and a current of burning flesh drifted over from a dead goat on the fire. Its horns were melting and flies droned stupidly in the smoke.

A tall man, thin as a shadow, went down to the fire, with one hand covering his genitals from the heat. He prodded and turned the goat and eventually pulled it from the flames. He took off his wrist knife to release the glistening entrails and dismembered the animal with such economy of movement that he seemed hardly to touch it. He tossed a leg through the midday air to the man nearest him, who bit a piece of meat off and heaved the remainder to the next man, about fifteen feet away. It missed and landed on a rock with a wet thud. The man stretched out his foot and, catching a bit of skin between his toes, idly pulled the meat towards him. Other cuts of goat were being flung along the line like rugby balls in a lazy warm-up. Nobody said anything and so a lot of the meat went unheeded among the rocks until the thrower bestirred himself to pass it on. Occasionally someone passed a knife or a spear, or threw a slow stone at a dog, but despite the sun no one sought out the shade.

The man beside Laroi handed him a lump of yellow fat and

a spear. Laroi cut the fat on the spear and gave me the largest piece.

"Ha. Ha. Goat fat. My favourite. Looks delicious. My word yes." I didn't say it but my expression must have indicated something very nasty being held under my nose. I brushed off the worst of the detritus clinging to my morsel, bit and gulped. The taste was less repulsive than the texture, like a cross between burnt toast and warm lard. Laroi was ready with the next lump, this time a piece of ragged and bloody meat in blackened skin. I gave a sickly smile and reached for a knife. I had noticed that the others took a bite on their meat and then hacked off the rest at their mouths. I ought to be doing that too. The trouble was that without having the eyes of a chameleon you couldn't see where you were cutting. I felt the knife carving off my top lip, luckily protected by a very greasy moustache. The blade skidded into position, sliced through the gripped viand and on into my bottom lip. I managed to avoid serious self mutilation and after a manful struggle swallowed the meat, washing it down with a fair splash of my own blood. Patting my stomach like a fat rotarian to indicate near repletion, I allowed the next piece to last out the rest of the feast.

Gregory kicked away a small cur which trotted off behind two women who had come from the huts to collect the goat's entrails and its head. The men had eaten and one by one they wandered off across the boulder-strewn terrain. Some just stood up and looked about them contentedly, slowly digging out their teeth with acacia thorns. One or two broke wind and slept like exhausted fakirs folded over the bare rocks with their heads cradled on wooden pillows to protect their hairdos.

Laroi took a moist ball of tobacco from behind his ear and chased it round his mouth with his tongue. He spoke briefly to the family headman beside him who said that although he had a few donkeys, they were not for sale. He was moving his family to a new pasture soon and he would need the donkeys to carry their gear. We climbed back up the cliff and walked about a mile into the middle of nowhere. I was amazed that people actually lived out here in the nothingness, but I became accustomed to it rapidly.

Sitting in the shade of a lone acacia with a couple of glossy crows for company was a wrinkled old woman. She was sewing up holes in her leather apron with a needle of acacia thorn and twine rolled from inner bark. Laroi called out to her and I tried a surreptitious "Ejok" which she ignored. She held her hands out to him, palms upwards, one in the other, in a gesture with which I was to become exasperatingly familiar. It meant "give me"—anything—but tobacco would be perfect. Laroi untied the rag in which he kept his stash and gave her a pinch to chew, explaining what we wanted. She spat, picked her nose and said that her husband was absent. I looked beyond her tree and with a twinge of frustration saw a small herd of donkeys dangling their lower lips in the sun.

We went to two more places with no luck. The huts were difficult to see against the rocks and scrub and I would have missed them on my own. We were now about seven miles north of Loyangalani and there were only a few families left to visit because at this season with plenty of grazing the herds could concentrate in a small area close to the town. I wondered what lay beyond this pale of settlement, but my rather wild imaginings were interrupted by Gregory. He pointed.

"Ah, yes," he said, having presumably found something significant in the landscape ahead, "over there, by that black tree. Maybe we will get it."

We walked well over a mile before I could even see the tree but on the way I spotted several donkeys against the lava. A herd of more than 50 watched us reach the tree and flop down in its welcome shade. Just beyond us were four crude shelters and far in the distance we could make out scattered sheep and goats, some camels and a few cattle.

A woman approached. She was built like a tall male gymnast and her hands were enormous. Her brow was puckered in a frown against the sun and her eyes held an aggressive gleam. When she smiled she looked wicked. Her leather apron was decorated with white shells and beads, but, apart from a small brass plug in her lower lip, she wore no jewellery or bangles. Her name was Lopuran and she was the second of six women belonging to Ekai Lour, the owner of all the huts and livestock that we could see. Two of her co-wives emerged from their shelters and came to sit with us, their aprons and leather cloaks slapping rhythmically against their legs. They both wore a heavy mass of beads round their necks, from chin to shoulder, indicating their wealth and their status as married women.

Laroi launched into his "I-want-a-donkey" speech. I think that he liked talking to women, and he must have been persuasive as Lopuran soon summoned a young girl to call Ekai home. While we waited, Laroi chatted up the wives and made them laugh. They were all for selling donkeys by the time their husband arrived. He was well over six feet tall, thin as a rake, and looked absolutely senile. His lower lip hung down in a lump over his ivory lip plug, and tobacco juice dribbled onto his chest as he bent his shanks to his stool. He listened to his wives and he listened to Laroi and every few minutes he shut his mouth with a grunt. He ran his long thin hands over his head.

"Why," he asked, "can't you get donkeys in Loyangalani?" I had no idea why we had walked all the way out here, but it hadn't occurred to me to try in Loyangalani first.

"And what do you want them for?" he continued.

Gregory assured him that the donkeys were not to be ridden. Turkanas do not like their donkeys to be overstrained and never ride them. Ekai conferred with his women and much to my surprise and delight agreed to part with two beasts. After some haggling we reached a price of 120/- for each donkey, but this was on the understanding that I would give them back to Ekai at the end of the journey.

"What if they die?" asked Gregory.

"That is in God's hand," said Ekai. "If they return, they return."

I counted out the money which he folded precisely and handed to each of the two wives sitting with him. The donkeys' services as pack animals and their milk, meat and skins belonged to the women, but the right to sell or dispose of them belonged to Ekai. I gave him a little tobacco to confirm the deal, which he accepted with outstretched hands.

"By the way," he added, "when you bring the donkeys back, perhaps you could pay me 30/- more for each one because they will be tired." It was neatly done.

A dirty child was despatched to fetch the animals. We followed its progress behind the distant rise until it reappeared, like a Javanese puppet show on the skyline, with an epileptic cast of kicking, plunging donkeys. The child ran about frantically waving its arms and yelling, and the herd came nearer, tacking across the hillside. Lopuran and another woman moved to meet them, shouting out the names of the two to be sold which they caught by the nose and corralled. Laroi had done some fast talking to a third wife who had watched the money changing hands very closely and he eventually persuaded her to sell us our third donkey. They were all three males: Komote, named after a river; Lobrolei which is the word for the cap on a gourd; and Lokarangan meaning red in Turkana after the reddish tinge in his coat. Komote and Lobrolei were gnarled old warriors but insofar as donkeys ever look young Lokarangan was adolescent. I hoped that the wisdom of his elders would quickly rub off on him.

To my complete astonishment it had taken less than 24 hours in Loyangalani to arrange the journey: I had men, animals and supplies. There were a few odd things left to get but we could easily be ready by the morning to start our recce. I rose to go but Gregory and Laroi motioned me down.

"We are waiting for milk," they said.

I dozed off under the tree but was startled awake by a horde of goats converging around me. The women and their daughters were diving into the smelly herd and dragging out their own animals by the back legs. The remaining beasts stood packed tight and panting beneath the tree with us sitting among them like lone policemen in a restless crowd. Ekai sat up and said something to Gregory. Although he was only a couple of yards away I could hardly hear him above the ever-increasing herds.

"Why is it," shouted Gregory, "that Ekai see lots of aeroplanes flying north, but none ever come back?"

A lot of international flights fly over the lake and on up the Nile valley. I assured Ekai that they did come back, and I described the size of a jumbo jet to him. He clucked his teeth and asked what happened if they crashed, and so I told him about the tragedy in the Canary Islands when two jets collided, killing more than 500 people. He was astounded.

"God," he said, "that's more than the shifta ever kill. Just in one time! Terrible!"

I brushed a hot muzzle from my ear to hear his questions about the cost of tickets and the distance from Nairobi to London which I equated to laps of the lake. A goat trod between my legs, tripped and kneed me daintily in the crutch; another defecated down my back. I was beginning to doubt if I would reach the starting post for my one single lap.

"And what," continued Ekai, "is the moving star?"

He meant the satellites which passed overhead every night. Being a curious man he wanted to know why they did not fall down when I told him that they had no wings. That took us on to a discussion of gravity and to the difficult concept of a round earth. Ekai was a traditionalist in these matters, and would have been a pillar of the Turkana Flat Earth Society. At that moment he was unbalanced by the goats and fell on his backside with a thud, amply demonstrating the principle that large bodies attract smaller ones. Nevertheless I struggled to my feet with a handful of dust and let it trickle onto the hairy backs and shoulders at my waist. "Why does it fall?" I asked. Ekai's head reappeared between the heaving flanks of his milk supply. "Because the earth is flat," was his uncompromising reply. The extraordinary conversation continued among the bleats and grunts until Laroi, fed up with having his hair eaten, went off to get the milk from Lopuran whose container was nearly full.

The pear-shaped gourd was old and imparted a delicious smoky flavour to the thick creamy milk. We drank and wiped our mouths on my tee shirt. Ekai handed Laroi the donkeys' ropes and wished us the best of luck and gave us his blessing. He waved us goodbye, still sitting among the goats, his bony arm sticking up above the bobbing backs like a twisted stick in a stream.

Towing the reluctant donkeys back to Loyangalani was slow work and it was nearly dark before we arrived. Laroi tied them to large rocks near his house and then we went to buy spears. Men with weapons slowly gathered in the twilit courtyard of the Amani. I could not really see what they were like in the dark but I dismissed several hopeful salesmen offering crudely repaired or broken spears, and eventually bought a fairly well balanced one, about six-and-a-half feet long, which I presented to Laroi. He was delighted and ran about in the moonlight killing lions and beating off wild Rendille and Shangalla raiders like a small boy. I left him reliving his days as a warrior, and went with Gregory to buy cooking fat and torch batteries which I had forgotten to get in Maralal. At Gregory's suggestion

I bought several pairs of sandals cut from old tyres which he said one could barter for goats further north. We dumped the kit in a heap in the courtyard, deciding to leave the packing until the next day.

The Amani's public room was packed as Laroi, Greg and I blew on our tea in the lamplight and discussed the plan. We would follow the lake shore northwards to Allia Bay which people thought to be about a week's walk, and where there was some sort of police or army post. That seemed an ideal way to reconnoitre the ground and to discover any unforeseen problems before returning to prepare the expedition proper. One of my main failings is that I tend to rush into things but I was determined to do this journey sanely and logically, step by step.

Laroi and Greg went off to sleep leaving me excited and happy that all was ready, but with doubts that I could not shake off. Travelling without the usual European accoutrements is fine but if things go wrong one lays oneself open to valid and embarrassing criticism. Would I stand the heat or would I need to be rescued, lobster red and feverish, from a walk I should never have attempted? Could I trust Gregory and Laroi, and how would they handle the donkeys? I had an intense vision of all three of us stranded, the donkeys having run off with the loads, staggering back to Loyangalani with our feet in shreds. Apart from these tangible problems I had a deeper worry. How would I cope mentally with being totally isolated from my own culture without even a book for company? Apart from a Swahili grammar I had decided not to take books but to concentrate as much as possible on the people and events around me. I had not come all this way to read English poetry and prose although I knew that having nothing to read would take some getting used to. I fell asleep with an uneasy feeling that I might have bitten off more than I could chew.

4

"KUMI!" CHANTED the crowd.

"Kumi na moja!" retorted Joseph, bent over his hot chappati pan. He recounted the floppy pile beside the fire, turning each one in his flour-dusted hands. Confused, he scratched his head a ghostly white before agreeing that the majority were right.

"Ndiyo," he grunted, "kumi tu."

Production was excruciatingly slow for I had ordered twenty chappatis the night before and here we were, ready to go, with only ten finished. The onlookers turned on Joseph with fatuous advice, but their hungry eyes were soon diverted from the broiling kitchen stones to the dust outside where Laroi was giving the sort of performance that children remember long after the circus has gone. He was actually trying to reload the donkeys, although a better imitation of octopi on honeymoon I have yet to see.

The trick was to start with two sacks loaded equally so that they balanced each other over the donkey's back. In the bemusing hour of dawn the sacks had been hastily filled and paired at random and now a ton of rice and beans was remorselessly pulling a bulging but weightless sack of clothes up over Komote's spine. The donkey's ears were laid well back and I could see a hoof going through the lot, but did not interfere with Laroi's delicate manoeuvres. He untied the load which dangled obscenely between Komote's legs, but as he lifted the sacks to shove them forward again, Komote sauntered forth with a casual nibble at the grass and Laroi put the full weight down on thin air, collapsing in a sudden heap. Bruised but still determined he crept about bent in a sort of Groucho Marx stoop, darting minnow-like at cocked ears and trailing harness until Joseph's voice came triumphant through the compound fencing.

"Kumi na tatu!" He had reached number thirteen. Laroi turned sharply.

"We want twenty," he commanded, and trod on a rope,

alarming the donkey tied to the other end, which set off briskly, jerking Laroi into a fresh dung pat. He kept his temper remarkably but went up to the spring to wash off while Greg and I reloaded from scratch.

We rolled the necks of each pair of sacks tightly over a rope, whipping the free ends under the collar of sacking and tying hard. Firmly joined, the sacks were a nuisance to undo and it was an advantage to check beforehand that nothing vital had been left in (like cigarettes and matches) and that no jagged edges protruded which would chafe the donkeys' flanks. Positioning a load on the goatskin saddle blanket was easy with two people and Greg and I had soon roped up the first donkey. A band of sisal three inches across passed from one sack to the other under the belly like a girth, then back round the haunches and forward to the opposite sack. I took a very minor part in the operation, as rope-puller and donkey-steadier, for I had no idea of how things were done; but Greg worked steadily and had all three animals retied before Laroi came back from the spring.

Rain was in the air, and the gusty breeze swung the orange windsock towards the lake. In a last-minute gesture to orthodoxy I had bought a ragged bush hat from an onlooker's head with a piece of violet fishing line to keep it on. The crown was rotten and tore convincingly as I pulled it on but the brim was all right and kept the sun out of my eyes and off most of my nose. Greg's mother and father came with us to the edge of the airstrip: he tall and proud in a red blanket, busying himself with a slipping load; and she quiet, and, I felt, apprehensive. Half-way across the airstrip Laroi and I had to stop as the empty jerry cans were falling off Lokarangan's back, and while Laroi retied I adjusted my dress.

Above a very old pair of khaki shorts (thin of seat but of great sentimental value) I wore a tee shirt which I now removed and stuffed through my belt, a piece of cotton string whose principal function was to retain my penknife. Scudding clouds blew off Kulal and safe from the near mid-day sun I tucked my hat in beside the tee shirt. I began to feel like a walking clothes line but was reassured by my feet in their prim brown ankle socks and desert boots tied with sensible double bows. I carried my fishing rod in its white-cloth case like a magic wand, but

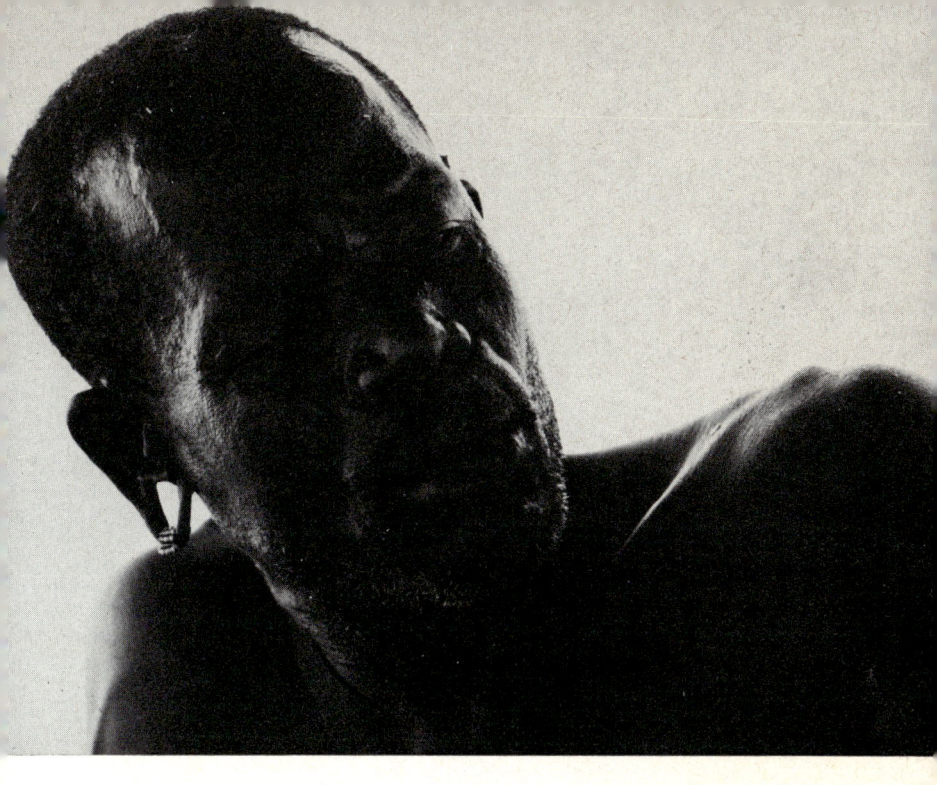

Laroi

Day 1. Loading up. *Right to left* Greg, Laroi, Greg's mother and father. Their house behind

"The Luos had long since dragged the lagoon . . ." p. 82

Esenyon plodding towards Ileret in his hat

Orip stirring blood

The women in Loolim's Manyatta

Goodbyes in Ileret. Laroi with Natiekwaan and his younger brother

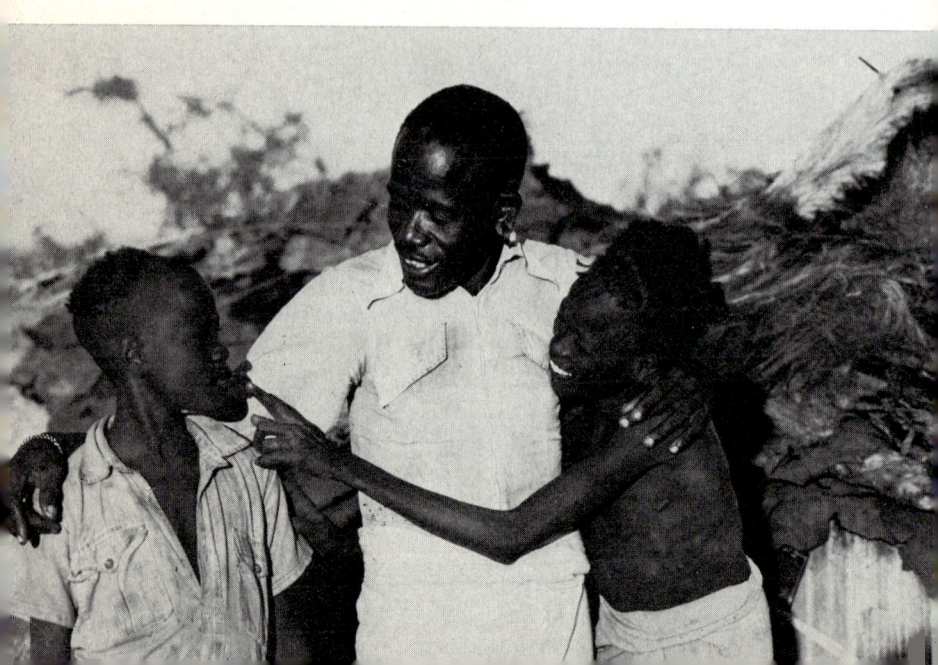

Natiant—the Moran with TB

A good day's catch, two snout fish carried off the Omo river bank by a Shangalla youth

Shangalla herdboy and his charges

A dugout on the Omo below Geleb

Dandel, one of the police guards at Geleb

An old Shangalla walking through Geleb Post

as Laroi caught up the donkeys' head ropes I swopped it for his Rendille cow stick—the whittled heart of a desert tree with an iron hard knob. He was happy enough as he had his spear to carry. Turning to wave goodbye I saw Greg taking leave of his parents. A scuttling figure rushed past him. It was Joseph and he cantered up to Laroi like a hermit crab in a hurry, handing over the parcelled chappatis with a flourish. We were off.

In their youth most Turkana donkeys have their noses pierced and a ring of grass or rope is inserted. This sign of the covenant between man and beast tends to go bad in time and fall away. The rotting process does little to enhance a donkey's breath, and in Komote's case it was well advanced. The poor animal had galloping halitosis and we agreed to replace his nose ring at the first opportunity. Laroi led off down the runway tugging the reluctant beast in the direction of the lake. Greg and I came behind, herding the other two with what sounded to me like pretty good donkey talk. We got well past the windsock before the little one's jerry cans fell off again. As they slipped under his belly he pricked up his ears and clattered away sharply, banging the gross udder on his ankles. My mind was a seething ferment of calculations and I dismally concluded that at the present rate of progress the lake would have dried up before we were half-way round.

We had just set off for the third time when the fruit-cake-and-whisky people came down the road in a swirl of dust. They had been camping further up the shore and were on their way home to Nairobi. I was strongly attracted to one of the girls and, oh heaven, she gave me an orange. Resisting the temptation to swagger nonchalantly I waved goodbye feeling a little bit forlorn. It was almost like having old friends and family seeing one off. We split the orange three miles further up the track after our fourth reload and sat rather dazed under a tree. We had a small plastic water bottle which we polished off in the shade.

"Greg," I said, "where actually d'you think we'll get to today? I mean there's no real hurry these first few days while we settle down."

"Not far," said Greg, "there is one manyatta soon, then the manyattas get to finished."

"No more manyattas?" I asked.

"No, finish until Etopia. People afraid of raiders at this time. Also they can come close to Loyangalani because of good grazings."

We followed the North Horr track for another three miles, and then turned inland up a dry stream bed which became gradually more steep sided until it developed into a hidden canyon similar to the place where we had eaten meat the day before. The appalling braying of a donkey broke the stillness of the late afternoon and soon we heard bleating goats from just ahead. Three groups of huts stood on rocky bluffs above the stream, loosely positioned round a venerable old acacia.

"El Tepes al Narokushu," announced Laroi and he began to unload. We had obviously reached the last manyatta, about six miles north of Loyangalani as the crow flies. Not having a vastly complicated baggage train, unloading was more or less synonymous with pitching camp, a simple operation once the donkeys had been persuaded to stand still. Lokarangan, the young one, gave us a little trouble as he ran off over the boulders and thorns with the half-unloaded jerry cans streaming out behind him, but he was caught with the help of a couple of people from the manyatta. Being so close to home we took no chances with the donkeys and anchored them firmly to large rocks after a couple of hours' closely supervised grazing. They drank from a hole dug in the stream bed below, and while Laroi filled a jerry can Greg collected bits of firewood from the flotsam left stranded among the boulders. I cleared a flat space and arranged our canvas and skins on the ground and while Laroi went off to greet the manyatta people I aired my feet and watched Greg making tea. I was starving.

"How about a chappati Greg?" He undid the bag.

"Very thin," he said shuffling through them. "Only thirteen? Bastard! He only give us thirteen. Mbaya sana dis man Joseph —you pay for twenty and remaining seven. Well we see him when we coming back." Joseph would be called to account even if it had to wait on a walk. The water was seething and I passed Greg the tea. He examined the plastic container. "This only small tea," he said, "not enough to Ileret, but if we try hard maybe we get it at Allia Bay."

The tea leaves boiled away merrily. "Give me maziwa Steevan," asked Greg and I pushed over the tin of dried milk. He mixed up a little paste with water and stirred in into the tea. I produced the bag of sugar and Greg dipped in our largest cup to the brim. He took the milky stew off the fire and mixed in the sugar by repeatedly filling and emptying the cup from the pot. He seemed to use an awful lot of it but I said nothing. Laroi returned and tossing over our enamel mugs he announced that this would be a good place to buy our first goat. He had the usual Rendille aversion to fish and so I had promised to supplement what I supposed would be a daily catch with meat of either goat or sheep, cut and dried into biltong.

The tea had cooled sufficiently for the leaves to have sunk and Greg poured it from the pot. Tea-making was to become a ritual of revivification, repeated three or more times a day. It was the first thing we did every morning and the sweet reward at the end of a march. Our mutual appreciation of a brew was often a silent admission of ennui and fatigue which bound us together as companions who had endured a little without draining each other's morale.

Gregory and I walked down to the lake later in the afternoon. Behind us Mount Kulal was hidden in the towering clouds. Black squalls drifted down on the water but the sun shone all around us picking out a dozen huts on a dark island just off shore. Through the binoculars I could see a few goats and some logs pulled up on the beach. There were no trees to be seen but because of the rain there was plenty of short grass which thickened as we reached the shore. Standing well above the grass a kori bustard watched us approach and moved off sedately on strong, gently striding legs, his black crown feathers well out to the rear. A male kori can weigh upwards of twenty pounds and I rather regretted not having a shotgun. A handful of little ringed plovers scuttled down the beach under the lazy eye and deadly beak of a sleek grey heron, and a pair of Egyptian geese allowed us within 30 yards before taking off with loud squawks of alarm.

"Mambas?" I asked Greg.

"No mambas," he said, "those El Molo on the island keep all crocodiles away."

"OK. I'll put the rod together and we'll get some fish," I said confidently.

Greg took a keen interest in the gear and I showed him how to set it up. We stripped and waded into the pleasantly tepid, elephant-grey water to cast the hook. A Goliath heron watched from one leg as I untangled the spinner caught on the flooded grasses bobbing further out in the water. I had no enthusiasm for fishing that afternoon and I was happy to hand the rod to Greg with brief instructions on how to work the reel. I lay back and wallowed, just a little speck on the enormous landscape. I felt pleased and thought how lucky I had been to be able to start the recce so quickly. Apart from idiot mistakes like not having enough tea the kit seemed about right, and although the rains were heavy and prolonged local opinion was that they would soon stop, justifying my decision not to carry a tent. We were going to be rather short of food but, strangely enough, that did not worry me much. I just blithely assumed that whatever was at Allia Bay would supply our needs.

I could see no signs of activity on the offshore islands. Four pelicans flew away in a dipping line, following each other on an invisible roller coaster over the dark water. The far shore was low lying and hidden in the haze but over there I knew that the Turkwell and the Kerio rivers had risen and inundated an enormous area, cutting off the township of Lodwar, some 40 miles from the lake. I hoped that if we ever reached there the waters would have subsided.

My dissipated thoughts were suddenly congealed by Greg's triumphant whoop and the splashes as he began to dart about the shallows. He had hooked a fish and in his excitement was running after the line instead of reeling it in. It turned out to be a small tilapia and we returned to El Tepes with heads held high. Laroi had been waiting for us and we followed him over to a tall and rather haughty-looking man wrapped in a black sheet. Leaning on his spear he pointed out a goat the size of a small poodle.

"One hundred and twenty shillings," he said, with an indifferent finger up his nose.

I sat down sharply, wondering how even a large goat could cost the same as a donkey. After a protracted bargaining session I bought a stunted sheep for 70/-. Some days later I discovered that the owner was Laroi's brother-in-law which may have had something to do with the extortionate price. We held the animal down over the rocks. Blood followed the knife like dark earth curling off the plough—Laroi's deft slice had opened the white hairs of the neck and crimson life bubbled out of the sheep's throat into a wooden bowl.

Laroi had promised the offal and the skin to another of his relatives in the camp and he came over to collect it. His name was Lkees and he offered us a much larger sheep than the one we had for only 30/-. I refused with some regret, but I could hardly return the first one which lay about us in gory piles. I followed Lkees back through a thorny fence to a rough shelter where his second wife Nesere sat shivering in a blanket beside the fire. There was an open discussion of her symptoms and after a cross-examination with Gregory translating I diagnosed her problem as either malaria or flu. She could of course have had anything but not being a doctor I relied on guesswork. My aim at brief consultations like this was always to cheer the sick person up, to give them a little hope, and if ever possible to point them in the direction of a clinic or a dispensary. I gave her some Aspirins and Nivaquine and a few vitamin tablets to add a dash of colour.

Smoke drifted among the huts where cattle stood quietly in the fading light. The few camels brought into camp for the night looked about disdainfully as the lower orders, the sheep and goats, were driven bleating to their enclosures. Twelve or fifteen donkeys came down the rocky slope and shattered the evening peace with their noisesome braying. Having kicked each other about a bit they settled down and soon the only sound I could hear was Laroi's grunting as he dismembered the sheep. Gregory took the stomach, washed it and cut it into small pieces with the liver and kidneys to simmer over our fire. I just sat thinking how peaceful everything was. It was about the right time for an arrow to slice the air and land with a quivering thud by my ear. Instead two El Molos came staggering down the cliffside, each with a long palm tree carried crossways on his shoulders. Despite the heavy weight they walked well past the huts before they stopped to ease the logs. Then they moved on into the gathering night, down to their island in the lake. They had cut the logs from the slopes of Mount Kulal in order to make a raft. To me the Turkana encampment at El Tepes looked so much a part of the natural landscape as to be almost remarkable, but the El Molo displaced it all as they stalked through, old and mysterious fish eaters among the brash and bloodstained cattlemen.

A hyena woke the whole camp during the night and Laroi was stung on the leg by a scorpion. Nesere, the sick woman, continued to shiver and vomit and in the morning I advised her husband to take her to the mission hospital at Loyangalani. I bought a spear for Greg from another man and we left El Tepes at about eight o'clock. We had retied each load three times in the first two miles before the lake shore but I had expected the early days to be slow as not only had the donkeys to become accustomed to us, but we had to get to know each other. Despite the sacks and the goat skins that we used for saddle cloths and padding, the donkeys developed sores very quickly, especially on their rumps where the ropes rubbed the most. Lokarangan was rather crudely branded down one haunch and his light load had re-opened the scar.

Grey clouds and cool scudded dancing from the east and a few spots of rain fell as we reached the lake and turned west to follow the line of the bay. The shore was confused by low sandspits, some broken and others enclosing long shallow lakes of rain-water. Fresh, very slippery mud showed clearly that the water was evaporating, but we could see from the extent of the dried mud, curling up in flakes like brittle leaves, that the whole area had been very wet that year. There were plenty of birds to watch: herons standing in the shallows, immaculate plovers on the sand, fat geese in squawking pairs and cormorants having fun out on the water.

A little fog was coming nearer, approaching from the north, where the broken lava was overlain by windblown sands baked into a hard flat pan by the sun and the rain.

"Here comes a bus," said Greg, and indeed it was—a closely packed group raising their own dust all the way down 40 miles from North Horr. The driver had no need to follow a definite track but could pick his line at will. He chose to pass quite close by us and as the Mercedes came nearer we could hear the dry mud crunched beneath the dusty tyres and the tick and throb of hot injectors. I wondered how conditions were inside behind the diesel, where fumbled film and long black lenses were in hasty preparation. As the tourists passed they ran out their cameras and we waved to a broadside of clicks.

We plodded on towards a line of trees in the distance, which marked a spring called Balo. By temperate standards the vegetation was sparse, consisting of occasional bushes and shrubs, thin grasses and some low succulents, but there had seldom been as much growth in the area as in this exceptional season. All the plants seemed to be in flower, from delicate fronds of waving grass to some minute red and scarlet petals stuck like beads of coloured glass on the little creepers near the ground. There were even two sorts of mushrooms poking through the sand.

We stopped near Balo at mid-day. Laroi had become fed up with adjusting the loads and had been telling us that he would fix everything during our halt. While Gregory brewed tea Laroi wandered off with the machete. I rubbed antihistamine cream on the donkeys' raw skin and watched them roll ecstatically in the sand, then I went to join Laroi. I found him digging up the long supple roots of an acacia tree which grow on or near the surface. He cut six lengths of about eight feet, stripped off the bark and tied them into circles. He and I then searched in the thorny branches for suitable Y-shaped sticks to tie across the circles making a pear-shaped peace sign like this.
We rolled the inner bark across our thighs to make fairly strong cord which we tied across the frame, backwards and forwards until the whole thing resembled a medieval tennis racquet. The roots had a pungent and rather unpleasant smell about them which, according to Laroi, just proved what good medicine they were, especially for cases of dysentery and gonorrhoea. 'We must smell like oversexed gourmets,' I thought. The frames were tied firmly against the donkeys' flanks with the loads piled between them. This arrangement worked well with proper frames, customarily made by the women from pliant stems and leather thongs, but Laroi's efforts were not very successful. Three frames broke as we were reloading and one snapped when Komote trod on it.

Gregory had produced a good meal of roast mutton and ugali which we demolished, then slept until mid-afternoon while the donkeys were grazing. As we packed up to move on I asked Laroi why there were no more manyattas ahead.

According to him the whole country up to Ileret on the Ethiopian border was deserted, although at this time there was an abundance of food and water.

"Because of raiders," he explained. "Plenty of water all about now so those Shangalla raiders move easy in the bush at this time. Also enough grass close to Loyangalani and we like to come together just talking and making sociables." Shangalla is actually an Abyssinian term for the people of the areas west and south of the highlands, and is applied also to the tribes of the lower Omo river at the north end of the lake. A word of explanation may be appropriate.

To the nomadic peoples of East Africa cattle raiding and the killing that goes with it is, or was, just another of life's hazards or benefits depending on which side one was on. The pleasures of livestock thieving are not enjoyed exclusively by Africans, one has only to read accounts of life in the Scottish highlands before the seventeenth century, or appreciate the interest North American Indians took in each other's horses to understand that.

In Kenya two other factors have amplified the endemic level of violence. First is the ancient practice of the Ethiopian Habash of descending from their mountain fastness in Abyssinia to plague the Galla and the smaller tribes of their Kenyan and Sudanese marchlands. Under the Emperor Menelek II (Menelek I was the legendary son of Solomon, King of Israel, and Belkis, Queen of the Habashat or Sheba) they expanded south, conquering the Galla peoples but never effectively administering their conquests. Menelek died in 1913, leaving his own heartland in its normal state of chaos, (the Addis Ababa railway which first rolled up from the Red Sea coast in 1918 took three days to arrive because night travel was too dangerous), and complete anarchy in his new empire which he had acquired largely with the aid of French advisers and expertise.

As late as 1962 Habash raiders were killing Samburu in the Loyangalani area, leaving their grisly trademark behind them. Ethiopia has an old established Christian church and many facets of Ethiopian culture reflect the dark and violent days of the kings of Israel. It may be remembered that King Saul was envious of David's success in battle against the Philistines.

David, a poor commoner, was invited by Saul to become his son-in-law and absolved of the obligation to provide a dowry. Instead Saul asked him for the foreskins of 100 Philistines, hoping that David would die in the harvesting. In the event he did rather well and got 200 which he duly presented to Saul who handed over Michal his daughter to be David's wife. The Habash continue David's work, although at the level of souvenir hunting.

The second source of violence springs from the first, and it is a result of the chaotic state of the conquered lands, and of the geometric national boundaries, ruled with notably firm but myopic hands, through them. Northern Somaliland was occupied by the British in 1890 and a year later the Somali nation, an exceptionally large and culturally homogeneous group by African standards, was dismembered and divided between Italy, France and the rapacious and debased power of Ethiopia. The Somalis fought back but resistance was eventually confined to the Ogaden, that region of Somaliland ceded to Ethiopia, where, because of the lack of effective control, the fighters were relatively safe. Dissidents and outlaws from Ethiopia itself based themselves in Ogaden province as well, which became a lawless area with the Ethiopian Tigre and Somali Shiftas looting across the frontier. Between 1941 and 1948 almost the whole of the Somali nation was under British rule but because of Ethiopian objections and Soviet veto, a proposal to establish Greater Somaliland as a Trust Territory was abandoned. Instead Ethiopia was handed the Ogaden and Eritrea under feeble federal arrangements. I quote Ernest Bevin, who was then the British Foreign Secretary, addressing the House of Commons on the subject on 4 June 1946: "In the latter part of the last century the Horn of Africa was divided between Great Britain, France and Italy. At about the time we occupied our part the Ethiopians occupied an inland area which is the grazing ground for nearly half the nomads of British Somaliland for six months of the year. Similarly the nomads of Italian Somaliland must cross existing frontiers in search of grass."

Despite this early demonstration of the illogicality of retaining a dismembered Somaliland, Harold Macmillan, the Emperor Hailie Selasse and Jomo Kenyatta all agreed that the

Northern Frontier District should remain within an independent Kenya and that the Ogaden should be retained by Ethiopia. In 1962 the reports of two regional boundary commissions were published. Both reported a homogeneous Somali region in the Northern Frontier District (a semi-desert area one quarter the size of Kenya) with some 250,000 Somalis, almost unanimous in wishing to join with Somalia. Needless to say that when Kenya became an independent country on 12 December 1963, she retained the Northern Frontier District. The Somalis were aggrieved and have remained so, expressing their natural desire for self-determination firstly through the Ogaden Liberation movements (begun in 1936) then through support for the shifta raiders, and lastly in an abortive attempt at all-out war with the treacherous support of the Russians.

Gregory, Laroi and I were walking north at the time that the Somalis had reached Harar, and the Ethiopians were regrouping with new-found Russian support, recently withdrawn from the advancing Somalis. I was of the opinion that any shifta worth his salt would be up north with the rest battering the traditional foe. I digress into history and politics, not because I have an axe to grind but to make the unsettled nature of the Northern Frontier District and southern Ethiopia a little clearer, and to show that because a war was going on in the front garden the back garden was probably safer to play in. Laroi and Greg disagreed.

"Shangallas all about at this time," said Laroi. "Now they miss Loyangalani because of the police there got guns, but from here they can take any person." We had stopped for a drink and Laroi and I shared a cigarette. "You say what that laibon tell you," he muttered at Greg.

Before we left Loyangalani Greg had consulted a man who was said to have powers of prediction. The Turkana and other pastoralists hold these people in great esteem. They are called laibons, and the one in Loyangalani was quite well known.

"I saw him and told him maybe I am going to journey with the Wazungu but what will happen? He said, 'You just sit down.' I sit down and waiting two hours he just smoking and sitting quiet. Then he say 'Hokay, it a long travel and bad man will look down from the hills when you pass. But don't worry, they not kill you, only watching. But still you go very carefully.'

So this man my huncle say tomorrow better we start to do guard at night when we sleeping."

This talk of raids and death made me jittery. Every bush concealed a murderous savage, and I glanced up at the trees ahead to check for ambush or traps. I calmed down as we walked on through a belt of shady acacias and past several abandoned manyattas. Ahead of us rose a perfect cone of volcanic ash, tinged with pink in the late-afternoon light. Easily visible from Loyangalani it marked the western limit of El Molo Bay. We left the trees and the ground became rocky again as the lava reappeared on the surface. I was walking about 200 yards in front of the others when I saw a man with a spear in his hand hurrying away from me along the shore. He had seen me first and I could only watch him out of sight over the dry Akamusune river and round a boulder-strewn headland.

The sun was falling into a grave of mighty clouds behind the black mass of the Loriu plateau on the western shore. As the light faded the sun gave a dying gasp and it seemed as if the whole world was swelling with colour, produced from somewhere within. Each blade of grass was vibrantly green and the air was crystal clear. Behind us the clouds on Mount Kulal were smoking across the darkening ridge. The whole mountain was burning. Reds, roses, blacks and greys shot through the billowy cloud-smoke and away over the northern desert, tinging the lonely storm clouds like a prairie fire. The effect was at the same time exhilarating and exhausting, but only lasted for about five minutes. I had noticed this phenomenon of increased light just before sunset in West Africa although never as richly as this evening. I called it the rosy time.

We reached the headland and as we unloaded the donkeys we again saw the man with the spear still walking fast and by now far away. Both Laroi and Gregory were suspicious because, as they explained, raiders normally send scouts ahead to spy out the land. I took all this in and uneasy feelings returned as I picked my way down over the rocks to the lake. The wind was rising as I cast into the gloom. The spinner got stuck very soon and eventually I had to abandon it to the soaking shivering waves. It poured with rain during the night. Gregory and I huddled under the groundsheet with the kit between us, but Laroi just covered his face with his sheet and lay on his sack like a wet log. It was a miserably grey morning but as the sky grew lighter I could see that what I had taken to be just small pebbles and stones on which we had lain that night was actually a heap of sheep shit in the wet light of dawn. Gregory performed a miracle with a piece of flaming polythene and some wet sticks, and so we were able to drink tea before we left the dung heap.

The donkeys began to steam as the sun came out. We passed over the flank of Porr, the ash cone in whose shadow we had walked the day before. I climbed the hill a little way with my soft paper and the binoculars and let the others go ahead; I could hear them still discussing raiders.

"Very bad," I heard Laroi muttering, "bad people in the hills."

"Yes," replied Gregory, "we'll have a guard tonight."

I remained up above, hoping that I wouldn't get the middle watch. To the south I followed the sweep of El Molo Bay and the backdrop of Kulal, and on past Loyangalani to South Island. These now familiar features would be out of sight once we were over the ridge and I had a feeling that the recce had started in earnest. I soon caught up with the donkeys. They did a fairly steady two miles an hour which meant that one could drop behind but catch up easily, or go ahead and scout around without having to gallop. It was less of a struggle to catch them by now, and it was also the first morning we had not had to stop and reload. As we descended the grassy slope towards the lake shore Gregory pointed out an abandoned manyatta.

"I used to live near here," he said, "but we went away. It was in 1963." I had noticed that he was always very precise about dates. "Shangalla raided a big manyatta over there," he continued, indicating the dry water course below us. "They take all cattles and kill many people. We hear the guns and we just take our brothers and run to police in Loyangalani. We stay there but police come here. They miss the Shangallas but they bring some goats back. We never returned to this place."

We were walking about half a mile in from the lake shore. In places the old shorelines were clearly visible as raised beaches terraced into the lava which sloped up to a broken ridge, rising into low hills to the east. There was a police vehicle track running north for another five or six miles, but it was old and washed out and we did not follow it. The vegetation was occasionally thick enough to slow us down, but in general the walking conditions were good, with clouds and a light breeze coming from the east.

I was pressing through a rise of coarse grass with thorn bushes up to my waist when I saw what looked like a lollipop on a stick running far away. It was a male ostrich cantering off at top speed, and was soon joined by another one. When we reached the spot I looked back to where I had been and estimated the distance to be about 2,000 yards. Only my upper body was visible above the grass, and since my head was in an old canvas hat and my chest is puny those ostriches must have had marvellous eyesight. They hadn't heard us because, unusually, none of us were talking. We crossed over the braided course of the Serentomia river, only ankle deep but about 30 yards wide. Gregory and Laroi sloshed across in their tyres but I had to go through the boring procedure of taking off my desert boots and drying my feet on the other bank. It did at least give me a chance to get the burrs out of my socks. Laroi found a broken ostrich egg at the water's edge and carefully scooped up the pieces into his shirt. The Turkanas make necklaces out of them by stringing together farthing-sized pieces on leather thongs. Laroi reckoned to sell the shell on the other side of the lake, which confidence in our arrival there made me suspect that the Shangalla menace was perhaps less immediate than I had been led to believe.

Eight gazelles appeared. They stood stock still until we were within 300 yards, then bounded off like sandy fauns. A large male with fair-sized horns kept turning to look at us. They were all quite curious and when we stopped to rest two of them returned to within a stone's throw of our tree, a twisted acacia which hung down over a sandy wadi, providing a deep but insect-ridden shade.

We put our kit out to dry in the blisteringly hot sun with the remaining mutton hung in strips over the lower branches. It had not dried properly and was getting smelly, but Laroi kept a close watch over it as a couple of oily crows flapped down from their perch. We were only 50 yards from the water, and Gregory and I followed the donkeys down to watch out for hungry crocodiles while they drank. We saw a few basking with their mouths wide open on a sandbank, but they slid into the water very quickly. I disturbed a roosting fish eagle from the top of the tree as I ran back up the sand, too hot for shoeless feet, into the shade where Laroi had already made tea and was preparing rice and beans for our mid-day meal.

Another little ceremony had evolved besides tea-making and it was called Checking the Map. I am a poor map reader and Checking the Map always lasted for at least a cup of tea and a cigarette while I estimated our position and the distance we had covered since the previous halt. There was often a heated debate over our mileage while I worked it out, but my announcements were always taken as correct. An average day's march was about fourteen miles, roughly five hours in the morning and two in the late afternoon, but our routine was highly flexible.

Walking that afternoon was sheer delight. We swished knee deep through miles of mauve flowers, an endless and sweet-scented meadow covering the stones. Our legs were heavily dusted with the ochre-yellow pollen which hung from drooping anthers like sherbet on wet liquorice. In the stream beds we saw tracks of oryx and hippo and Laroi picked up a few crystals of quartz. He and Gregory had cleared an airstrip here in 1975 for some gem hunters with whom they were working and, as we crossed the old bush runway, a battalion of frogs opened up from a marshy area on the far side. We waded through the tepid bog and down to the lake, where Greg and Laroi had slept in their prospecting days. They called the area Sandy Bay. The ground was littered with lovely stones of the semi-precious variety used to make ash trays and eggs and other mantelpiece knick-knacks. The land was glowing in the late-afternoon light which touched the dark-blue lump of Moite Hill, two days' march to the north. We could no longer see Mount Kulal.

We stopped for the night just above the lake shore, and I held Komote still for Gregory to loosen his ropes. Komote's nose band must have been in place for months and every time he sneezed we ducked and held our breath. Gregory was about to cut the band and replace it when he stopped suddenly and looked up.

"People with a tent," he whispered to Laroi.

"It's the man from yesterday," said Laroi, "they must be Shangallas."

"Not with a tent," said Gregory, "what shall we do?"

I couldn't be bothered to take evasive action but if we remained where we were and the people in the distance (who I could not see) were hostile it would be wrong to light a fire and advertise our presence. And that meant no tea. I decided to go over and find them, for if they were friendly we should have our tea and a full night's sleep because there would be no need to mount a guard.

We plodded along the thin soft beach. The odd crocodile hoicked itself to its toes and scuttled into the lake like a clockwork toy. The water was calm as lakes in the sunset are, and reflected the spiky grasses of the shore and the rosy sky. Things were turning to grey and black and becoming indistinct and grainy except in the western sky where a slow postcard sunset was evolving. It became slowly darker until the eastern horizon sank beneath a swaying boat with yellow sails gliding over the hill. As she rose the golden moon burned bronze then cooled through silver to an arctic white.

We got within hailing distance of the campfires in the darkness ahead and I called out a hearty greeting. I wondered at Gregory's ability to have seen the people at such a distance. His eyesight was evidently better than that of the people before us, as on my cheery "hallo" there was a surprised rush from the fires to the lake where their canoes were pulled up. A few stout hearts stood their ground and called the others back when they saw me walking forward. They turned out to be a party of Luos and their gang of fishermen from Loyangalani. The man we had seen the day before was one of them and had reported our presence as possible raiders. There was general relief and rejoicing as Laroi and Gregory came in with the donkeys and greeted some of their friends who were there.

I lay in the sand with my tea and a cigarette and felt weariness draining down my legs. Five or six young Turkanas came over from their tent which had actually been given to Gregory by his brother, who in turn had had it from Wilfred Thesiger, the traveller: a fact I did not discover until much later. Gregory had sold it to the consortium beside the fire, who were watching my cigarette hand closely. They had been here for a week and had run out of tobacco, and so we traded a packet of Sportsman for some tea and a few tilapia. Gregory rubbed salt into the fish and balanced them over the fire. The sweet flesh and burnt skin made a delicious supper.

The bright moon and the boys' talk precluded sleep, and so I lay back stargazing with the binoculars. A curious little boy had once spent an hour alone with my binoculars. They have never been the same since, and despite my attempts to mend them I could always see two of everything. I handed them over to Laroi and helped him to find the moon with one eye. When he did finally get it he let out a high-pitched grunt of surprise and sat back on his haunches.

"It's full of holes," he said. A long discussion of meteors, the earth's atmosphere and friction followed while the Turkana boys from the tent squabbled over who was going to have the next go with the binos. One of them, a youth of about sixteen, had been talking earnestly to Gregory. He had been captured from a manyatta near Loyangalani by a Shangalla raiding party in 1968 and had spent eight years in the deserts, near Moyale he thought, tending his captors' herds. He had lately left or escaped and was earning 2/- a day fishing.

"Was it true," he asked, "what the Turkanas say, that fire smoke rises into the air and mixes with the dust, making the rain?" I asked him how many campfires there were before last night's downpour. "Just ours," he said.

"How could so much rain come from only a few fires?" I asked. He took the point. "You are right," he replied in a quiet voice, "the smoke must have blown here from the camps across the lake."

5

THE SUN WAS already yellow and the sea was blue and I could feel starbursts of heat through tiny holes in the weave of my cotton sheet. I stretched my body out tight on the yielding sand.

"Hm," I thought, "a late start. Not many clouds about. It's going to be hot." I turned over and caught Laroi's opening eye. He yawned mightily.

"How was the night?"

"OK, did you sleep well?"

"Ver' naice," he said, but hesitated. "Steebon, the donkeys are very tired."

"How the hell do you know? You haven't seen them for nine hours!"

"Yes, tired, and we have been walking now three days. Dis place is ver' naice." He glanced about. "Plenty of fish for you and Gregory and lot of grass for the donkeys. Just no food for me but I don't mind if you want rest here today." I was nonplussed.

"Er, well, yes, actually I did say that we would take it slowly at the start so, yes, yes, OK, we'll rest here for a day." I snuggled back until the sun drove me out.

Due to an oversight by one of the minor gods, the European summer of 1977 was lousy. In consequence my skin required protection and for the purpose I had had that sheet cut and stitched in Nairobi. My beard was too short to say the effect was biblical, but when I wound on a turban of blazing white cheesecloth and strode forth as I had in the previous days, I could have been described as an Amos Camembert. Now I sat primly with the sheet over my knees. I felt like a nudist in a nettle bed. Rubbing spinanch-green antihistamine cream onto Komote's raw back, I pointed out my scarlet legs.

"Komote, old boy, we'll have to ration this stuff. Maybe you could make do with some nice Vaseline till my skin gets brown?" He thought very little of that and breathed heavily all over me.

The bare sandspit on which we were camped enclosed a lagoon and some small ponds. Fresh green *sporobolus* grass had colonized and fixed the dunes but not one tree broke the horizon, limited inland by the ancient beaches, but shimmering north to where lake met sky and cloud in a haze of white and blue. Only in the far distance could we see Moite, the first of the hills which ran parallel to the shore up to Allia Bay. I walked out along the white sand, turned grey where the wavelets splashed over the bar. The Luos had long since dragged the lagoon, and were sorting out the nets from their gaily painted canoes pulled up on the beach. A couple of them were re-caulking a plank with cotton waste rammed home with a piece of stick. Their skins were deep blue-black, hipless men with hollow backs and deep chests, enormously muscled round the shoulder and upper arm. They smoked their cigarettes with splendid energy, breathing smoke down fast and expelling it with a rush in twin clouds, like negroid dragons.

Spiky handprints and drag marks of crocodiles' tails were scattered everywhere, but only the birds remained in the daylight, hunting over the water. Least shy were the crows, sleek as thoroughbreds, but harsh and with the manners of a vulture. They were constantly after the fish drying out in the sun, and would hop skip and flutter gradually nearer until driven off with a shout. Solitary black-backed gulls stood isolated on the smaller spits, ignoring the undignified cries of their grey and black-headed cousins. Clusters of elegant terns flew by on delicate wings, erratic in flight and making sudden dives into the water for fish. Flamingoes and pelicans from the soupy green ponds behind us took off in a rushing cloud and performed a lazy circuit every so often, alarming the scampering hunters of small fry and insects whose sharp eyes and nimble feet kept them always one step ahead of the coming wave. A pair of marsh sandpipers preceded me along the spit, rising with a characteristic "tweet" as I came within danger range and settling a little further up the beach. Dunlins and stints probing and stabbing, never still, hunted the wet flotsam of the foreshore. Many of the birds found on the lake are Palaearctic winter visitors, returning north to breed in the European summer. Some, like the little stint hunting out in the sun, breed so far north, in Spitzbergen and in the delta of the river

Ob in Siberia, that they delay their journey until late May or June, and return to Africa by mid August. I reached the soaked point of the spit, turned and met Greg coming behind me with the rod.

"I'll try the inside," he said, "lake side too rough, and no fishes coming close there."

The lagoon side was shallow, luke warm and leaping with small tilapia, but the lakeside fell steeply down into the choppy waves. Greg still had problems casting and we practised together for a while. His lower lip was blistered by the sun, and my legs were uncomfortable, and so I went back to our camp where Laroi had rigged some shade with the groundsheet and sticks.

With my head propped on a pot I could see the ponds lying down, and I spent the rest of the morning watching a group of eight pelicans. They were odd-looking creatures, probably, I thought, the result of unnatural intimacy between a pterodactyl and a swan, and they seemed particularly buoyant in water. The group bobbed sedately about their pond like a clutch of old spinsters on a summer promenade. They may have been humming a few bars from the "Pelican Chorus" by Edward Lear.

> King and Queen of the Pelicans we;
> No other birds so grand we see!
> None but we have feet like fins!
> With lovely leathery throats and chins!
> Ploffskin, Pluffskin, Pelican jee!
> We think no birds so happy as we!
> Plumpskin, Ploshskin, Pelican jill!
> We think so then, and we thought so still!

Every 30 seconds or so the pelicans performed a strange evolution. The lead bird would spin round, and the group behind her followed with a sharp inwards turn so they formed a circle. Their heads then dipped smartly together and their tails like gale-blown petticoats automatically stuck up in the air. Five to eight seconds of this and the tails came down, the heads resumed their solemn carriage and off they paddled again all fiddle-dee-dee and titty-fa-la. I could make out no regular leader nor could I see how their very slick drill was controlled.

I assumed that by swimming about in the shallows as a group they disturbed enough food to trap by their sudden disciplined plunge.

Some of the lads on the Luos' payroll decided to drag the lagoon on their own account. Three of them paddled off in a wide arc, playing out the net on polystyrene floats as they went. Hauling it inshore was a long job and I gave them a hand, glad to be standing in the balmy water. Plenty of small tilapia came bouncing in, and eventually when the whole net was untangled on the sand the catch included a turtle and a couple of sluggish brown catfish. Theirs was an undignified end for, having been dispatched, they were hung up by their long whiskers outside the Luos' tent.

An outboard canoe buzzed up from Loyangalani at mid-day with new nets, food and recruits. Half-a-dozen impish creatures leapt ashore in torn sports jackets and blazers. They did not have a great deal else with them, just a couple of nets and some line, a bundle of spear shafts and the back end of a small crocodile. They were El Molo hunters and had been given a lift by the Luos from their islands in El Molo Bay. They were heading north up the coast after hippo. Four of the hunters were under the instruction of Tringa, the leader, who wore oval earrings of fish bone, which signified that he had killed hippo before. His father had been chief of the El Molo during colonial times.

Tringa explained that the way to catch hippo was to ambush them at night as they left the lake to feed. Within range of a long-handled harpoon the hippo would be struck hard and with the barbs well embedded the average victim would spin like a monstrous jelly and head back to the lake, dragging along the tree or rock or whatever it was attached to the harpoon. In hot pursuit the ambush party would rise up with long pliable spears and stab the hippo to death. Thus a maximum of danger and excitement is combined with a minimum of noise in a land of many game scouts, and of course successful hunters get plenty of kudos with the women back home. A certain amount of maize meal changed hands and they told Laroi where they were going. I threw in a packet of cigarettes and they invited us to go along, but since they were not hunting that night we arranged to meet them further up the coast on the following morning. They walked off smiling and were soon away in the long grass.

The Luos were glad to have El Molo people about, because they granted them a certain immunity from attack. "No one ever killed or even just disturbed El Molo," said Greg, "because they are very poor. Also if any man kill one El Molo that man will die before he reach to his home. He would just die out on the road. No one kill El Molo in the whole lake, not even Ethiopians or people on the other side." The Luo foreman and his gang had been attacked and robbed four months before, encamped 20 miles up the coast below Moite. No one had been killed but the raiders had taken everything except the canoes. There was quite a run on trousers when the debagged victims finally paddled back to Loyangalani.

Hundreds of flamingoes came in to settle for the night, and the evening sun caught a sky seemingly full of scrap paper the colour of milk and roses. Paul, the foreman, came over and stood in amused silence as Laroi turned out a steaming mess of ugali from the pot. He bungled the job and Paul took control. He knew all about making ugali. It was a source of constant wonder and not a little ridicule to the Turkana how much posho the Luo got through. Walking past their tent, Greg had pointed out two large sacks of it.

"That's only why they have a tent, just to keep their posho dry," he said. I never saw a Turkana refuse a good feed though. A rather stout and jolly looking fellow joined us. He wore a pair of ancient shorts and a straw cowboy hat, which I believe was welded to his head. He had a long chat to Gregory while we ate.

"This man is called Esenyon," translated Greg. He licked the ugali from his fingers and continued. "He is a good man because I know him long time in Loyangalani. His name it means 'dust' in Turkana language. His manyatta is on the other side, up near Todenyang where his family is even up to now. He's sad now and wants to return to his brothers. He's been here this side for one year and a half and now he wants to return back so he asks you if he can come through Etopia." Esenyon gave me a vacuous grin and scratched his stomach.

"Has he got shoes?" I asked, wise to the essentials of expeditionary work.

"No."
"A spoon?"
"No."
"A shirt, a knife, a cup?"
"No."
"A belt, string, needles, buttons, food, money . . . No?"

Esenyon said something in Turkana which had everyone rolling in the sand.

"He say," said Greg, "he say just he want go to Todenyang, not trading or getting married only making small journey, and also you only got three donkeys." He and Laroi launched into a long dialogue about the enormous dangers from Shangalla raiders and lions in the country ahead. Instant death lurked behind every rock and bush and sleep was out of the question. In this atmosphere of anxiety it seemed right to increase our strength, especially by one who neither smoked nor took snuff. Esenyon was hired and at once our two-week recce had turned into the real thing. So much for the sane and logical step by step approach, I reflected wryly.

The pelicans twittered at intervals during the night. Lear must have known the birds well because verse two of the chorus is a very good description of pelican night life.

> We live on the Nile. The Nile we love.
> By night we sleep on the cliffs above.
> By day we fish and at eve we stand
> On long bare islands of yellow sand.
> And when the sun sinks slowly down
> And the great rock walls grow dark and brown,
> Where the purple river flows fast and dim
> And the Ivory Ibis starlike skim
> Wing to wing we dance around,
> Stamping our feet with a flumpy sound
> Opening our mouths as Pelicans ought
> And this is the song we nightly snort:
> Ploffskin, Pluffskin, Pelican jee,
> We think no birds so happy as we!
> Plumpskin, Ploshskin, Pelican jill,
> We think so then and we thought so still!

We rose and were gone in the blood-red dawn. Brittle flamingoes stood in the half light, their supple necks curving down into the still water. Esenyon took upon himself the tedious job of towing the lead donkey over the damp grass and the cloying sand. He was the first man I had met whose patience exceeded a donkey's stubbornness. There was no mud, but until the heat joined the light, the flat grassland held the dank, lonely spirit of an Essex marsh. Nothing moved but the colours changed and birds began to sing and four miles on we saw the El Molos waving in the distance. They were camped on the landward side of a narrow sand bar with their handlines cast out into the bay. As we approached I could see five good-sized tiger fish lying dead on the sand. Elterewa, the youngest there, was cleaning them. He extracted a small tilapia from the stomach of the largest tiger fish and neatly tucked its entrails back through the gills. The others were hacking bits off the crocodile which had been part-roasted some days before. They had not found fresh enough hippo tracks, and Tringa reckoned they might have to search for two more days. Our food would have run out or, as I perhaps cynically suspected, fresh hippo tracks would not appear until it did. Esenyon and Laroi went on with the animals, while Greg and I sat by the fire eating our bits of crocodile which tasted like chicken might, simmered in boiling rubber.

Tiger fish can weigh ten or fifteen kilos and have vicious teeth which grow directly from their equivalent of lips. For some reason the El Molos do not carry them about when hunting, and so they either eat them immediately or chuck them away, dead. It is not worth the risk to one's fingers to unhook them while they are still alive. As we rinsed our hands of crocodile fat in the sand, Tringa jerked in his line. A poor turtle emerged on the beach, bemused and gasping. Tringa flipped it over and stabbed it through the heart. Thick blood oozed out over the soft white underbelly. It was all very sad and made me feel a bit gooey inside. The nasty treatment had no effect on the turtle though. It continued its swimming motion and silent gasping. I made to pick it up but Tringa knocked my hand away.

"Leave it," he said. "If it bites you you'll carry it beyond Moite."

The idea of walking for two days with a turtle dangling from my finger was unattractive. Tringa took a stick and thrust it down the animal's gaping mouth. Then he cut its head off and threw it back into the lake like a raw kebab. The flippers waved a weak goodbye as we moved off.

It was overcast and breezy and comfortable walking across the hard sand and through the feathery calf-high grasses. Moite stood out ahead like a winning post. A number of doum palms appeared, at which Laroi threw things in an attempt to bring down the fruits which hung like clusters of squashed apples high among the palmate leaves. We stopped at mid-day beside a shallow rain pool about a mile from the lake shore. Being large, slow-moving objects, the donkeys had attracted flocks of light-brown almost gingery horseflies. These squat creatures were sluggish and easily caught, but survived our squeezing and slapping by being flexible. You had to squeeze until they popped to be sure of a kill. I thought them sinister little beasts and they caused the donkeys considerable discomfort, especially when standing still.

We unloaded Komote and Lobrolei quickly, as they were restless, shivering and stamping off the flies. Being the youngest and least-burdened, Lokarangan was last to be relieved. The sight of his peers trotting down to the lake was too much. He laid back his ears, sent Esenyon flying and galloped off after them. He intelligently shook off his load into a bush en route, which included my camera and the binoculars. Looking forward as one did to one's mid-day rest with tea and fags beneath a shady bough, it was particularly aggravating to have to chase back after a silly juvenile. Esenyon set off in pursuit and I got up to help him. Laroi stopped me.

"He can fetch them," he said, "you just rest."

Esenyon returned fifteen minutes later. "I can't catch them," he panted. "The bastards are too clever."

I was worried in case they decided to return to Loyangalani like the three kings with gifts of our rice, posho and sugar.

"They won't," said Laroi, "they got brains. Wana akili." He tapped his temple knowingly. "Only if zebras come they might run away with them but you see tonight they not make noise. They just keep quiet and not tell lion and hyena where they are. We can tie up two and the other he won't run, only grazing near the place we are. Ver' clever, these donkeys."

Greg remained cooking lunch and the three of us went to round up the geniuses, now barely discernible dots by the shore. Laroi found my camera bag as we drove the animals back to camp. We tied them to a tree.

There was lush grass beside the pool, a few acacias and a well-developed toothbrush tree. *Salvadora persica* is an unusual plant on an arid landscape. It bears neither thorns nor spiky twigs, but soft young shoots and branches and bright apple-green foliage. It grows up to about ten feet high and as the ends of the branches tend to droop like willows, it provides a very good shade. The youngest branches have greenish bark but just below that is a length of grey-blue bark which powders off in your hands. Chewed for a couple of minutes, the soft wood frays out and makes a first-class toothbrush. I used to chew bits to help cut down my smoking. Greg had cut a length of branch and was hacking away at it with the machete. Chips flew and he eventually ended up with a decent-sized spatula for stirring the rice and ugali, a considerable advance on the bits of stick we had been using.

I had an enormous gutful of rice and tea and lay helpless, my head on a root and my feet in the pond. I was looking way into the east when on over the skyline came seven Grant's gazelles, grazing peacefully. Two of them came down to the water, both large males, and they had not seen us. They were about 100 yards apart, and 150 yards from us when one charged the other. There was a clack as their horns met and the dust rose from their straining hooves. Laroi was making excited shooting gestures and Greg stared intently through the good half of the binos as the combatants pushed back and forth. They were about the height of a Shetland pony, perhaps a yard at the shoulder, and a sandy fawn colour, lighter below and white on the rump. As the two milled about over the pool we could see the black bands on their thighs and black tail tips in the billowing dust. They disengaged after three minutes and the challenger stalked off, to be suddenly and treacherously pursued by the other. He whirled about and we heard the clear bang as their horns crashed together. They wrestled a while longer until Lobrolei gave a loud hee-haw and scared them off. The other five had remained grazing up on the hill and now moved slowly back over the rise.

Laroi had picked up several lumps of blue chalcedony during the morning. Stones littered the sand, washed down from the hills, and some were quite beautiful. I found myself walking for hours with my eyes not much beyond my feet, stopping to examine likely specimens. I got fed up with carrying them but Laroi persisted and packed away his treasures in a sack.

That afternoon we saw several mixed groups of Roan antelope and zebra, whether Grevy's or Grant's or both I could not tell. Roan antelope are about the size of a horse with long backward curving scimitar-shaped horns. They have very long, tufted ears, that from a distance can look like another pair of horns. I have a soft spot for Roans. A stylized head was used as the symbol for the Game Department in North-eastern Nigeria for which I used to work.

One of the reserves that I lived on for a time had 25 miles of arrow-straight hard-surfaced road leading in from the entrance to the visitors' camp, an irresistible temptation to the average Land-Rover driver who may have spent a couple of days sweating on plastic seats in the heat and dust and the corrugations of a normal earth road. Despite numerous warning signs, accidents occurred from time to time. A short while before I left, the head driver thundered back to camp with a spanking new forward control Land-Rover he had just been sent to collect. He hit a Roan antelope at what he admitted was about 50, but more likely 70 miles an hour. He and his cabin passenger received minor cuts, and the near-side wing was stove in. None of the passengers in the back was hurt but they were all shaken up when the vehicle finally crawled into camp.

We had no weapons in the reserve, despite their occasional usefulness, and so I grabbed a bow and some confiscated poisoned arrows, got some chaps together and drove back to find the injured animal. It had crawled about 30 yards off through the bush and snorted defiantly, tossing its head as we approached. I could not see where it was injured and called Juji, the head game scout, over with a chain and canvas. We were going to try and smother the horns and hold its head still, then cut its throat. Juji escaped instant death by a very nimble backward somersault as he tried to get the canvas sheet over the head. It was a bull with wicked horns and needle sharp points, and he tossed the canvas and chain away like chaff on the wind. He moved further into the bush and we saw the horrible extent of his injuries. His back legs were both shattered and he was crawling on stumps of splintered bone. I put four arrows into his neck at point blank range and we had to wait twenty minutes for the poison to take effect. It did its work and the head dropped slowly. We tried three times to hold him down but he recovered and fought back until at last the knife hit his jugular. I felt entirely inadequate and humbled and although I have had to dispatch several injured or diseased creatures since then, the proud head always comes back into my mind. One hopes to face pain and death with the same defiance.

A chain of rocky hills runs north from Moite to Allia Bay, stopping short of the lake in a 3,500-foot peak called Jarigole. The hills drop sharply to the lake in a series of forelands and sheer cliffs unsuitable for donkeys, and Laroi advised us to pass east of the hills which we now did, leaving the shore and walking directly north over the open plain. From the point when we left it the lake runs north-westwards until it recurves east under Moite peak, where it reaches its narrowest point, just twelve miles across, opposite the Turkwell delta. It seems probable that with continuing desiccation and the slow advance of the delta, the lake will one day be cut in two. We breasted a low rise, finally losing sight of the lake, as we crossed the braided course of the Tass river. Although everything was in leaf and blooming the ground was pretty bare with anything like dense growth only near the water courses. Once out of sight there was no hint of the lake for the waterbirds did not wander far.

Moite peak is called Longondoti in books and maps. Greg, Laroi and the local people I had met all insisted that Longondoti was a figment of some early cartographer's imagination. The name was Moite, Big Moite and Small Moite for the twin summits. Far beyond on the horizon a black pimple of a hill appeared. Laroi reckoned that it was Sibilot, 25 miles north of us and overlooking Allia Bay.

"D'you reckon we'll get some sugar and stuff at Allia Bay?" I asked Greg.

"Yes. We get anything at the police canteen there." I was

quite looking forward to arriving. The police would be sure to
give us an accurate picture of the path ahead and even,
perhaps, some information about Ethiopia. And the canteen
sounded too good to be true.

"Shall we fill up the jerry cans here?" I asked. We had
crossed a trickling stream and filling up now would allow us to
continue and camp without being tied by having to look for
water.

"No," said Laroi. "Plenty of water ahead. We just move on
and we get it."

"OK," I said.

It was becoming cold and quite dark in the east, but still
remained light over the hills. We had spread out in extended
line ahead of Esenyon and the donkeys to examine the frequent
dry stream beds for signs of water. By plunging a spear into a
likely spot and feeling the resistance of the sand one could tell
if water was close to the surface. We had a long hunt and I
could hardly see the others, nearly a mile away through the
gloom. I was thinking about loneliness when Laroi gave a
shout. By the time I reached him the donkeys were unloaded
and he and Esenyon were digging rapidly. They had to make
four holes before one yielded water as they kept hitting a hard
pan about a foot below the surface. There was just enough
water for tea and ugali, prepared by Esenyon, whose ability
to produce food when we were tired I was beginning to
appreciate.

The spears beside the fire crowned a sandy hill, surrounded
on three sides by the stream bed and clear of vegetation. The
swarming flies left us and followed the thirsty donkeys browsing
in the formless shrubs below. Laroi arranged the loads around
the fire, and as we settled the red moon rose silently over the
Tulugalas plateau. It soon turned to a harsh white, snowing
out the stars and silhouetting the weapons stuck into the sand
by their hafts like nodding black sunflowers. Nightjars flicked
over the bushes and between the low trees, and out in the
darkness we heard the screeching cough of a hyena.

We agreed to do two-hour stages on guard duty, starting at
2200 and finishing at 0600, the last man was to make tea and
then wake the others. While I explained the watch to Esenyon,
Laroi and Greg bickered over who should take which stage.

The searchlight moon beaming down and the whining mosquitoes made sleep difficult. The net had not been necessary before, but we rigged it up that night between the spears so that three of us could get our upper bodies and heads in. I eventually fell asleep against Esenyon's back. Laroi woke me at 0200.

"Fookin' mousakeetoes," he said as he handed me the torch, spear and watch. "Ver' fookin' mousakeetoes," he slapped himself all over.

I giggled insanely as he crawled under the net still cursing in his extraordinary but recognizable English. He had picked up his expletives from my stream of invective when the donkeys had run off at mid-day. I checked the donkeys' ropes and walked slowly round the hillock. The sand shone like snow in the moonlight and every so often the belling hoot of a stone partridge came tunnelling over the silent bush. A sweet warbling night bird poured velvet wine down my ears as I watched all around for creeping shadows and distant fires, but nothing moved. A fox yapped as I woke Esenyon for the last stage and I fell gratefully asleep.

"No tea, Steebon," said Greg, shaking me awake.

"No tea?"

"Maji hapana," said Esenyon in halting Swahili. The holes had dried up and there was no water.

We packed in record time and sped over the first few thirsty miles in search of our chai. The going was rougher than before due to many small luggas with their thick fringes of bush across our way. A group of sleek gerenuks broke cover ahead weaving through the shrubs, their long necks stretched out in front as they ran. Their russet coats looked well against the green of the river bank. By mid-morning we had filled the water cans again and were directly east of Moite Kitok, the larger peak. Ahead of us lay a broad and much-dissected valley between the hills hiding the lake shore and the lava fields out in the desert. At mid-day we reached a sandy tributary of the Moite river and stopped to rest. Débris stranded high in the branches of acacia trees on the channel side marked how the river had risen in spate. Although it had ceased to flow above ground, I dug a bath-sized hole in the sand and wallowed luxuriously in the tepid water which soon seeped in to fill it.

Greg dug one beside me and then Laroi, and we lay there in a short row passing the soap and razor blades between us. Dead skin was beginning to flake off my shoulders and the burning had stopped as the lobster red had turned to brown.

At my insistence Esenyon filled the jerry cans and hung them over Lokarangan's back. I need my morning tea! Lokarangan accepted his load without grace, but his gait that afternoon was less than carefree, and his minor forays at passing succulents ceased. We walked easily over the dissected plain, following the interfluves as best we could. Crossing the main Moite river, which was still flowing, we found the skeleton of an oryx, with the long black horns still needle sharp nearby. It had most likely been killed by a lion. A big male ostrich galloped across our front towards Opori Hill, the dark mass Laroi had mistaken for Sibilot the evening before. The two females with him dithered and ran the other way. Although cover was close by they changed their minds and turned to follow the male, crossing about 400 yards ahead of us. Laroi said ostriches prefer to escape out into the desert rather than be trapped against the hills or the lake shore.

There were plenty of Grant's gazelles about. One pair retreated before us for over half a mile at a distance of 30 to 100 yards, before finally breaking off at a delicate canter. I found a tiny lark crouched below a bush on watery pink legs, its small feathers ruffled in the breeze. Larks have always been brown birds that fill my heart with the gladness of summer, but the lovely freshness of that chick's mottled coat has made me appreciate their form as well as their song. Swallows dived in sweeping bursts between the columns of lark song, an exhilarating ballet of free movement on an enormous and uninhibited landscape. Between the streams the lava rose in gentle swells and from the crests we could see strange hills, misty blue on the horizon. Above these tiny battlements hooked wisps of cirrus cloud were blown like wool on a shimmering fence, and high up beyond the point of solid vision two neutral vultures hung. Below them a bee-black eagle turned in the vastness on oiled wings to face the softly roaring wind. Outside it the silence was almost holy.

The moon did not rise until eight o'clock, and so for the first hour after sunset we were treated to a sparkling light show of the stars and planets. Esenyon cooked rice under the direction of Gregory, who lay back with his mug of tea. My cup was the largest and so we used Gregory's as a standard measure. There was no cup for Esenyon but he used a baked-bean tin instead. Our one spoon was reserved for my exclusive use when we ate rice; it was always offered to me before we ate but I seldom used it, preferring to eat with my hands like the others. The cooking fat, trade name Cowboy, melted when the can was opened, and as we had no bottle Laroi carried the open tin on a string, like a little boy with tadpoles in a jar. Esenyon stirred fat and salt into the rice then quickly lifted the steaming pot off the fire, snapping his fingers to lose the hot sting. He shook Laroi awake and we settled round the pot.

"OK," I said, taking the first spoonful of rice, "let's eat."

Even at our hungriest we exercised a certain self-control in eating and our meals tended to be leisurely affairs, but without much talking. Rinsing one's hands indicated a full belly and it was left to the last man to scrape the pot, usually Esenyon. He did most of the washing-up too, but after a few days' subtle exploitation I redressed the balance of chores. I did not want him to become a general dogsbody. He spoke very little Swahili and no English and so our conversations were simple affairs, except through Gregory.

Esenyon had the first duty that night and Greg gave him another lesson in telling the time. We had a good laugh as Greg described his pupil wandering about the camp the night before, peering uselessly through the binoculars into the darkness, wondering why he could not see anything except the luminous watch face he was clutching but did not know how to read. The mosquitoes were annoying, and I spent most of my duty crouched in the smoke of the fire to keep them off. A mouse the size of a hamster with a very long tail kept me company, scuttling about our gear for food and keeping well into the shadows, out of the owl-haunted moonlight.

6

The wind cut, pressing tingling heat into our dull bodies. Wrapped in our sheets held open to the fire we numbly extinguished the coldest hour, sluggishly watching the water pot, but mostly listening for the thousand bubbles which speed from boiling water like crowds through a turnstile. The tea produced in me the feeling of greasy inertia that follows a heavy breakfast. I walked on and up a small western hill, laid my cigarettes on a suitable rock, the binoculars and soft paper on another, and massaged my knees in the thin gloom. The grey band passed by below, marked well by the two white jerry cans. Light dew on a small euphorbia twinkled red and green beside me, its shadow hardened and I rose. Damp flies were already moving in.

The narrowing valley rose to a low divide from which the country drained south from whence we came, and north to Allia Bay. No waterbirds were to be seen here six miles from the lake shore, only stone-coloured creatures and thorny trees and several sandy foxes slinking on their guilty way. Gregory and I walked ahead to pick a route, shouting back directions and waving the baggage train round the steeper places. We overreached ourselves occasionally and had to wait in patient strain for confirmation that the others followed. Near misses would have been easy in the choppy terrain. The bald bare ground grew fringes only round the luggas and the species of acacia had changed, now less than trees and branching directly from the surface, like upsidedown wigwams with green carpets. Walking was slow, tiring work.

Teleki had lost four men in his first eleven days by the lake. Our path now followed his but he had been here in a time of drought. He had shot a rhino the day before he reached our present position. "Our men, no longer able to quench their thirst whenever they liked, seemed weaker than ever, and the effect on them of want of water was illustrated by the eagerness with which they fought for the loathsome, dull-green contents of the rhinoceros's stomach." There are no rhinos in the western Northern Frontier District any more, nor any elephants of which Teleki shot at least seven near Allia Bay and wounded several more. Nor buffalo neither. Returning to the coast the Austrians came upon a large herd of buffalo, about 200 paces from them. "We waited until they were yet another fifty paces nearer and then . . . fired shot after shot into the closely packed mass of bodies." At least 24 rounds. They actually followed up and killed only one animal, a bull. "On our way to him we had an opportunity of killing two rhinoceroses, so that our game bag today included five big animals. As this was more than enough, we gave up the dangerous task of following the other wounded buffaloes into the thicket."

The count's legions had to be fed and the costs of expeditions like his were partly defrayed by the sale of the ivory they returned with. Activities of "sportsmen" like Teleki or self-professed hunters like Neumann no doubt accelerated the demise of East Africa's larger mammals, especially in areas where game was less plentiful anyway. But fierce competition for the scarce resources of arid lands and the subsequent or concurrent degradation of the flora and the soil are what turn rhino fields to dust, whether that pressure comes from the forester or the goat. It is a fact that the Sahel, that great east-west band of arid land below the Sahara is drier than before; and humans have advanced the wastes by omitting to foresee the disastrous effects of over-grazing and averting them by adopting alternative livelihoods and styles for the populations so joyously fostered. We may see in these new deserts what will slowly come to all of us, unless in our finite and delicate world lust gives way to love, the soldier to the husbandman and the many to the few.

We were now less than fifteen miles from Allia Bay as we crossed the divide and followed down the Sibilot river, which as it grew descended a small canyon. Where it cut through, the basalt house-sized boulders had been broken off and high columns of rock were exposed, looking quite like the Giant's Causeway in Antrim. Beyond the gorge the land flattened out, but the water was thigh-deep and flowing quite strongly. On our right the sheer cliffs of Sibilot Hill rose dry and colourless in the sun and on the left the rugged and scrubby Jarigole Hills separated us from the lake. We swung west away from the river across the flat, baking levels and into a confusion of dry watercourses and sandy gulches called Lobok and Karsa. As we dropped down into Lobok we could see the lake glistening ahead. I was not sure where the police post was exactly because it was not marked on the map and Laroi's memory had faded. I swept the shore with the binos but could see nothing except a few brown rocks.

"Steevan," said Greg with his mid-day snuff. "When we reach to Ileret those Luos say sometimes we get a boat to Todenyang."

"What, a ferry?"

"Yes sort of fairy. They say there is a white man there with a big irrigshun and a boat going on the north end of the lake."

"A big what?"

"Irrigshun. When they put showers like at school on the plants."

"Irrigation! An irrigation scheme." I thought for a moment. "Maybe Esenyon and Laroi could go by boat with the donkeys and we could quickly walk across the Omo delta and meet them again in Todenyang?"

"Yes, OK we maybe do that." We were all getting impatient to discover exactly what lay ahead. The tedious morning's walk had tested our patience. I was slightly worried about my shortage of funds and I only had one roll of colour slides. I hoped I could buy more at the Allia Bay post, a naïve expectation as it turned out.

We trudged towards the lake shore in the late afternoon, scanning forwards for signs of the post. Gregory saw it first, just a radio mast sticking up above the bushes in the foreground. It turned out to be about three miles away over absolutely treeless grassland. The post itself, which could now be seen clearly, was built on a small peninsula jutting out into the water, and consisted of half-a-dozen cabins and some large tents. Laroi stopped.

"Kuni Steebon, no Kuni," he said.

"Kuni?"

"Kuni, Kuni, Kuni!" he said, picking up bits of stick. "Dis Kuni."

"What d'you want bits of wood for?" I asked. "Let's get going, the sun's about finished."

"He say to get firewood—no trees there. Here last bush and trees before the water."

"Sorry, Laroi," I said, "I didn't think of that." We loaded up Lokarangan until he looked like a thicket out for a stroll. A solitary topi watched us with mournful stance from the crest of an old beach line, and behind him zebras were grazing peacefully.

The evening air was damp and heavy over the lake shore where an oily swell rose and fell beneath a jumble of rotting flotsam. Bits of cloth and dead fish were caught between the flooded grasses and the ground was soggy underfoot. We reached the vehicle track running from Allia Bay to North Horr and followed it with some relief to the camp entrance, marked by white-washed stones leading up past the flag post and into the compound. In three days of walking since the Luo camp we had covered about 50 miles and we all felt a little weary.

"OK chaps, hang on here, I'll go and suss things out," I said, putting on my hat and a pair of shorts. "Better have a tee shirt too. Don't want these guys to think we are a bunch of hippies."

A group of indifferently dressed men had gathered on the hillock by the flag. Their absolute silence was less than neutral, but I strode in and raised my hat.

"Good evening, gentlemen," I said, loudly. The ranks were unmoved. "Hello chaps!" I continued, "my name's Livingstone . . . oh never mind, who's in charge?"

"OK, I'm Sarjant. Officer at his house," said one of the larger men and I was led through the darkening camp. Although I could not see very much the developing stink of diesel oil and urine spoke worlds. The officer was holding court on his verandah which faced west across the lake. He sat in the light of a kerosene lamp hung above a table, bare but for small piles of notes and coin and a few empty bottles. I introduced myself and briefly explained my presence. 'This man looks neither lean nor mean,' I thought, 'no bushman that's for sure.' The fat man leaned back on his chair with a despotic scowl.

"You are in a game reserve, my friend. This isn't police,

this game department. No police here, no army, these my people all game department."

"Oh sorry, I thought it was a police post."

"Wrong my friend. This East Rudolph National Park, Allia Bay station. You see? You got a ticket? A permit? No. So we have this question of park fees."

"Of course," I said, with plenty of bonhomie, "park fees, absolutely."

"Park entrance fees, game-viewing fees, camping fees, perhaps guide fees and vehicle fees." He assumed I was a normal tourist with a vehicle, and I explained myself at greater length.

"Donkeys?" he said. "No vehicle?"

"Yes, just my three chaps and our donkeys. We don't actually need game-viewing trips or guides or anything. Funnily enough I didn't realize that I was in a game reserve. Must have missed the signs. Doesn't seem to be on the maps either."

The assistant game warden in charge, East Rudolph National Park, rubbed his fair round belly and smiled a podgy smile. He had reached a generous decision.

"You just pay camping fees. You see, we don't like many tourists to come here because this is scientific reserve. So we don't have bar or cookhouse. Just place to camp. Five shillings each per night." I handed over one night's ground rent. "Also," said the sweating cherub, for it was hot, "also the question of walking on in continuation. I am not informed of you and I think you cannot pass through here."

"Oh! What a pity," I said in a sickly voice, "that would be a shame," and I went on to explain that the journey had not been done before, that our food might run out and that we would be a general liability if held up in his camp for long.

"OK, you just rest. Come back at nine o'clock."

Laroi, Gregory and Esenyon had settled down and were brewing tea behind the bungalow. They were appalled and indignant when I told them I had had to pay.

"Fookin'," said Laroi, "no water, no Kuni, no shitoose. What we pay for?" Even the lake water was dirty with thick brown scum in the reeds.

I presented myself at nine o'clock with the maps. The staff had gone and I was kindly offered a beer. Then the officer talked, and I mustered my thin tact to keep an amicable conversation going. He explained that the reserve, now called the Turkana Reserve, had been opened in 1974, and was off the main tourist routes. We studied the map.

"The boundaries? Yes, well, in this region then around here and across up here." He was imprecise, and did not actually trace the boundary on the paper. "When you go back you take this road to North Horr then up to Ileret, just follow the tracks, they won't be too washed out. You see my friend, this is a scientific reserve, for fossils and studying, not for people visiting on safaris." My heart sank at the thought of going back and I jollied him along with questions about the reserve.

"You know this Olduvai in Tanzania?" he asked. Olduvai gorge is the site of Dr L. S. B. Leakey's famous finds of remains and artefacts of early man. "This Turkana is more important than Olduvai you know. We don't want people here stealing all the fossils like they did at Olduvai so we don't encourage them to come here. Up from here there is Koobi Fora, two days' walkings north. I will send a radio about you to the people there." My hopes rose.

"What's Koobi Fora?" I asked.

"This is scientific camp of scientists." Science was the thing.

"Do you get a chance to do much research?" I asked, sweetly. "It must be very dangerous with all the shifta and the animals."

"No, shifta finished now," he said. Before I left England I had been warned by an expatriate adviser to the Kenya Game department, then home on leave, that the whole area of East Rudolph was "swarming with Somalis". He had omitted to tell me about the reserve, but was adamant that I would not make it round the lake. I told my host who rapidly lost his rag. He wobbled to his feet like a Christmas turkey.

"You see, you see, these people. You go to museum and game department but they do not tell you. They do not inform me. I am here, if you are killed it is me that gets the trouble." He had a point. "Ah! These wrong things people tell you. There are no police here, just game. And no Somalis. The Somalis are far. You have been deluded. Yes, misled and deluded and now you are here. You see there are many expatriates in Kenya deluding people. The Kenya government is looking at these people very closely. These are second-class brains, my friend.

These so-called experts, why do they come? Because there is no job in England or America. They would not work in Africa if they could get a job at home. Yes, these second-class brains, we know them, we are watching them." I agreed with him. What he said was partially true. High wages, low taxes and cheap commodities, with indifferent local competition on the labour market give many expatriates a rocket-propelled boost which leaves some a little wobbly. He then ripped the various United Nations agencies to shreds.

"This is job for the boys, in the international civil service," he said, "you just see these experts come to Kenya, they write a report and go away. Plenty of money but no facts on the ground. We need facts on the ground."

'This man should be in the Israeli cabinet,' I thought, but again I felt that he was right.

A wet snap and the sound of a splash came up from the water beyond the mosquito screens.

"Crocs," said the fat man. "You know this Rudolph crocs pretty big. You like my camp?"

I lied.

"Yes, pretty good, isn't it? I designed it myself so that it can't be seen from away—this process of camouflage."

"Really?" I said, "camouflage!" The huts and tents were indeed quite nicely built without the glaring wriggly tin normally used to roof government buildings.

"Anyway, you say you don't see my guards out in the reserve? They are there, yes, they are there, but we only move when we hear there is trouble." I wondered what the Swahili for a stable door was. "You see, here we have the personal security problem. My friend I have been game warden for so many years. These my scouts know the bush. When they camp they don't make fires, or except just small ones, thus achieving surprise elements. I have seen many accidents with these so-called experts leaving the Land-Rover in the park and getting killed on foot. So many, therefore I am in a way responsible for your personal security question here."

It was time to demonstrate a certain competence, albeit verbally. Words, I sensed, were the warden's chosen medium anyway. I told him about my time in West Africa working for various wildlife units; and I threw in a couple of lion and elephant stories for good measure. We discovered that he and my Nigerian superior had been students together at Moshi, the wildlife school in Tanzania. I got all the mileage I could out of that and I began to feel more confident of being allowed to continue. "Anyway, I will send message to Koobi Fora and also Nairobi so come back tomorrow for answering," he said finally.

"Thank you very much," I said. "Goodnight."

Laroi had cooked ugali long since, but they were waiting for me by the dying fire so we could all eat together. A few scouts were squatting round the embers, trying to cadge cigarettes from Laroi. He was wheedling tea and sugar from them. An old school friend of Gregory's, now in the game service, brought in a slab of Grant's gazelle. The post was allowed a quota of game for the pot, and having eaten the roasted meat I rather wished I was too. It was quite delicious. Laroi almost ate his raw, for our smelly sheep had long since run out.

Greg's friend happened to be on guard duty that night, patrolling the camp with a flashlight and a .303. Lion and hyena commonly scavenged the area, on the lookout perhaps for the post's goats, or even some of the game guards. The risk of a raid was small, but Allia Bay was equipped to deal with that sort of thing. The guards were normally armed with .303 rifles, but had weapons of .270 and .480 calibre available. They also had sidearms and boxes of grenades. Poaching is a serious business in East Africa and shootouts between the game staff and poachers occur quite frequently. We rigged the net against a parked trailer and crawled in. A guard strolled past flashing his torch.

"Punda!" he hissed.

"What?" I asked. "Donkeys? Are they OK?"

"Punda, I say Punda, then you say Punda, then I just go on," he whispered.

"Ah," said Greg, "this the password. Punda." It had been chosen in honour of our donkeys, chomping away on the lakeside grasses.

When I woke up the next morning Laroi was already polishing his bits of rock and Greg had set up the rod and line.

"Morning!" I said. "Laroi, look I'm sorry but these people

will think your stones are fossils, or at least they might believe that we are prospectors, so would you mind leaving them in the sacks? And Greg, I think it might not be a bad idea to put the rod away because I just could be required to produce a fishing licence which I don't have. If we don't use the rod I can claim that it's only for self defence." They were both very good-natured about this negative start to their day. Indeed, Laroi took the fossils-for-science thing to heart, but I could not make him understand that they should be left *in situ*. He scoured the camp and came up with a couple of fossilized vertebrae, rich and shiny chocolate brown in colour. I handed them in to the assistant game warden and felt righteous.

A scrubbing party went out to the white speedboat anchored beyond the fetid shoreline. It had soft chairs and large twin outboards which were revved aggressively over the still water. As the boat roared out of sight one of the three-tonners started up. A Toyota and a Land-Rover buzzed about on errands, and I found a place to do my washing near the vehicle pit. The post's mechanic was a large man with very small feet in slim plimsolls. He was protruding from a lorry and looked like a brown pear, jammed beneath the radiator, giving a running commentary in rapid Swahili as he changed the engine oil. The spiel was punctuated by technical terms like "engine knock" pronounced in exquisite Oxford English. He was an affable sort of about 50 and emerged for a chat, adjusting his rect-angular, black-rimmed glasses as they slipped down the tripod of his long fat ears and bulbous nose. He had a couple of washers in the band of his camouflage cap.

"Do you come from?" he asked.

"England," I said.

"London Town?"

"Quite nearby. About 70 miles away."

"I bin everywhere the world. I was steam-pipe fitter seven years. Indian you see, but now since independence we all of us Kenyan. Ha! Ha! Yes, everything Kenyan. Nice." His home was in Malindi, down on the coast, but his wife was allowed to visit him in post a few times a year. There were no women living in the camp, but some of the guards had established their junior wives in North Horr or Marsabit.

If the officer in charge of the Allia Bay post was no bushman, he certainly did not mind dirtying his hands on the vehicles. He was doing something greasy to a brake drum.

"These vehicles are my priority responsibility," he said, "the number one job. Without them and the radio you are finished. Already we are broken down just two days and no Tuskers left, just Coke." Tusker is a bottled beer.

Hot and humid air built up beneath the thin clouds, a soporific blanket from which I escaped into the shade of the trailer. I watched the glossy crows and the camp goats grubbing around the water's edge and heard Esenyon snoring like a hippo beside me. He rolled over in my sheet. Things were gradually changing hands and settling down into a natural pattern. Laroi always seemed to carry the cooking fat and a spear, but was losing the rod to Greg. I rarely had anything to hand but the stick Laroi had given me, while Esenyon, who had joined us with nothing but his hat and a pair of shorts, wore an assortment of our clothes and sandals. Greg, as befitted an educated man, usually carried the binos and had recently taken to wearing my watch. In exchange I wore his sarong in camp. He had lost his snuff bottle, and I repacked some pills to give him an empty container. The vitamins which I took daily were consequently contaminated with Nivaquine, the ultimate in horrible medicine. Nivaquine stops you getting malaria.

In the evening I was again summoned to the verandah. I assumed that the answer had come from Nairobi. I had a Coca-Cola and we discussed the phenomenal rainfall and plant growth of that season. A torrent of scientific clichés fell about me.

"My friend, this Rudolph a very special reserve having unique flora and fauna supported by the Lacustrine Strip." He meant the perennial grass on the shore which supported more game than the deserts would alone. "Yes, the rain very heavy and the Population Dynamics of the reserve will change, but here we don't do Vegetation Manipulation (burning). No. At this time the protein in the grass goes down. It goes to the root. We got primary and secondary grazing, browsing and both. So now the animals eat at this time. I expect a very heavy calving season this year, fill all the Ecological Niches. This is good. The people out in the desert got grass so they don't want to come in now. So it is Minimal Pressure on the Periphery. Also not much commercial poaching here because it is remote. So remote. But you know my friend we have got it, the commercial poaching here in Kenya. Very sophisticated." He rambled on. Eventually I could stand no more.

"I want to go on tomorrow," I said, "did you get an answer over the radio?"

"No," he said, "the radio not get through. But I see you a bushman. You just go. Be careful the people outside don't mistake you for cattle raiders. Also the boat will tell my patrol post up the shore you are coming. You just call in there to report progress. Since you come so far I don't spoil your safari." I could have kissed the guy, but I gave him my biggest fishing lure instead.

7

THE ROAR OF a lion swept over the night-ridden grassland towards the echoing hills, rebounding out between the stars which hung picked against the black in icy clarity. Among those million lidless eyes the guttural challenge rang until it reached the bejewelled scabbard slung high on Orion's belt. The hunter's dogs quartered the sky behind him like twinkling razors following his smooth ascent up the face of the darkness and riding the slow curl down as the dawn broke in the east. We had packed and gone before the colours came, leaving the dismal camp, and struck across the flat grassland by the shore. A couple of grey topi galloped away then stopped to watch, two clumsy ungulates in the tinted sky.

Ahead of us the Sibilot river ran out into a glutinous bog before it reached the lake. Narrow pools lay hidden below the waist high grasses, which rippled and glistened in the sun and the incessant wind. Some were already dry and easy to cross, others remained a sticky and clinging mess into which the donkeys sank to their knees. Laroi and I walked ahead to scout out the easiest route. The wetter patches would give way to thick stretches of prickly sage bushes way above our heads which tore at skin and clothes alike, but smelt divinely of lavender and linseed. The wind sang like water from a hose across the open places, picking up tubes of yellow dust which swirled through our eyes and teeth then tumbled down to the shore. When the grass dies and the wind really blows the river's charge of sediments whips over the lake in a stinging mustard-coloured cloud that creams the water to a gritty broth, dusting the bush into old age and the eye into bloodshot pain.

Before mid-day we entered a particularly intricate maze of overgrown pools and water holes. I crashed through the bushes with Laroi fookin' away behind me, hoping not to tread on a lion. From just ahead came a rustle and a sudden splash, and soupy ripples in the next pool marked where a croc had gone under. Laroi and I sat on the overhanging bank with the spears.

I started prodding the water and soon found the animal's back. Out of curiosity I worked the point gently up and away from me towards what I assumed was the top end. It wasn't. The pool erupted instantly into flying mud and spray. I jumped out of my skin and fell over as two rows of nasty teeth set in a very determined jaw went galloping past, over a sand bar and into the next pool with a resounding splash. Laroi grabbed his spear and jabbed vigorously into the water.

"Steebon! Steebon! Look dis mamba mkubwa sana!" He was jumping up and down.

"I know it's a bloody big crocodile," my voice was shaking and my face was surely white, "for God's sake leave it alone. This is a game reserve," I added lamely, ignoring my own silliness in disturbing the creature. In West Africa at the end of the rains my head game guard and I used to check drying pools for crocodiles. They were always very small beasts and we would wade in happily to catch them and return them to the main river. I had not thought of the splash I had seen as anything other than a little wriggler, especially since we were a mile and a half from the open lake. Laroi saw my shaken state and laughed his head off.

"Never throw your spear into darkness," he said, subsiding into giggles. "The devil might throw it back."

Five more of Count Teleki's men had died by the time he reached the area where we stopped at mid-day, about seven miles north of Allia Bay Post. A few just disappeared but one poor man had eaten his ration of beans raw, presumably in extreme hunger and he died after a night of terrible agony. "Caravan people know perfectly well that eating raw beans often causes death," von Höhnel recorded priggishly. They lost their prefabricated boat as well. It had been head-loaded all the way from the coast and they assembled it to go after an elephant, wounded and standing in the shallows.

> The boat once more circled about the quarry . . . but the next moment the men in her jumped overboard for the elephant which had appeared rooted to the spot suddenly charged with inconceivable fury dashing the water around it into foam. In the twinkling of an eye he was upon the fragile craft which he first shoved before him for a little distance

then seized with his trunk. He shook it, crushed it, tossed it about and then contemptuously flung it aside. Finally ... he marched with slow and steady steps through the water and disappeared behind a peninsula.

I sat on a pile of soft red rocks which dug into my backside. On closer inspection they turned out to be a mass of shells stuck together in a matrix of sand and dried mud, accumulated in the waters of the lake and now left high and dry. I moved to a more comfortable perch and thought how lucky we were to have got across the soggy marsh, for it would have been impassable a week earlier. We had not walked far that morning but were through the worst of it and by now had nearly 100 miles under our belts. From our camp at the base of an old sand dune I could see Choro, as the North Island is called, and the Central Island standing clear in the evening sun and could just make out a rumour of mountains on the other side of the lake.

Before we stopped that evening a herd of about 30 zebras had given way before us. They were unalarmed but cautious and kept a fair gallop between us before easing out into the bush and away from the lake. They were in prime condition, rounded out and sleek as butter barrels. Grazing beside them were five gazelles whose grace was softened by a dumpy layer of fat. As the zebras moved off Laroi stopped dead.

"Steebon," he whispered, "look dis."

Six deadly black spikes broke the skyline, held high above the white muzzles of three bull oryx walking slowly across our path. They stopped at 100 yards and stared as we went by. I could see almost every hair of their coarse manes, and the rippling muscle beneath their rich, yellow grey coats. They were magnificent beasts and the first wild oryx I had ever seen.

Gregory moved slowly into my shadow. He carried the panga and began to dig a narrow trench with it in the sand. When it was about a foot deep he tied the donkeys' head ropes to a broken branch which he buried in the hole. We used this method of securing our beasts at night when there were no suitable rocks or trees to hitch them to. They rolled luxuriously in the sand, kicking like irate morris dancers and snorting the flies away. The rope sores which had opened in the first days were healing now although Lobrolei still had a raw patch on his back. I collected firewood to last the night and saw many tracks of lions, jackals and foxes in the sand. We had passed several victims to their predations bleaching in the swamp.

"Estoon," Esenyon could never pronounce my name, "kuja. Chakula tayari." Food was ready and he turned out a hot wedge of ugali on to a palm leaf. We were eating dehydrated vegetables as a relish with the dough, boiled and mixed with cooking fat. With plenty of curry powder it tasted fine, but we ate fast and dived under the net to escape the mosquitoes, all except Greg who had drawn the first guard duty. Above the low-level droning of our tormentors came the cough of a lion. The donkeys stood silently in the smoke of the fire, but they were suffering badly. Sleep was impossible. The lion coughed again, and Laroi sat up cursing.

"Fookin' mousakitos." He lit a cigarette. "Simba too many in dis place, mingi hapa—like goats. Ndyio, simba mingi hapa kama mbuzi, na fookin' mousakitos kama mvua." Lions are common as goats, he said, and the mosquitoes are like rain, he had added with a sigh. I laughed and said that he should take his spear and kill one of the lions.

"He killed before, what is small lion with black spots? Duma in Swahili language—yes, leopard." Laroi stood up at Greg's remark.

"Ha! yes I killed it one duma. I was a moran just looking with my father's goats on Kulal. It was pure day and a leopard took a goat from the herd." Laroi crouched in the darkness with a spear. He had lost twenty years. "He run with the goat but I see for him. I just take my spear and the stick and I go running so fast to him. He stop and he dropping the goat making up his mouth he spit." A dark bundle of sinew sprang from a bush spitting and snarling, raking the air with its claws. Laroi was a tremendous actor. "Then I come near still running. I take my sheet and I put it round my hand and when I reach that leopard so close it run at me I give the hand to his mouth when he hit me."

Laroi leant back, his body down, almost squatting on wide-spread legs. The spear was up vibrating against the stars.

"He come, ugh, bite with mouth, whip the claws like man in

a thorn tree. I snap the spear down, shhooo, stab, spear him in throat. He turn like snake on spear and the blood come through his mouth. I pull the spear but that leopard biting still and he get my arm here." Laroi sprang back and withdrew the spear. At the same time his right arm was pulled forward and he gave a gurgling cough.

"That leopard he cough once more, release my hand, and then he just die there on the ground." Laroi's eyes were shining and sweat stood on his face, sparkling in the firelight as he showed his scars from the fight.

"Then he run and run to his home," Gregory finished the story off, "and his father say, my son, you have killed a leopard. And they had a feast and killed two goats. And the women they like Laroi too much." Esenyon and I gave admiring grunts.

During my period of guard duty the mosquitoes seemed to intensify their attacks. I watched the nightjars hunting in pairs above the chapparal like little ghosts on owl-soft wings. I hoped that they were catching plenty of the blood-sucking demons whining round my ears. The donkeys rolled and stamped in torment and Komote nearly strangled himself on his rope before I could cut him free. At dawn we could see how badly they had been bitten. Their heads and withers were cobbled with raised lumps and with the sun the flies continued the torture.

It was a calm morning and the lake was blue. A shiny brown hippo grazed down by the shore like a fat boy looking for sweets on a cricket pitch, and a topi snorted as it cantered off towards a low rise ahead. The donkeys picked their way unhurriedly through the euphorbias and the low commiphora trees with their papery bark and sweet-smelling leaves. A pair of dik-diks sped like hares through the dry bush and over the stony lava, which swung away from the lake and across our path in a low, dissected rise, from which we could see the roofs of Koobi Fora camp and the vehicles' dazzling reflections over the shimmering grass.

Greg and I drew ahead. I noticed the camp buildings were neatly thatched and cool, with walls of hewn stone and wide, airy verandahs. 'Bit of money gone into this place,' I thought. A couple of speedboats stood off the sandy beach. From the shade of the buildings came a pliant but bony youth of about twenty.

He had the most extraordinary hairdo. His head was shaven to well above the ears at the rear and several inches back from the hairline on his forehead, leaving an oval shaped skull cap of frizzy hair. The rear portion of this grew up in a crest running fanwise across his head, and the front fell forward over his temples and forehead in a series of tightly plaited rats' tails which swung as he walked towards us over the hot sand.

"Shangalla," whispered Greg. "He's blind. He can't see." I could now see that the chap's eyes were clouded over by a milky growth. He greeted us loudly but instead of leading us back to the huts he stood, waiting.

"What about the others?" he said.

"What others?" asked Greg.

"The others with you," he replied. Although the donkeys were half a mile behind he had sensed that Greg and I were not alone. I do not know how.

We sat with him and a handful of other men, mostly Kikuyus. Two of them wore white shirts and were peeling potatoes into a saucepan. There seemed to be more room in the camp than people to occupy it for several empty huts were hung with mosquito nets over bare bed springs.

"You want the Wazungu," said one of the potato peelers.

"Yes," I said, "OK," but I was really quite happy as I was. Greg had discovered an old classmate, also from Loyangalani, who was working here. I looked out over the sea-green grass and the bleached sand, across the glistening blue sheet to the sheer mountains of the north-western shore. Penetrating the blue in the zenith was Choro, bone dry and baking in the heat, the upper slopes white like snow on a summer alp. The sighing lake drifted back over the still grass on a slowly wafting air, its thousand mirrors flashing the millisecond glory of a burnished sun dance.

"Hello, how do you do?" said a geologist with long blond hair and a well-tanned face. He was about 35. He called for tea which was brought to the eating house, milky and sweet. "What, er, sort of um, that is, why actually . . ."

I gave a detailed account of the journey so far and explained that the general idea was to walk round the lake. He in turn was kind enough to show me some of the things that had been found at Koobi Fora. The expedition had been set up in the early seventies, in order to explore the enormous mileage of sediments exposed out in the deserts on the sides of the dried-up wadis and water courses, which, it was rightly assumed, might contain fossils and artefacts of early man, or his immediate ancestors. The work began with a resounding success, for very soon after digging had started someone unearthed the almost complete skull of an Australopithecine. There was a cast of it in the camp storeroom which the doctor kindly showed me. Many are the dreamless but irresistible naps I have taken to the somnolent drone of a lecturer in sequential bones, or physical anthropology as it was called. I felt rather sorry for the thousands of students who will have to store skull 1470 in their heads as just another example to be trotted out in essays or examinations, but actually being at Koobi Fora and handling the thing was so ridiculously simple and straightforward that the hours of debate as to whether it was in this direct line with man or that or not at all slipped irrelevantly away.

The geologist and I actually spent more time discussing the plane crashes there had been down on the airstrip than talking anthropological shop. He did tell me something useful about mosquitoes. I had noticed that their depredations were irregular through the night; sometimes attacks took place at dawn and dusk, sometimes at midnight and so on. This, apparently, was due to variations in local winds and air currents, the times of still air being the worst for bites. I thanked the geologist for the tea and said goodbye. He had actually been saying goodbye for a full ten minutes but I had not picked the hints up. Laroi and Esenyon had drunk tea and rested, and Greg had been given a kilo of sugar by his friend, an extremely generous and timely gift. We reloaded the donkeys and left the camp just after mid-day. The geologist reckoned we had about 30 miles to go before the border post of Ileret, or roughly two more days' walking.

Beyond Koobi Fora we crossed miles of flat, sandy grassland and we saw a red brown topi lying alone out on the airstrip. I thought that it was a rusty fuel drum until we got closer and could see its horns, like bent pitchforks stuck on its clumsy head. I wondered what it had died of, lying there in the open just a few yards from us. There were no vultures or storks about, because, said Greg, it was just asleep, not dead.

"Can't be," I said. "Must be dead. Shoo, hey, wake up." It remained dead. "Look, it's dead all right." I changed course and stretched out my hand to touch it. It looked fresh enough to eat. "Hey, Greg, bring a knife over, it looks fresh enough to ——" a roar and a snort and a clattering of hooves drowned my instructions, and the fresh meat leapt away, its eyes still half-closed and dozy. I turned round with my mouth open. Laroi and Esenyon were pissing themselves with laughter and Greg gave me a pitying smile. Even the donkeys were grinning.

"Christ, you bastards. I could have been run over then. Why didn't you stop me?"

"Sometimes they just sleep like that," said Gregory, "but white people never believe it." I felt about two feet tall.

There was another tiring stretch of drying pools and thick bush after the sand flats where the Koobi river came down off the lava and ran out in a maze of pools, sage brush and sand. We crossed that obstacle and stopped early near a litter of strange round boulders, some of them three men high, scattered at the water's edge like Cyclops' marbles. As I wrote up my diary Laroi looked at me over Lokarangan's back. He was unloading.

"You aren't as strong as you were when we started," he said. It took a few moments for me to get the message. He was telling me, in the nicest possible way, that I was not pulling my weight. "Gregory isn't strong either," he added. I had noticed that Greg had taken to looking at the maps a lot and standing around when the other two were doing the physical work. Although all three of them were in a sense my servants I had not intended to be waited on. Laroi's tact had made me feel ashamed and I resolved to pull my finger out.

It was a beautiful evening. The sun sank down behind Choro and just on the point of its disappearance a lion coughed and it was very very close by. I jumped, Laroi clutched his spear and Esenyon grabbed the donkeys. The lion was right behind us, somewhere in a jumble of rock and thorn within 30 yards of our fire. Greg and I showered the likely spot with stones but the invisible lion merely broke into a series of roars. Shouting loudly and throwing stones we retreated downhill to a defensive position in the sand dunes by the lake. In fact we had no trouble from the lion at all that night but the subtle beast had pressed us into the arms of its insect friends, whose pestilential kisses drove us mad.

We tried to settle down, and watched two satellites slip across the heavens. Esenyon attempted to follow them with the binoculars, but said that he could not see anything. Laroi gently pointed out that the lens caps were still on, and Esenyon had another go. Jupiter had risen, and I explained the difference between the stars and the planets to Greg. He had enough general knowledge to laugh when Esenyon asked if the moon was closer to Kenya than London, but perhaps not as much as he thought he had.

"How long does it take to get to Mars?" he asked.
"About three months," I said, "going pretty fast."
"Wow! Travelling day and night?"
"Day and night," I assured him.
"How long to the moon?"
"About four days."
"No stopping? Just take their food and go ahead? Wonderful!"

The lava reached the lake in a line of low, rocky cliffs just north of our camp. We followed the cliff top for an hour before we saw the patrol post of Kokoi nestling above the steely blue water and advertised by its glaring corrugated iron roofs and the tall water tower. We got there at about eight and had morning tea with the game guards. They pointed out our route to Ileret, north over the cliffs until we met the vehicle track that they had made.

Although it was muggy the walking that morning was a delight. All across the hills we waded ankle deep in the snow-white flowerlets of low *Heliotropium* bushes, borne in rows on the inside edge of the flower heads, bent like the tip of a recurved bow in the breeze. To the east the hills split and reformed then split again in a confusion of rock, dusted green away into the Chalbi. A pair of ostrich strutted miles below on mighty thighs and larks twittered in short, low bursts of flight. A large gull cruised through the hazy air as we descended to the lake shore, stumbling down a river of small stones. Esenyon's hat fell off, but not for long. He replaced it, cursing the sultry heat. I took over Komote's head rope and soon my upper body was covered with fine dust, etched into erratic brown channels by my running sweat. Fibrous débris, from which dried mud fell as we brushed past, hung in the lower branches of the trees on the banks of the Lugga Tulugalas. Nothing large moved in the whistling heat, and we were grateful for the shade of the toothbrush tree in which we had parked for lunch and a snooze.

I dug a bath out in the sun, had a shave and lay back. I still had no reliable information about the delta region beyond Ileret but I had decided to press on with the journey if I could. I reckoned that I had enough money to reach Lokitaung, the first township in Kenya on the far shore, and I could go back to Nairobi for more from there. The journey was going well; Laroi, Gregory and I worked happily together and Esenyon had made himself a member of the party very quickly. Our rations were low but I hoped that we could buy more at the duka in Ileret. I heaved my weary body back into the shade. After some general discussion we agreed to rest in Ileret for two or three days to be fresh for whatever Ethiopia might have in store for us.

Leaving our shady tree Laroi noticed a concentration of vultures north of us somewhere near the lake. He and I went off to investigate. The bare parched earth gave way to thick grass as we reached the shore and cast about for the birds. They had disappeared and so we followed the marshy lake shore north. After a few hundred yards the sound of a flapping scuffle broke from the reeds ahead and as we approached a coven of vultures creaked away into the nearby trees. Laroi splashed through the water, hoping for meat. I followed like an excited child at a lucky-dip stall, brushing aside the tall grasses in my hurry to catch up. Laroi gave a shout and I changed course to meet him. He had found the meat. A crocodile bobbed in the bloody grass. Its back legs and tail had been hacked off, leaving about three yards of upper body and the grotesque jaws floating in the shallow water. Little fish nibbled at the shredded flesh and water dribbed through the blunt teeth grown stale with an algal rind of dank green. Pieces of flotsam were caught in the jaws like crazy straws. Forward of the right arm were three deep stab wounds, and Laroi pointed to another cluster at the base of the skull.

"Kill him like dis." He mimed a man steering a canoe in the

shallow water. "Wait. Wait. Waiting all the time, but always the spear up." His spear was raised like a heron's beak. "Then mamba come and down! Bang! Canoe rock, maybe man fall out, maybe mamba escape. Other men spear fast. Mamba die!" His sad face brightened. "Then cut the meat and go before game comes to catch you!"

We left the rotting saurian and turned back on a course to rejoin Greg and Esenyon. Very soon we were floundering through a muddy bog, and could see little over the thick bush. We blundered on between the pools and across the soupy remains of the Tulugalas river. I could see a glint of water amongst the reeds and, hoping to find a clearer route, we pressed through the tangled undergrowth towards it. I was about to step out into an open patch when Laroi gave a warning shout and flung himself down. I followed suit, but just caught the end of a Shangalla spear shaft on my shoulder.

'Jesus Christ,' I remember thinking, 'what if there had been a head on it?'

Two naked men were scrambling up the far side of the pool. One fell back but the other dashed off into the reeds and was immediately out of sight. Laroi sprang to his feet.

"Mimi Rendille," he shouted. "Hapana game. Rendille. Rendille. Jambo Rafiki. Salam."

He jabbered on in a mixture of half a dozen languages, trying to calm the scrabbling man. As he reached the top of the bank the man turned hesitantly and shouted something to Laroi, who replied in the affirmative. The man stopped and a long loud exchange took place in which I caught only two words, "Game" and "Tombacco". He was tall, thin and dirty and as he came over the water to us in his canoe I could see his appalling teeth and gummy eyes, and his crudely arranged hair. He was a Shangalla from up the coast, fallen on hard times and taken to poaching crocodiles, not quite the thing for a proud young warrior to do. The man punted over to us, his arms outstretched for the pinch of tobacco Laroi gave him. Apparently there was an acute shortage of it in the area. He called out to his friend in the reeds and by the time he had rolled the tobacco and chewed out the first bitterness five men had converged on us from the bush all around.

Laroi had to do some fast talking to persuade them that I was nothing to do with the game department. Next to the poachers he looked almost urbane, even in his ragged shorts and torn shirt, like a country squire doling out largesse in the form of tobacco to a gang of coarse rustics who "oohed" and "arred" as Laroi introduced himself. In their hairdos they had mushroom-shaped pegs and little seed heads for decoration. A couple of them wore leather bracelets and small pouches hung from the neck containing herbs or talismans for good luck. Otherwise all six were naked. Laroi had adopted the English approach of shouting at foreigners to make himself understood but I gathered that the Shangalla dialect was similar to Turkana. One of the hunters offered to lead us on through the marsh and put us on the right track. As we left Laroi mentioned that we had found a crocodile, and although I speak neither Turkana nor Shangalla I understood their innocent replies perfectly.

"Gosh!" they said. "Really? How about that? Is it dead?"

Our guide pointed vaguely north from the edge of the marsh and waved goodbye after a final appeal for tobacco. We followed the direction through miles of thorny scrub both tedious and painful, but relieved by the sight of many chestnut gerenuks with their long maidenly necks and fluent legs. Eventually we came out on to an open, stony plain and far across it I could see our white jerry cans bobbing along on Lokarangan's back.

The heat was well out of the day as we climbed up a bone-dry wadi into an area of coarse red sandstone ridges, and crossed crest after crest looking wearily north for signs of habitation. Distances appear to increase at the end of the walking day, but we had done nearly 20 miles and it seemed that the darkness would fall to catch us without water. About half an hour after sunset I reached the top of a steep wadi side and found myself on a sandy plateau of short bushes and tussocky grass. Smoke rose from a manyatta just ahead, and I could see spears at the entrances of several huts pointing to the emerging stars.

A neat shed of corrugated iron stood incongruously on the skyline beneath the spider vanes and the pylon of a water pump, and beside them was a water tank and a standpipe. Hushed grey-blue haze rose from the bush down below, a dark three-mile-wide strip wrung from the sandstone upland. Thirty miles over in the grainy twilight stood the volcanic nipple of Lapurr on a black breast of hills. We had reached Ileret, and between us and Lapurr lay the uncertain lands of the Omo delta.

8

I LEANT AGAINST my stick, feeling good, while Laroi and the others came panting up the hillside. A younger man than I, of similar build but beardless and more graceful, approached on bare feet. He wore a folded sheet about his loins and he led us to his manyatta.

"Who is this guy?" I asked, for hardly a word had been spoken.

"His name it is Loolim, means a shadow in their language," said Greg.

"Yes, but why are we going with him?" I insisted.

"Just we rest in his manyatta. He said he wants we go to his place."

"But he doesn't know who we are or anything."

"No," said Greg, "he don't know. Just follow him."

I knew that I was 36° 15′ east of a point in the London borough of Greenwich, and 4° 19′ north of the equator. Where I was peoplewise I had no idea. I did not much care. Things might be explained later. Loolim pulled aside a spiky branch and we passed through the thorn perimeter and into his compound. We unloaded on the dung-bespattered ground between two of four huts. Facing us were three bristly enclosures heaving with livestock. The goats in one were being milked and were restless, but the cattle and donkeys in the others hardly stirred as Lobrolei, Komote and Lokarangan were driven in for the night. We stacked the gear against a hut under the close scrutiny of Loolim's family. Some of the smaller things, like the spoon and my washing kit, fell off the pile and slipped through the domed side of the hut. A skinny lad crawled out and put them back.

I rummaged through the stuff for a towel and the Daz and sauntered over to the standpipe with some sweaty clothes and an orphan, smiling little tragedy called Ali. He soaped and I rubbed, rinsed and wrung out to dry. We were both pretty clean ourselves after that and I felt most refreshed. Ali told me all the important things about Ileret. There was a police post about two miles away and beyond that, down by the lake, was a duka and a fish store where you could get posho and sweets. A Protestant mission had sunk the bore and built the pump and an American flew in each week or so to hold a service. A group of five catechists kept the rudimentary school and the Catholic church near the police post. Ali did not think that there were more than 30 manyattas in the area, or about 500 people. He himself was ten and spoke very attractive English.

Our tea had been monotonously black since Allia Bay and until our re-supply of sugar at Koobi Fora it had become less and less sweet. The tea Greg had prepared was creamy sweet and steaming and I savoured it to the full, stretched out and clean on the tarpaulin, with a cigarette and all right with the world.

The sick parade marched on. About four adult women and three men, a smattering of kids at the scampering age but already in charge of babies, and one old crone moved aside as Loolim's father emerged from the hut on our immediate left. It seems to be a general rule among East African pastoralists that from the ascetic heights of moranship—of fierce bachelorhood where a diet of blood and pride feed the warrior who disdains tobacco and ignores alcohol in heady pursuit of cattle and glory—from these arrogant years the moran turned elder descends the slippery path to fatherhood and even grandfatherhood, indulging himself in all manner of sin, avariciousness and gluttony being the least, until premature senility completely obliterates the once frightful youth. So it was with the father of Loolim, a man of over six feet four, whose final nine or ten inches seemed to contain little but noise and spittle. Esetiel, a long streak of all that horrid old men can be, well into his seventh age and loving every minute of it. He crawled out and uncurled before me, shaking his stool in mock salute before sitting. His dribbling lower lip was handsomely plugged with ivory and his hair grown grey and wild was tied about with a dirty cotton headcloth. A titter ran through the family and I sensed that Esetiel was held in no great esteem.

From his wooden stool the old man established a long wail of complaint. There was no tobacco to be had in Ileret. Did I have any? Why not? Running out of tobacco was dangerous.

Everyone had bad heads and their insides would rot. Look at my eyes. Are they not in terrible pain? Ah, my head is so painful. No supplies had come through from Marsabit for some time because of the appalling state of the track.

Besides its narcotic properties, tobacco is a medium of social intercourse. A pinch given here and there as a mark of courtesy and respect establishes a friendly atmosphere. Our own lack of it would be a problem, for it was the one thing which would certainly ease our way through Ethiopia, far more useful than money or even bullets. All I had were 'Sportsman' tipped cigarettes and I gave Esetiel a few. He was unfamiliar with burnt tobacco and smoked like a schoolgirl. It made him cough and so I split a couple and gave him the tobacco to chew. He thought that was pretty good, and spat appreciatively, his eyes following the struggle of a goat his elder son had selected and dragged from the enclosure.

Loolim killed the goat and his wife caught the blood throbbing out in a gourd. Out past the firelight and the sick, two boys grunted through the butchery in the darkness. A girl sat near the flames wrapped and shivering with a fever, and some others had colds and heavy chests. They said the rains brought this kind of sickness. I always tried to give out my medicines with a certain formality, or even ceremony. This stopped them being wolfed in one go, and a little mystery added to the hope value of an insufficiently protracted course of most drugs. Instead of giving someone nine Aspirin, for example, and saying "Here, take three of these a day for three days," I would give Greg one and mime the sunrise. He would translate and help the act along, and then pass the sunrise pill over. Next the mid-day, then the evening pill and so on.

Lightning flickered out in the desert and a few drops of rain fell, but the cloud soon dispersed and the children's lovely voices, muted and slightly husky, drifted over from an expectant circle by the cooking fire. A lonely bleat for mother's soft answer came from the inky goat run, and over left wooden cow bells sounded, like clogs on cobbled streets, as the cattle shifted in the smoke. Dried dung was piled in smouldering heaps inside the pens to keep mosquitoes away, but it was the night wind that discouraged them most. Loolim's wife, Tuode, knelt with the other women beside Laroi. He was in his element, revelling in an attentive and unsophisticated audience as he poured out and expanded his sufferings of the last eleven days.

"Oh, yes," said Laroi, "a lot of lion and many hyena," and he growled, menacingly. Before we left Loyangalani I had bought several extra pairs of sandals on Greg's advice to trade for goats up here. I would have been better advised to bring tobacco, but after some considerable discussion as to whose was whose and a lot of searching down scarcely opened sacks with the torch, I found a pair to fit Loolim and presented them. He adjusted the straps with a stone, a knife and his teeth, and seemed very pleased.

Laroi's continued narrative was interrupted in full flow by the arrival of the goat, cooked and dismembered on a sack. The giggling kids fell silent as they were given meat, crunching bones and sucking marrow out beyond the firelight. Esetiel came staggering out of his hut again to greet me as I ate. I supposed this to be the noisy old decrepit's *maître d'hôtel* act, just checking if the food was up to standard. He ate nothing but re-entered the hut, his belches and groans gleefully imitated by the women and children as he eased himself back to sleep. Loolim and the boys smiled despite themselves and tried to hide their laughter behind bowls of goat soup. Slowly the family dispersed to sleep, except Loolim who checked all the fences and talked quietly to the young boys sleeping amongst the goats where, they believed, there were fewer mosquitoes. My head fell back on a pillow of dry rice and beans, the old man's delirious snoring in my sleepy ears.

Inspector Kariithi of the Kenya police sat in his bare office. He looked at me. 'Cool Dude,' I thought. We had walked down from the manyatta early that morning and passed through the tattered perimeter wire while the day was still cool. It was a difficult moment for me. Although I had a valid tourist visa for Ethiopia, I knew that the Kenya police could stop me and send me back to a higher authority in Marsabit, or even back to Nairobi, for any number of reasons. Nothing like a few stamps and heavy documents to get you through remote bureaux, but I had none. The inspector looked at my maps and did not say much. He was a thin, finely drawn man of deliberate speech. He checked my passport and had tea made on his verandah overlooking the lake. He had beautiful hands and brooding eyes and most exquisite manners. An altogether pleasing presence to be in, whatever he had to say. We chatted and discovered mutual interests, including donkeys.

"These Turkanas, they have a lot of donkeys," he said. "Shangallas not so many but Turks—oh so many."

"Yes, I have three myself," I said.

"Three? These men, they have herds, hundreds. They don't use them. The donkeys only eat food and live free. Goats they eat. Camels and cattle are good for presents and to make a man rich. But donkeys. What's the use of them? They are useless. I hate them. Come and see my trees."

He led the way out into the compound to where a couple of prisoners were carrying water from a standpipe to the trees planted in attractive positions between the lines.

"Today is Saturday. Tomorrow after church you are going to. . . ?" I nodded vehemently.

"Oh yes, I meant to ask you what time the service was."

"Nine o'clock. Afterwards you come here and I'll tell you about the trees. Except the dates I tell you now. Here are dates. I love them. Hate donkeys but love dates." During his two years at Ileret, the inspector had carefully tended a couple of dozen date palms in the compound, the budding fruits of which he had tied in hessian to prevent thefts before the fruit ripened.

"Also you need a guide. I will try for you. Good morning."

He had hardly mentioned my journey, but there seemed no question of stopping us. His calm manner and quiet dignity were quite a treat as I had come mentally prepared for the long wrangles or at very least the polite indifference which we had faced in Allia Bay and Koobi Fora.

Just below the sandy bluff on which the police post was built lay Ileret city, a motley collection of rude shelters which housed the seasonally variable population. Laroi was down there in deep conversation with the headman, a large Shangalla called Rantale. Laroi was after pack skins and ropes to replace our worn-out stuff, and he wanted goats as well. Since we were resting for two or three days I decided to dry two goats, to provide enough meat for contingencies which might arise over the border. Idling between the 40 or so huts reminded me of the rubbish dump I had had the privilege of clearing after a NATO exercise near Trondheim in Norway. Mounds of empty compo ration boxes stood on the heather among the delicate birches. No heather here but blistering sand and boxes used to roof the huts, hand-me-downs from the police above. His business with Rantale finished, Laroi paid social calls. He took me for elevenses to the hut of a Samburu woman of his tribal section called Ngerei. Her husband was a local-authority policeman away east in Moyale.

I bent my sun-coated back in through the low opening. Smoke from a small fire by the door had turned everything a dark tar brown and the bare earth was laid with stiff goat skins which Ngerei rearranged for Laroi and me. She was giving suck to her youngest child, but was obviously pleased to see Laroi. I held the baby while she prepared tea in opaque glasses. Two other women crawled in, and disturbed the flies, but they took the baby back, much to my relief. Laroi stretched himself out to sleep and the women chatted about their shambas and the millet crop which was going to be a good one. They had just returned from the cultivations and their breasts glistened where flecks of sunlight pierced the thin hut frame and dappled the smoky gloom. I tried to ignore my increased heart beat and the hollow feeling in my abdomen, but my eyes wandered to the point of ill manners. I lit a cigarette and studied the hut to distract myself.

Poles like bean sticks had been planted in a circle and bent inwards then lashed together to form the frame of a dome about eight feet across and five feet high. Limited standing room for children and dwarfs only. Thorns, sticks and grass were woven into the frame providing a certain privacy. Cow hides were tied down over the top half of the hut to keep off the scanty rain. A variation on the compo-box theme were flattened kerosene cans which I had seen on some huts, but this one was strictly traditional. We had passed old manyattas on the journey which had stood for nine or ten seasons whose skeletons still held firm, where corrugated iron would have long since been battered to death. The huts are very easy to erect and disassemble and the frames can be used over again. This hut was lined inside with greasy old donkey panniers of the kind Laroi had tried to make and a tiny kid crouched behind one, panting in the heat. A few dark lumps of dried meat were wedged among the twigs above our heads. The buzzing flies were so loud that they impeded conversation, and many of them died, hot, wet and lonely in my tea. I had to get outside.

I left Laroi spinning a yarn to the laughing women and went in search of Greg. I found him with two of the catechists, who happened to have been at school with him in Marsabit. As we spoke, Rantale, the chief, came to us with a pigeon-chested Somali youth with shifty eyes and a foxy face. He was the boy for us, Rantale informed me, waxing eloquent on the boy's uncanny sense of direction in the bush, and on the many solo journeys he had undertaken through the Omo delta. Gregory and the catechists interrogated the lad who wilted under the pressure. After five minutes or so Greg turned to me and surprised me by saying that the chap was very good.

"Good, Steebon," he said, "this man very good. He can take us to the border."

"Great," I said, "when did he last do the journey? How many days does he reckon it will take?"

"In 1971 he passed through to Todenyang, but now he just take us to the border. About two hours."

"Amazing," I muttered. "Thank him very much but I can get to the border myself. I can almost see it from here. We need a guide for all the way."

"OK, we will get it."

The Somali went off smiling, he took his rejection in good part. Greg worked on the principle that something was always better than nothing, but we needed to get a little beyond the border. Rantale did not seem unhappy either, and said that he would still help us to buy the goats. He escorted us down to a wooden cattle crush where several herds had been brought into the shade for the morning milking. We sat on the rails like rodeo hands and I eventually bought two rather sick looking males. Rantale explained that the big goats were away in the bush, leaving only the milk herd with a few of the weaker brethren destined for the chop. Feeling like the fourth shepherd in a nativity play I walked the two miles back to Loolim's manyatta with a goat over my shoulder and I fell down a few times on the way. The goat expressed its feelings all down my neck and I was grateful when the water pump came in sight.

Laroi took charge of the livestock and I went off to wash and rest through a fly-ridden afternoon.

There was only one duka at Ileret, and it lay three miles away on the lake shore. Greg and I took our empty food bags down there in the evening to see what we could buy. A babbling mob of women spilt out of the breeze-block store as we approached and the wooden door slammed shut. The women sat in the dusk hurling abuse through the cracks. They gave suck to their babies and consolidated the settling dust of the day with long streams of spit to the left and right. They were mightily disgruntled because as Greg explained, there was no tobacco to be had and they suspected the shopkeepers of hoarding it. They complained of headaches and fever and mimed fainting spells and weak legs as they turned to me and begged for medicine.

"Dawa, dawa, give us dawa. Our heads are light. We cannot sleep and we do not take food. You are a white man. Give us medicine and tobacco." It was worse than being the manager of a busy launderette with no washing powder. I turned the bags inside out and shook them dramatically.

"We are poor. We have nothing, but we have far to go." Corny stuff, but at that moment the duka re-opened and they all rushed back inside. Fisticuffs broke out when two young ones got stuck in the doorway. Greg and I and the other men there stood well back, feeling a little sorry for the two chaps serving inside. A tall, distinguished-looking man strode up, his greying hair neatly combed back over his forehead and his olive-green safari jacket pressed to a knife edge. He barked out something authoritative and the scuffles instantly ceased. A line of humbled women shuffled past and the man motioned me into the shop.

"I am Laurienne ex-army," he declared. "I to be your guide." His effort with the angry ladies was so impressive that I hired him on the spot. He had been over the delta many times and seemed just the sort of chap we needed. He frowned when he heard that we had no tobacco but suggested that we might get by with posho and sugar, which the bush Shangallas also regarded as luxuries. We filled our bags with maize meal and sugar, but there was little else to buy. I got a kilo of tea in small packets and ten cans of baked beans, an unexpected treat. The store had one other surprise, a case of tinned orange juice and Greg, Laurienne and I demolished a tin each outside in the evening air. It was superb.

On the way back up the hill with the food Laurienne went over the route ahead. He reckoned that it would take about ten days to reach Todenyang, the first Kenyan settlement south of the western border. Studying the maps I had thought four days would be ample. I had agreed to pay a daily rate, and the longer we took the more money he stood to make. A tiny mouse of suspicion ran through my head.

"OK, Laurienne," I said. "We walk every day, I think about four days. I will pay you for eight days so you can return, but you don't get the money until Todenyang. If it takes two weeks you still only get eight days' money."

The speed with which he accepted the offer accelerated the mouse to a rat, but, after all, I thought, he was resolute with the women and no one could blame him for trying it on with an unknowing white man. He had two annoying habits though, which would have precluded him from the permanent staff anyway. One was his constant and deferential reference to me as "Bawana Satibon". He said it with the ingratiating tones of a self-important butler. I usually turned out in underpants and plimsolls and so I felt very under-dressed to be a Bwana. The other thing was the way he combed his hair, and the frequency with which he did it. At every opportunity out would come his comb to be run through the well-loved thatch ironed straight back over his forehead, followed up with a vain caress and a pat from the other hand. All a bit odd from a man of about 45 and over six-foot-three-inches tall. I put it down to his army background.

That night I drank my first bowl of blood. It had been brought over from the next manyatta and was slightly congealed, but Orip, a daughter of the house, had kept it for me. She mixed in a little milk and offered it to me with a grin. I sealed off my sensibilities and shut my eyes. It slid down my throat in a rush and I was wiping my beard, smiling and saying how good it was. I did not mind it at all really, but I did find the soup Orip had made pretty nauseating. Pieces of offal were cut and boiled together with the goat's chopped but unwashed stomach. The result was a hot green morass with oily blobs floating in the steam. Stomachless soup was fine for me but like chips without vinegar for the Shangalla. I stuck to tea and milk.

Esetiel sat with us in the first hours of night and asked about England. With Gregory's help I tried to describe to him a land where nearly everyone lives in a town but where there is no wild bush. He found this a strange paradox. I told him about my home and the farm but he was not very impressed by our herd of only 60 cows. He did not believe that it was possible for a cow to yield as much milk as ours did, and rather than plod on with lots of "amazing but true" facts about England I steered the conversation round to his family.

He had two wives. The senior, Walame, was an ugly old squaw who sat outside her hut all day mumbling. By her he had four sons: Natiekwaan, a boy of 16; Loolim, just emerged from moranhood with his first wife; and two older boys, Toros and Loki, who were married and living away in the bush with their wives and small herds. Esetiel's other wife, Asale, was much younger and lived in a manyatta about eight miles away across the Nangole river. She had about four small children, Esetiel was not exactly sure of the number. I asked him why his eldest boys lived away.

"Because of the raids and the grazing. This is how we do. The sons take the big goats out to the bush. Just here are only ones to give milk for our food. Also the cattles if there are many we divide it and take it far away for the good grazings and the no raiders. Just if I need some cows then I send for it with Natiekwaan, he run to bring me the animals." Esetiel was describing a complex system of management in simple terms, but I was beginning to see the animals around me not just as a food supply but also as the currency in which one man's relationship to another was expressed. I asked Esetiel what happened if one of his sons lost some cattle or killed a goat.

"I would know," he said.

"How?" I asked.

"Just I got to look and I see it has gone." Gregory had told me before that Turkana herdsmen do not count their livestock by number but merely by looking over the herds they can see if even one goat in 200 is gone. As a man grows older and his herds increase and divide, so his accounting becomes more complicated and a system of sub-contracted management evolves whereby, for example, a son in charge of a quarter of the family herds in turn gives out animals into the care of his children and relatives. I did not understand how sons became owners of cattle in their own right.

"When I die then all the animals go to some other people," Esetiel explained. I never did discover to whom or in what proportion, but he went on, "and in the life a man and womans too get animals. When child is born or if he do a good something he get animals. When she is married the woman gets donkeys and goats. But the best way of getting cows for young man to start his own herd is by raiding. If not his father can give some. And the old men they mostly get cattle from their sons and from husbands of their daughters. In a herd a man should know which cows are his and which are ones of his father, or of his brother. He should know every cow like the European mans know every star. And the man who knows the pastures before other men, the man with sons who keep off the leopard, with the wife to stay with him for many children, with the friends and good relatives to stop raiders and the guns to get cattle, he a good man. But some men get sick, the cattle stolen and the bush dry. Then he die and his family finish. That is how it is!"

Esenyon and Gregory walked back to Ileret with Loolim to dance in the black night, but Laroi and I slept with the flies. And in the morning the goats were let out and stormed over us, a bleating, urinating stampede through our gear with stupid cold eyes only for the dewy bush. The cattle passed above the early goat-stirred dust and the willowy boys went too, their thin blankets wrapped in flimsy and individual fashion and held close by a warm hand inside. The other, cold, hand grasped a stick or spear and the mouth chewed slowly on a frayed twig to rid white teeth of soft rind come in the night. The family herds were moving into another dawn.

Greg and I went to church at nine o'clock. About 40 people attended, over half of them children, and only one adult man, an old Shangalla who sat on the top of the pews watching intently. The service was taken by Greg's one-eyed classmate who glared the fidgeting children into silence. After church I went to tea with Inspector Kariithi. We walked very slowly up the hill to his house with a grubby child clutching each of our index fingers. We tarried awhile among his trees while he described the planting and the struggle each one had had through repeated droughts and floods. He made tea and compo-biscuit sandwiches while the kids bounced on his armchair. He brought the old Second World War map of the area with the refreshments and we studied it together, amused by some of the cryptic little warnings the surveyors had written about the terrain. We found a "Puckoon ridge", lots of "Motorable with difficulties" and several "liable to floods".

"I like maps," said the inspector. "No need of books if there are maps."

"I like them too," I said, and I do.

Laurienne turned up. He wanted a letter to say that he was on an official mission which he could present to the Ethiopian authorities.

"Laurienne," said the inspector. "The best thing for you to do is to take them round the border post at Kalam. You know the police there keep everyone delayed while checking the visa, so the wise road is not to go there at all." Kalam was about 20 miles up the Omo river from the lake and to avoid it we would have to cut across the thick bush of the delta.

"OK," said Laurienne, pulling out his comb. "OK. But this not correct procedure."

Oh God! I thought, I've recruited my first natural bureaucrat.

We bought the rope and skins we needed from women in the settlement and began a hot walk back up the hill, when a very angry old lady came panting after us and snatched one of the skins away with shrill abuse. Apparently her daughter, a little short of cash, had sold it without her permission. We got the money back and with another skin returned to Loolim's manyatta. There was a good rain storm at mid-day which cleared the air and relieved the humidity. The lake turned muddy brown, then, as the rain cleared, it went blue. The Lapurr range over the water looked so near one could almost touch it, and I could see a low line of hills on the northeastern horizon, well inside Ethiopia. I took shelter in Tuode's hut, with Laroi and all the flies for miles around. I swear they were tame. I felt like Gulliver in a Lilliputian riot. My brothel creepers had dried out the wrong shape and the result was a wriggling blister on my left big toe. I abandoned them for light gym shoes with no socks, a perfectly satisfactory arrangement which lasted for the rest of the journey.

Esenyon had been detailed off to look after our goat meat during the morning and after the rain I went to see how he was. About a third of the meat was missing and the severed heads lay under the tree with their tongues hanging out and their brains still in. Esenyon was asleep. Having had our first goat ruined by rain, I was annoyed at the prospect of meatless days ahead. A voluble and exceedingly angry Laroi woke Esenyon and he emerged from his wet sheet like an owl to face summary trial. He had not a clue where the meat was except to show us a pot in which he had crammed the offal for supper. He had forgotten about splitting and drying the heads. I gave him a stern look and a warning but there was absolutely no malice in the man and I felt ashamed of my original suspicion that he had stolen the meat. We built a good fire to roast and dry what was left.

That night we all went down to the dance. Loolim and his young brother Natiekwaan set off with us walking rapidly down the dark path to Ileret. We reached the outskirts of the black but still murmuring village, but nobody was dancing. Loolim and his brother began to sing, a haunting song of starlit praise to their cattle. Esenyon and Gregory picked up the rhythm with their bodies, casually expressing a freedom we have forgotten to even miss.

People gradually drifted over from the huts to join us. A chorus rose and fell behind one solo voice after another and when twenty people were there Loolim stopped singing. He and his brother began to stamp out a rhythm on the ground, slowly increasing the tempo until they were jumping with both feet off the ground, higher and higher, coming down together with a shock and a "Hooo!" from the stomach. Two more lithe jumpers took over as Loolim tired, urged on by stamping feet and clapping hands. Esenyon and Gregory jumped together, complete strangers to the company but equal in this physical celebration of joy. I had a quiet go myself. Old men came out and sat on the edge of the circle, watching and occasionally shouting out comments at poor performances.

The girls began to move, dancing against the men, their shoulders draped in long white shawls. Soon the whole crowd was leaping against itself, laughing, clapping and singing, the girls' shrill cries twining like tendrils about the solid, atavistic grunts from the warriors' bellies. After a couple of hours the dance died fast, and we walked back like exhausted wraiths over the colourless sand. Before we slept Laroi turned to me.

"This Esenyon. He is a good man. Very polite and work hard. Now he do wrong thing with meat, but not bad. I ask can you forgive this man?"

I had already dismissed the incident but thought it odd that Laroi, who seemed most angry that afternoon, should think that I held a grudge. Travelling in disharmony clouds the mind, and may eventually spoil the chorus which supports the individual voice.

9

THE BOMA THORNS jumped sharply black against the rich dawn sky, sweet light to lift a body from fly-ridden sleep. I staggered over to the standpipe for a wash and had just filled my mouth with peppermint toothpaste when Laurienne strolled up, empty-handed. My heart sank as I had expected him to come with at least a few things for the journey. Had he changed his mind?

"No, of course not, Bawana Satibon," he said. I swilled out my mouth and spat. Looking up I saw his wife sweating up the hill with a large bundle on her head. It was Laurienne's load. I normally give a small advance to guides to give to their families, and in order to pay Laurienne I asked him to find change for a 100/- note. Carrying enough small change in the bush is always a problem.

"But 100/- is enough, Bawana Satibon," he said. A con man too, I thought, and told him to forget the advance.

"Hokay. Hapana mbaya. It is not bad," he said smiling. He knew that I knew.

Loolim's wife, Tuode, had wanted to come with us as far as her mother's manyatta, but changed her mind at the last minute. Instead Laurienne's five-year-old daughter Edekoi came along, a tiny figure scuttling down the path, clutching an empty tin of Bimbo cooking fat. The cornea of her right eye was clouded and she had been partially blind for a year, but her father had done nothing about it except to have her thighs nicked in the traditional manner of cure, a double row of cicatrix running from hip to knee on both legs. His lack of initiative in getting her to hospital annoyed me, and he agreed to bring her to the mission hospital at Lokitaung instead of leaving her with her mother in the delta. Passing the police post I said goodbye to the inspector, then hurried on to catch the others.

Esenyon led the donkeys north among white flowers and low trees full of twittering birds and heavy with the parasitic vine

Cissus quadrangularis, a swaying green crown of fleshy, quadrangular arms, with ivy-shaped leaves and red berry fruits. The vine is commonly associated with species of acacia and *grewia* in dry bush country where it usually grows without producing leaves. Where there are no trees to embrace, *Cissus* can form a pendant mat, hanging down over cliffs and rock faces. The Turkana call it Egis and use an infusion of the pounded stems in water to cure calves of diarrhoea.

Termite mounds appeared and became a regular feature of the endless meadow land through which we walked with crested larks singing at our feet. They hovered tantalizingly close in shrill song then made off behind the slender chimneys and gaunt cones of earth thrown up by the mound-building termites. The colonies live in barrel-shaped piles beneath tall ventilating chimneys where they tend their fungus gardens and their queen, and store the food brought in by foragers from the outside. Waist-high squadrons of black *Brachythemis leucostictas* patrolled the damper patches of the plain. These small dragon flies have dark bands across their otherwise transparent wings which vibrate so fast that each body appears to be a wingless zeppelin escorted by two black outriders.

We drew nearer to the water and left the flowers for a band of whiskered white-green grass like ripening barley on the shore, rustled by a hungry young wind from the lake. The mountains on the far side were rugged in full daylight and lightly iced by flimsy cloud low in the blue arc which turned over us from the west and tucked down into the rising haze away in the eastern scrub. Below it all the full lake lay, a bowl of grey-brown waves and limited sparkles, with now and then a touch of blood and a wider reddish tinge. A Shangalla and three donkeys drew near, passed and went on south in silence with two loaded wives. They were moving to safer ground in Kenya with the skins and gourds balanced on the women and the spear and stool with the man. There were no children but two dogs, which remained for a while in the dry bed of the Sabare river, digging out the putrid remains of an oryx.

We halted at mid-day beside another dry river, just short of the border. A handful of Shangalla morans hung about in aloof curiosity, but the flies took a more personal interest in us and there was little rest. Four women approached us with milk for sale, and so we had good tea. They were disappointed that I had no tobacco, and soon went away. The young men drifted back to their cattle and we went on for a couple of hours in the late afternoon. The border markers were white concrete triangles, and our path lay about 500 yards from the nearest one. Greg took a photograph of us all posing unreasonably on the green plain and then we were into the mysterious land, walking beside a pea-grey sea in the spangly afternoon. Distant herds were spread to the horizon attended by boys and men who seemed not to have spears.

"Why don't they have spears?" I asked.

Laurienne looked down at me. "Because, Bawana Satibon, they all got guns. Some they carry, some they leave in the manyatta but you see if bad thing happen they get the gun at all times."

I walked hand in hand with Edekoi for the rest of the afternoon. She kept up with us manfully but did tend to fall behind after a while. Laurienne occasionally called back to her and she would break into a silent trot. She had no sandals and every so often she stopped to remove a thorn or burr from her tiny feet. Her hair and shoulders had been smeared with fat and ochre-coloured clay for the journey and her leather apron was decorated with shells and beads. I was sure no one would shoot me strolling along innocently with a little girl as sweet as her.

Dead acacia trees stood out in the lake, some about a mile from the flooded shore. I estimated our position by taking bearings from Lapurr peak, because the map was so inaccurate, having been drawn in drier times. About five miles north of the border Laurienne stripped off and walked into the lake for a wash. We quickly followed suit and found to our delight that the water was fresh, probably a lagoon or a marsh of rain water.

Three or four hundred yards inland, beyond a belt of tall acacias, fires were showing against the darkening land. We arrived to a handsome welcome by the manyatta headman, Asupaiteea, meaning a bull following female cows, translated, presumably, as Randy. Immediately they had been unloaded the donkeys doubled off to interview the local herds and could not be found, but I bowed to the general consensus that they would be easily recovered in the morning. We were invited to sleep between the huts and so we moved the kit inside the fence and brewed tea, quite a lot of it, as Asupaiteea's people loved sugar. Edekoi was taken into a hut by the women and made a fuss of and Laurienne went off to greet his relatives. The headman stayed to talk with me, and his opening gambit was to ask if I knew Bwana someone who had been the district officer here in colonial times. I stared into the fire and remembered a Fulani village clinging to a desolate, rocky hill on the border between Nigeria and the Cameroons. Up there in the cold hills a pastoralist like Asupaiteea had once asked me the same thing.

"You know this man?" he had asked. "He was British. You are British? True British? Then welcome." It is worth recording the esteem in which these district officers were generally held, not for their power or riches, not even for the imperial might which they represented, but for their fairness, and incorruptibility and their sense of justice. They left behind a reputation which one feels obliged to live up to, the light of which is sometimes humbling. I always try to increase the capital of goodwill and trust that the old DOs left, for it is all too easy to draw on the account, nibbling away at it until, one day, there will be nothing left.

"No," I told Asupaiteea, "I do not know him."

I held a sick parade and doled out quantities of Aspirin and malaria pills. There were no dispensaries east of the Omo river I was told, no schools, no dukas, no nothing. I asked what services the Ethiopian government did provide.

"None," the men said. "And what taxes do you pay?" I asked.

"None," they said. "And what of raiding, who protects you?"

"Ah," they said, "we raid, but no one protects us except if we go to Kenya."

An old woman knelt in the firelight. She began to sing. Everyone fell quiet and her voice was clear in the free night air. A thin man of enormous grace eased himself like a flamingo into the firelight. He wove a reply as gentle as bird song to his mother's chant. She was asking him when he would bring cattle home from a raid. When would he kill the enemies?

"Soon, Mother," he sang, "soon. But remember the raids I have been on. Remember the cattle I have taken and the food I have brought you." Other men nodded, slender and deadly in repose. The beautiful duet continued for only a few moments more, the mother's sad face against the shy smiles and recalling eyes of the son. Moments which touch the soul are always short but they echo pleasantly afterwards.

The rhythmic swishing of milk in a swinging gourd broke the thin silence of dawn. A child was making butter and we could hear it even across the stones where Laroi and I were looking for the donkeys. They were corralled with about a hundred others packed tight inside a prickly fence, and I invited Laroi, who had been so confident the night before, to cut ours from the herd. Most of the camels and donkeys I had seen were branded in some way, either by fire or a knife. Ours had had their right ears docked, except Lokarangan who had obscure marks on his rump. The Shangalla donkeys had also had the tips of their ears clipped, some right, some left and some both. Laroi doubled around the boma and stirred them up a little. He passed in amongst them like a prophet but the divinity was not with him. The sky lost its chocolate box colours soon after sunrise, and Laroi began to curse lightly. Bad thoughts snaked through my head, but then Laroi found Komote and allayed them. I hung on to his head rope and called Lobrolei's name, and like a magnet pulling iron splinters, he came out of the throng with a smiling Laroi. I stopped frowning.

"Great," I said, "we just need little Lokarangan." He was not there. We searched again, releasing the penned donkeys one by one. The sun was fully up and I feared that all the tea was drunk. I was at the "God-dammit-where's-that-bloody-animal" stage and Laroi was fookin' away softly. We decided to take the senior pair to Esenyon and Greg for loading, then to make further enquiries. As we walked over Laroi glanced west and there was Lokarangan standing completely in the open with his head rope caught on a shrub. My relief was great. His was too as he was half-suffocated and lucky not to have been killed by a hyena during the night.

There were cattle everywhere that morning. We were moving north, skirting the flooded delta and every mile or so we crossed a dry river bed. Laurienne would then tick the name off and recite those which lay ahead. He suggested resting at ten o'clock under a shady tree, which annoyed Gregory as it more or less confirmed his suspicions that Laurienne was going to try and spin the journey out. We carried on. Moran would join us for a while, to chat or simply stare and then drift off. The in thing seemed to be a strip of fluorescent orange material along the edge of your blanket, which is all that most men wore, and even then they were naked with a blanket rather than naked but for one.

The lake still shimmered in the west but the shoreline was turning and by mid-day we had reached the north-eastern tip. The countryside was park-like where we rested under a tall and shady acacia, watching the herds of cattle being brought down to drink. A very skinny youth had followed us in to rest and sat a little bit apart. He wanted medicine for his lungs and he was coughing up blood. I wondered if he had TB. His name was Natiant and he told us that the Ethiopian border post at Kalam was no more.

"All the soldiers gone," he said, "no police there now!" I wondered if this was because of the Somali war. "No hospital now," he continued. "White men run away."

"What white men?" I asked.

"Kalam men with the ferry," he said.

I was confused by all the rumours we had heard about irrigation projects and ferries and police who came and went, and I decided to just wait and see. Greg and Laroi had been instilling into Laurienne the wisdom of avoiding the post at Kalam, and he had agreed to cross the river south of the town. He had not really helped us with the chores, but seemed pretty free with his advice. I had a word with him, which improved matters but he was definitely an old soldier, a depot hero.

We had a bag of white flour which Greg turned into chappatis, rolled out on the jerry can with a biro. The hot flour and fat was delicious. A few children had congregated under our tree, to watch this curious man who smoked tobacco with hair on his legs. A dusty hand stole gently down my shins and I looked round into four pairs of shy brown eyes. It often happened that knee-level people, who all like furry things, were drawn to stroke my thin but hairy legs. I used to caress a bedraggled bit of rabbit fur myself as a child but African children are less inhibited than we. They tend not to express gratitude formally, but the joy and pleasure on the face of a small Shangalla with a boiled sweet stuck in its cheek is worth a million hollow thank-yous. We normally had a sweet at mid-day, waiting for the food to cook, but I always carried a few in my pockets for people on the way. Laurienne had sent little Edekoi down to the lake for water. She tottered back like a doll, an exact miniature of an adult and when she slept it was with the abandon of a toy left forgotten on the nursery floor.

A rolling herd came dripping from the lake as Edekoi returned. One of the cattle men strolled over to the tree with his gun. He was quite proud to show it to me, although when I opened the breech and saw the dirt inside it was evident that he rarely used or cleaned it. The parts were dry and worn with age and the round-nosed bullets lay tarnished in a leather pouch. I was surprised that the weapon looked so obsolete, but Greg told me that these men were all dead-eye shots none the less. I did not believe it and asked the rifleman for a demonstration, which invitation he declined on the grounds that bullets were expensive. The water Edekoi had brought was brackish but not salty like the lake. It was from the great sheet of flood water we had skirted called the Ado Nagul, the place of many oases. Normally the Shangallas make shambas and grow pumpkins and millet in the area, but they had lost their farms to the lake this year.

The donkeys were as stupefied as I by the prospect of a hot walk on a full stomach, because from now on there was no lake nor any open water in which to stand and cool off. We were about twenty miles inside Ethiopia and at last had turned to walk westwards towards the Omo river. We left the Ado Nagul soon after three o'clock, the dull aspect of the country being relieved by many steep-sided luggas which we had to cross. The bush was sparse except for clusters of tall doum palms and acacias along the rivers, and there was little game but for small scurrying mammals of the underbrush like mongooses and ground squirrels. Lovely red-and-green bee eaters and irridescent starlings flew among the riverside trees while eccentric hornbills cackled between bushes in the drier areas. They have a curious dipping flight as if perpetually correcting a nose dive and an insane piping cry to match.

That evening we came to the manyatta of Loote, a local chief and Laurienne's cousin. He was welcoming but disappointed that we had no tobacco. I tried to make up for it with medicines, dispensing first to the women and then to the few men who waited with dignity for the rabble of lesser beings to clear. Finally an old crone was carried out and laid down before me. Her face was wizened with sickness and pain and her time of dying was near. She could hardly speak and her husband reckoned that her liver had packed up. There was little that I could do except to give her a placebo of Aspirin in water, over which I squirted a little curry powder. She was about twenty years old.

"Why don't you take her to Ileret?" I asked. There was no dispensary nearer.

"It is in Kenya, it is far away and she is sick," they said.

"But you graze your cattle in Kenya, you raid all over the place and she will certainly die if you don't take her."

"Yes, she will die, but in Ileret there is no medicine." They were right. The dispensary at Ileret was empty and there was no doctor there anyway. The bundle of skin and bone was carried away.

"Couldn't you all get together, sell a few cows, and build a dispensary?" It was a stupid question. There is no open market for livestock in Gemmu Gofar province east of the Omo river. The Shangallas have no schools and no roads and no tradition of co-operation, for their nomadic existence breeds individuals and loose family groupings, with not even a regular cycle of planting and harvesting to follow. They are, moreover, only a small and insignificant group of backward nomads, far from Addis Ababa, the capital of an empire not noted for its benevolent treatment of peripheral groups. Dr Donaldson Smith, an American who travelled through south-eastern Abyssinia in 1894 and 1895 wrote a fairly crushing condemnation of the *ancien régime*, which has now been replaced by something more sinister.

There are moral considerations which should compel all the civilized people of the world to lend their support to the

crushing out of the Abyssinian power and to the substitution
of a humane government in place of Menelek's brutal rule.
Never have the evils of slavery shown themselves in a more
terrible light than that in which they are now manifesting
themselves in Abyssinia, nor could as cruel a government be
found in the world as that which is in store for the tribes
among whom I journeyed, if Menelek be not checked.

He was not checked, but there has been a popular revolution
since then. *Plus ça change.* As Arnold Weinholt Hodson, one of
his Britannic Majesty's consuls for Ethiopia, wrote of the
Borana province in 1925:

> As for the future of the province under the existing corrupt
> and inefficient administration, I content myself with quoting
> the following verse:
>
>> If seven maids with seven mops
>> Swept it for half a year,
>> "Do you suppose," the Walrus said,
>> "That they would get it clear?"
>> "I doubt it" said the Carpenter,
>> And shed a bitter tear.

Dusty Loote's feet described hopeless circles in the sand.
His skin was dry, like crinkly old leather. There could be few
resources to divert from the Ogaden, or from Eritrea where
festering sores were gnawing into the imperial body. Loote's
people had no voice in the towns anyway because the district
officer had been shot by soldiers the year before. At least, as
Loote said, they had stopped paying taxes as the dead official
had not been replaced.

"We should build," said Loote, "but we do not know. We
are helpless. We know only our cattle, not even enough each
other."

It was a bad night. I was stung on the arm by a scorpion, and
groping for the antihistamine tablets I saw an endless mass of
silent cattle in the torchlight, like ash-grey snowmen chewing
gum. Laroi said their silence was because of the hyenas, but I
reckoned that the mosquitoes had bitten out their tongues.

We had chappatis with our tea that morning and set off before the itching started. I had a string of bites under the waistband of my shorts and walked on in underpants. I only wore shorts again in company. Greg had taken over my hat and by now my skin was dark enough for me to stand in the shade and not be noticed, but I still showed up slightly at night. Laroi stuck to his ragged shorts in which he kept the matches and the cigarettes, with my penknife and a few sweets. Greg still wore the binoculars and carried the fishing rod and Esenyon had taken over the cooking fat. The donkeys carried everything else but their loads were very light. Worrisome lumps ran in clusters down their necks and flanks, their only relief coming with the penetrating dust of a thorough roll. The two animals following whoever was in the lead developed a graze-and-run technique by allowing the leader to get a little in advance while they ripped a quick snack of grass from passing clumps before jogging on to catch up, jolting and dislodging their loads in the process.

Young men going out with the cattle stopped to beg medicine while we were loading. They were most impressed with Laurienne's spear, a fearsome piece of blacksmithying about seven feet long, from Rendille armourers in Marsabit. It was passed to and fro in slim-boned hands, and balanced on thin fingers as cool as sleeping toads. Gleaming eyes and open smiles belied the bird-like twitterings of appreciation that the morans made, like doves discussing death.

Our westerly path continued a good ten miles north of the lake, and for the first part of the morning we crossed an area of relatively dense population. The bush was certainly well trampled by cattle and in many of the denser groves patches of the triffid-like *Calotropis procera* grew, a curious plant whose vernacular name of the Sodom Apple describes its extraordinary fruit. It grows on hollow stems up to ten feet high like the European hogweed, and the stems collapse with the same satisfying plop when you thwack them with a stick. There the resemblance ends. *Calotropis* produces little purple flowers which are pollinated by small ants. The ripe fruits grow into hollow green balloons about the size of small pineapples, but full of loose white fibres with the seed pods in the middle, borne away on the wind when the fruit is ripe. The fibre is used for stuffing pillows in some areas, and the fibrous green stems make reasonable rope, but otherwise the plant is rather a disappointment. It grows well in degraded scrub, particularly where the bush has been disturbed by cattle, and also in dry river beds where it indicates the presence of subterranean water. The roots have some obscure use in Turkana veterinary medicine, but no one seemed to know exactly what it was.

We had all picked up the Shangalla mode of greeting, the first part of which was a nasal braying "naa" to which the reply was "pya". You had to say it several times over, six repetitions seemed about average good manners. The "naa" and "pya" mode is also used in Turkana, but rarely, and Esenyon experimented happily with his new words, hailing dogs, cattle and women as we strolled on. There was little reaction to the caravan as it passed through each manyatta unless the white man was spotted, and then people would come to us, or wave us to them, follow, shout or stare. Quite a few children just screamed. I decided not to stop at each invitation because my supply of medicine was diminishing and we had no tobacco anyway, which was what most people really wanted. A running interview continued for a little distance beyond each manyatta as the inhabitants, mostly old men and eager at first, fell away and returned to the sun.

Early on we saw a whole settlement decamping. The women had dismantled most of the huts and were loading the poles onto harnessed donkeys. Everything seemed tanned and treacly brown, touched by smoke and grease, from the leather skirts and dry breasts of the women to the smoke-blackened pots and gourds and the house poles, all sticky with tars and carbon from the cooking fires. Later, with manyattas on our left and right, a young kudu suddenly burst from the trees and bounded across the open space, a leggy calf with wild eyes in an uncertain head. It leapt a thorn fence and careered off between the huts, its big round ears held out against its head like twin frisbees. Otherwise we saw no game at all.

According to the maps the Omo should divide into a number of distributaries before the lake. When we came to a meandering ditch across our path I assumed that we had struck the first one, although it had been dry for some time, if the trees growing in the bed were any indication. We followed the ditch for a few miles behind the khaki shorts and clacking knees of our guide until we struck a distinct path leading west, to the main river so Laurienne said. A green patch of bullrush millet, high as a cavalier's feather, swayed in the intermittent air and a number of crude platforms stood above the ripening grain from which small boys threw stones at the hungry birds. A light shelter of dry corn stalks rustled beside the path and Laurienne spoke with the four beings crouched inside it. They were naked, dirty and exceedingly thin, the skin of their bellies a dull loose curtain hung from inadequate ribs. Agricultural conditions in the region of Murle, which we were now in, seem to have changed little since 1895 when Neumann was here shooting elephants. "The people of these districts live from hand to mouth," he wrote, "beginning to eat the green millet as soon as the grain is formed, so that, though they keep on planting crop after crop as each is reaped, not only have they none to spare for sale but they are themselves often in straits for food."

The eldest of the men in the shade was blind because his eyelids were so encrusted. Clouded tears seeped down his grey cheeks in a damp track to the corner of his whining mouth. His gums had receded to the roots of his teeth, broken, filthy and few. Bits of mud and grass decorated his unkempt hair, and spittle flecked the sparse beard. Every few seconds his long bony hand went down between his insect legs to give his ample testicles a swing, brushing the flies from his penis which lay flaccid in the dust. An adolescent with distended gut filled the blind man's wringing hands with raw millet grains from time to time and they spilt down into the squatting crutch as he crammed the food into his mouth. I bathed his eyes with Optrex solution and got them open leaving a dab of Vaseline for him to apply when the ointment that I smeared on his eyelids had dried. He and the others were called Merille people by Laurienne and they belonged to the section of their tribe called Fargar, closely related to Laurienne's own section of the Shangalla. I was quite shocked by their degenerate state, but reflected that a walk through the Bowery would have shocked Laurienne even more.

The least decrepit led us out of the river bed and walked ahead for a short way. Laurienne put his hand on my shoulder and I stopped. The millet man was crouching at the side of the track and he drew a line across it with a stick. He looked up and Laurienne and Edekoi went forward. As they crossed the line the man took a little dust and threw it to catch them about the knee and thigh. He repeated the ceremony for everyone including the donkeys, then turned back to his shelter.

"What was that for?" I asked the others.

"Just his custom, Bawana Satibon, Merille custom to say you to arrive the place you go in safety. Turkana do not do this, just some sections of Merille people." Greg could add nothing himself to Laurienne's explanation, but, whatever the origins of the dust-throwing, that little patch of Africa on my leg boosted my morale considerably and gave me confidence that we would cross the Omo river successfully; but my trust was not in Laurienne.

That we were approaching water was obvious, and what light air did blow was a relief and a delight among the thickening and increasingly humid bush. Small plots of cleared land became larger and patches of millet continued as we moved steadily west. The rickety platforms of vociferous bird-scarers became more frequent among the crops and soon the dusty bush gave way entirely to damp and partly tame greenery. The track became wider and rutted where vehicles had passed. Can't be much of a river after all, I thought, as I knew that there was no bridge.

Ahead of us above the trees two white and shining reflectors beckoned. I assumed that they were radio dishes on masts near Kalam, but Laurienne said they were not and flailed his arms about in an explanation that we did not understand. Our impatience to see the river for ourselves was increased by our curiosity at the things in the trees. We hurried and poor Edekoi was left behind. We realized that she was missing and I went back for her. She tottered round a bend on tired legs and I carried her until we caught up, then Laurienne put her on his shoulders.

Picking up Edekoi must have jogged my memory, as I suddenly realized what the white things were. Eighty years before me Arthur Neumann had been struck with a good idea when he reached Reshiat, as the area of grain cultivation was then called. He was trying to buy food supplies for his caravan.

I found these people satisfactory to deal with: it is a treat—and a rare one nowadays even in Africa—to meet with simple, unspoiled savages. They cultivate nothing but millet and even that only to a very limited extent, just along the damp margin of the lake. It appears that the uncertain rainfall deters these not at all energetic cultivators from extending their operations, though the soil is alluvial and probably fertile all over these flats. It often struck me, while sojourning in Reshiat, that the lake water might be used for purposes of irrigation by means of windmills, for there is generally a good strong breeze blowing from a south-westerly direction.

Windmills. Of course. I had read an article about the delta in a popular travel magazine which has done as much as most to elevate the commonplace and sell cheap airline tickets. The article described the work of the Reverend Robert Swart, who had established an irrigation scheme using wind pumps to lift water from the river. Because of the low rainfall, cultivation in the delta depends upon annual floods to leave sufficiently moist areas to germinate the millet. The erratic nature of the river's course and régime means that in some years there are no floods, in others the highland rains sweep down and inundate everything, and in others the river banks cave in or the channels change course. The wind pumps would allow cultivation all year round, for the inlet pipes could be lowered as the water level fell. I now understood Laurienne's thrashing about earlier.

We were turned back several times by irate and woolly farmers complaining that the donkeys would damage the crops and so we made short detours round the fields, tightly fenced with thorns against the roaming cattle. We had been walking for over six hours without a break when we passed the silver wind pumps about half-a-mile away to our right. Ten minutes later we reached the river. We had been walking for fifteen days although it felt to me as if we had been travelling for years.

10

I SENT UP a modest Hallelujah, Laroi had a smoke and Greg and Esenyon shook hands. Laurienne, for once, unloaded the donkeys but he stopped short of preparing our ugali. We celebrated our arrival at the river with a tin of baked beans and one by one we fell asleep in sweaty bundles on the grass. I dreamt that I was a speedway motorbike driver. Waking in mid-afternoon is especially unpleasant on a hot day and I emerged from the shade like a bemused slug to crawl to the river for a wash.

The fawn-coloured water was hardly flowing against the contrary wind blowing little wavelets up the stream which was about 150 yards wide at this point. Beyond the bare sloping banks on the other side and far across the open yellow plains the mountain ranges of Lorionetom and Kangamanang stood out of the haze like a distant coast from the open sea. They lay well behind the Sudanese border and south of them, in Kenya, the high northern flanks of the Lapurr range showed up on the skyline, a reassuring and familiar outline.

I sat on the crumbling river bank, my mind somewhere down the dusty tubes of my binoculars. The drop into the water was sheer for eight feet and I fell with a plop into the sandy mud of the river bed. A sizable chunk of the bank came with me which was fortunate because due to the following horrific tale, I did not want to fall right in. The Omo river crocs are a meaner breed than the fat fellows of the lake as Arthur Neumann discovered. He records the scene.

> On my arrival here [about five miles north of our own position] . . . I had bathed in the river, standing up to my waist in the water which was deep close in to the bank, in spite of the crocodiles to be seen in the middle: for both I and the men had been in the constant habit of performing our ablutions in the lake where the reptiles were in plenty, and

so had come almost to disregard them, though I never went out of my depth, or even far from the bank.

Late in the afternoon I went down for another bathe, with Shebane (my servant) as usual carrying my chair, towels etc., and did the same thing again. It is a large river and deep, with a smooth surface and rather sluggish current [and] deepens rapidly so that a step or two is sufficient to bring it up to one's middle, while the bottom is black slimy mud. As we descended the bank towards the low muddy shore a native who was tending his crops said something to us, but knowing nothing of the language we could not understand him. Having bathed and dried myself, I was sitting on my chair, after pulling on my clothes by the water's edge, lacing up my boots. The sun was just about to set behind the high bank across the river, its level rays shining full upon us, rendering us conspicuous from the river, while preventing our seeing in that direction. Shebane had just gone a little way off along the brink and taken off his clothes to wash himself, a thing I had never known him to do before when with me: but my attention being then taken up with what I was doing I took no notice of him. I was still looking down when I heard a cry of alarm and raising my head got a glimpse of the most ghastly sight I ever witnessed. There was the head of a huge crocodile out of the water, just swinging over towards the deep with my poor Swahili boy in its awful jaws, held across the middle of his body like a fish in the beak of a heron. He had ceased to cry out, and with a horrible wriggle, a swirl and a splash all disappeared. One could do nothing. Shebane was gone.

I dragged myself back up the bank and Esenyon came over with a rope and a bucket to throw water over me and wash off the mud. Laurienne returned from a short recce south in the direction of more windmills, some rigged with sails above the tall river-side grasses. He had been to hire a canoe.

"OK, Bawana Satibon, everything is OK, let's go and cross now."

"Good bloke," I said. We loaded the donkeys quickly and followed him downstream and round a sharp bend. We were nearly there, for once across the river we could see our way fair for a dozen miles over the treeless plain, and back into Kenya. I even felt slightly cheated as I had been expecting much more delay and difficulty, and smugly congratulated myself on finding a guide of Laurienne's calibre. 'He wasn't such a bad chap after all,' I thought as we drew round the blind corner. 'At least he's done what he promised, got us here, and we're virtually across—miles from Kalam and the Ethiopian police.'

My thoughts dribbled on in this grateful vein and I was working out what sort of bonus to pay him when the river opened out ahead and there, slap bang opposite us was the police post. We all froze, except Laurienne who walked blithely on, shouting across to a knot of chaps with guns on the far side. The Ethiopian flag flew bravely from a white pole near a cluster of low buildings behind them.

"Fookin'!" said Laroi.

"Bastard," said I.

"Just we run?" said Greg. I turned and looked at Esenyon and the donkeys.

"Not a bloody hope, keep going. It's official channels men. Rubberstampsville."

It was a stunning afternoon. Laurienne crossed over in one of the dug-out canoes hauled up on the bank where we sat. He was trying to arrange for the police to ferry us across in their motorboat. He shouted over that it had broken down and walked off with a rifleman. A guard was posted whose English seemed restricted to two words.

"Go back," he yelled from the far bank as I walked downstream to observe the position. I carried on and he became agitated.

"Go back, GO BACK." I ignored him. His instructions floated across the river loud and clear until I saw him unsling his weapon and work the breach. My ears cleared instantly.

"What?" I shouted.

"Go back!"

"Oh! Go back? Right you are!" I went back.

Greg was in close conversation with a local youth making a contingency plan to take other canoes lying further downstream after dark, just in case the police refused to let us cross over. The only hitch was that Laurienne had left Edekoi with us. Cursing him to hellfire we decided to take her with us as far as Todenyang and leave her at the police post there until her idiot father came to get her. A cluster of small boys hung from the branches of a large tree leaning over the water where Laurienne had stepped ashore. They were fishing noisily, with nets and hand lines but as the sun marched to bed they drifted off to the manyattas on the open plain beyond the post. Half-naked women accumulated on our side, squatting with enormous bundles of firewood to wait for the return of Laurienne's canoe. There were no trees to be seen on the other side and gathering fuel must have been quite a chore for the women. Humped cattle came down between the millet gardens for their evening drink. As the sun went down the far-distant mountains beckoned, and the dozen or so wind pumps stood like mutant spiders waving a stiff *au revoir*.

We had a brew of tea just before seven o'clock when Laurienne paddled back through the gloom with a short soldier whose mission was to escort me to his leader. The small assault force leapt ashore and rushed the bank in fine style. I gave him nine out of ten as he darted between notional grenades and the whoosh of dripping flame throwers, right up to our position where the chip bag fell off his panting head. I reluctantly dropped the score to three as he neither fought through the objective, nor took cover, and I rose to greet him, cap in hand. Lokarangan farted rudely.

"Hallo old boy," I said, "have a cigarette?"

He took one and with the smoke came a deluge of words. The glowing tobacco leapt about his mouth.

"Is he talking to us?" I asked Gregory.

"I don't know. It's kind of Shangalla, but too fast. We don't understand."

The soldier adjusted his headgear and tried another channel.

"OK. OK. You coma wizame. Come wizmee. Wiziziz to coming."

"How kind," I said. "Thank you."

Laurienne explained that the officer in charge of the post across the river had been away for the day, but now he had returned and wanted to see me.

"Super," I said, "but we must all cross together."

The chip bag fell off again in the ensuing shouting match

with the soldiers on the far side. I thought that it might offend the little chap's dignity to offer him a hair clip. Eventually another canoe came gliding over and the soldier and I were ferried across towards the waiting torches of the reception party. The others were to follow with the donkeys and the kit. We stole over the water in the crooked dug-out. I tried to keep my backside off the wet floor, but felt the long puddle seeping through my shorts when the canoe rocked. I looked back over my shoulder but could no longer see the others through the gathering night. The chap at the back dug in his pole and we came swaying in under a loose covey of Ethiopian torches. The soldier jumped into mud but I sat tight. He took the hint and pulled the canoe in a little so that at least I could walk up the bank with dry feet.

An immensely tall young man with superb teeth stepped forward to greet me.

"Hi," he said, "how was the journey?"

"Oh! Fine," I said, raising my hat. I had decided on a formal approach, but the American accent surprised me. "My name is Stephen Pern. I am British. How do you do?"

"Sure. I'm George. Yeah, uh, British? Wow, er man, uh let's go meet the lootenant here." George fiddled nervously with his white turban as he turned to the group of men behind him. If anyone could have been described as black but comely it was he.

Lt Tafasa of the Ethiopian police dwarfed his little gendarmes who swarmed about in bits of uniform with stubby rifles. He was bearded but unarmed and in civilian clothes, a dark, heavily built man unlike the majority of his troops who were light skinned and clean shaven. The lieutenant stood impassively as I recounted the journey, with George translating from English into Amharic. He reminded me of a picture in my school Bible of one of the three Kings, but he seemed oddly retiring, as if he were not in complete charge of things, and I wondered if the revolution and the road to socialism had weakened his position as an officer. Before we left the river bank I called over to Laroi. All was well and the loads were being ferried over in the darkness.

"OK, Mr Steven, let's go to headquarters. Just to check out the papers, yeah?"

"Jolly good," I said, "lead on."

I followed George's Nilotic frame, with members of the people's police behind me. They wore jeans, but their tunics and caps and shambling boots were very Italian. Loud and ferocious shouts greeted us from across the compound. The challenging procedure was being well observed. The lieutenant's henchman gave an order and a generator hiccuped into life pouring neon light from an office window. Entering, I was immediately struck by the sparse but modern office furniture, the untorn mosquito frames across the windows and the display screens stacked neatly in one corner. It all seemed too sophisticated for a bush police post, but somehow unfinished. Lots of crudely designed posters were hung about the office walls, mostly in Amharic and concerning agricultural problems and the military. I noticed that only the front ranks in the pictures seemed to be armed.

The lieutenant, George and I sat at a round table and I produced my passport. This was handed over to an officious looking chap who had lots of papers on his desk. I learnt later that he was the company clerk, the sort of man for whom a properly completed document square on the table was as good as a woman in a crumpled bed. Three or four soldiers had followed us in and now slouched aggressively over a bench, cradling their weapons with disturbing incaution. They looked quite young when they took off their caps, and one of them helped himself to my last cigarette. I had left the packet on the table. The clerk clucked his teeth and scribbled away industriously, while George made a stab at polite conversation, but the night was hot. The clerk looked up. He spoke a little bit of English with a strong Italian accent.

"Why ezz ze lek acalled Rudols?" he asked, "end swear ezz yaour veeza?"

I explained about Count Teleki and his syphilitic prince, and then turned the pages of my passport to the rather grand visitor's visa stamped in by an Ethiopian embassy official in Nairobi. It had cost me 30/-. The clerk had a good read, glancing up at me meaningfully as he turned the pages.

"Zees veeza Amharic. 'ow you coming 'ere?"

"Ah, I see, I came from Kenya. Here is the visa." I showed him the small Kenyan stamp on page one, lying smugly between Police Nationale, Calais and Belgie Haven Oostende. He could not believe that it was so plain.

"Listen, clerk," I said, "Kenya is a sophisticated country. It's got a good bureaucracy left by us, the British. They have thousands of tourists a year and they don't waste their time with silly rubber stamps. You have the misfortune of inheriting an administration done up in red spaghetti." He did not understand the words, but he caught my tone of voice and meekly returned my passport. The lieutenant spoke through George.

"Right now, you can sleep in the compound," he said in a voice of honey and silk. "The lootenant is writing a message for the radio tomorrow morning real early to go to headquarters. Like the reply gonna come so soon and then you can go on. I mean no hassle man. So we're sorry you have to stay and we'll get the reply so early, maybe seven o'clock, but if you can come at nine OK." He smiled, all guava pink and ivory.

"Well fine," I said, "apart from the fact that I have a valid visa and was told in Nairobi by your embassy that everything was in order, but I had expected a short delay. Thank you for your help." I rose to go. I did not understand what actually needed to be checked with "headquarters" but buck-passing is a fairly common sport. "Perhaps you would be kind enough to tell the young soldier here that in my country we regard it as impolite to take without asking. It is just bad manners." I had decided to be slightly aggressive as the next thing to go could have been our food. George was immediately conciliatory.

"He's sorry. You see we're a socialist country now and everything belongs to the people. Yeah look have one of my cigarettes. It's like a free country now you see. Socialism, man. OK, he says he's very sorry."

"That's quite all right," I said to the lieutenant. "I'm sure that socialism and good manners go together. Since we are delayed here at your invitation and our food is low I'm glad to hear about justice and equality. I hope we get some." He smiled but did not reply.

George and the smoking soldier escorted me back across the compound.

"George," I said, "where actually are we?"

"Uh, in Geleb," he said, "it's near Kalam."

"Why are the police here?" I asked. "I thought they were supposed to be in Kalam."

"Well they like moved down here," he said.

"Yes but why? What's the point of being here?"

"Protecting the mission," he said. "This buildings was belong to the mission."

"Oh!" I said. "Where are the missionaries?"

"Just gone," he said.

"Gone? What for good?"

"Just gone away," he said. The subject seemed closed.

Guttural challenges split the night, to which I joined in the reply of "Ugh". Ughing our way through the dark I unexpectedly bumped into Gregory and three very fed-up donkeys. The others were at the rear.

"Steevan! OK, OK, all across except one man steal your bag."

'Oh no!' I thought. I kept my camera gear and compass in a canvas bag, hung on a donkey load so that it was accessible on the march. "Thank God I had my notebook and the maps with me," I said to Greg. "Never mind. We're sleeping here tonight to wait for permission to go on."

"Not bad," said Greg, "but your bag. Esenyon chase the man naked into the bush. He just drop the bag and everything spill out. We pick it all up but the man escape. It was when we trying to get the donkeys in the river he just creep out. Also Esenyon's tyres gone."

I thanked the bare-footed Esenyon. At least he still had his hat. While the others unloaded I checked my bag and found that the prismatic compass was missing. It was not a terrible loss as I still had a spare silvo compass in my kit, and navigation was the least of my worries across the open plain ahead, with such obvious landmarks as the mountains and the lake to guide us. My housewife had been opened and the thief had taken a plastic thimble, I do not know why, for he left the sail needles and thread and the safety pins, scissors and buttons which he could have used or sold.

George and the guards were genuinely concerned about the theft, said how awful it was and breathed vengeance and retribution on the thief. It surprised me that they should be so concerned. The ferrymen materialized from the darkness and it turned out that they knew who the thief was. I could not follow what was going on but eventually George said that I should pay them in the morning as they would get the compass back. 'Fat chance of that,' I thought as we tied the donkeys to a rotting lorry, parked under some black trees while Esenyon brewed tea. I spoke with the guards, sitting on half oil drums beneath the stars. Some of them had a smattering of English from school in Addis Ababa, which was where most of them came from. I thought how European they were, politely refusing the tea we offered but accepting a cup when pressed.

Twinkling fires flickered out in the blackness beyond the compound, and the cold blue afterglow of distant lightning briefly obliterated the stars. Snatches of verse from a childhood poem came into my mind and I recited aloud to Greg who lay under the net beside me.

> When awful darkness and silence reign
> Over the great Gromboolian plain ...
>   [can't remember what's next]
> When storm clouds brood on the towering heights
> Of the hills on the Chankly Bore.
> Then through the vast and gloomy dark
> There moves what seems a fiery spark
>   A lonely spark with silvery rays
>   Piercing the coal black night,
>   A meteor strange and bright
> Hither and thither the vision strays,
>   A single lurid light.

"Hm," said Greg, "that seems to be just as here. There is lightning going over the plain called Kang'kala from here to the Sudan. There! You see it touching behind Lorionetom and Kwanamoru mountains far in the middle of Turkana. And also the fires of Shangalla people you can see but not far, yes, red and dancing on the plain."

Needless to say there was no reply to the radio message the next morning. Using the blue peaks in the distance I worked out our position at dawn as roughly six miles south of Kalam, but without a compass I was not sure. Behind us the river slid on between steeply eroded banks dotted with wind pumps on both sides. I counted fifteen with sails and three larger ones with metal vanes. The garden beside me was irrigated by a big one which lifted the water out of the river and into little ditches running among paw paws, lemon trees and palms. Lush grass hung in dewy clumps over the ditches and a gossamer fuzz of fine roots was exposed along the river bank where the undercutting stream had collapsed the loose sediments above. The vanes and stiff legs of a drowning pump stood out of the water like a cold body and just beyond the garden the pylon of another hung doomed, waiting for the river to remove the crucial particle beneath its two supported legs.

A wall of swaying millet hid the bush on the far bank and small gardens of tobacco had been planted where the mud shelved out of the water. But away from the river and the watered gardens the western plain was a dry white sea, the home of snakes and goats. It has not always been so, for frogs once croaked where scorpions now lie. In the last full year of Queen Victoria's reign two Royal Engineers reached the area from Fashoda on the river Nile. Their survey had followed the course of the Sobat river and had brought them over the Lorionetom hills in the height of the rains. Fevered and terribly bogged down they struggled for a month in many directions before they were free of the swamps. They struck the lake shore at the northern point of an embayment they called Sanderson's Gulf. "We realized that it was of some magnitude [about thirty miles long and eight across]. It was therefore decided to call it after some distinguished personage, as hitherto it had received no name and with the kind permission of the Permanent Under Secretary of State for Foreign Affairs it was named after him." Both the gulf and the permanent under secretary have died long since, and we were, so to speak, sitting on the grave.

Laurienne strode over the open ground from the police lines, a double row of substantial huts, each with its courtyard fenced with grass mats, corn stalks and thorns. He sat down by the mashing tea and slicked back his hair, minutely examining the comb before putting it away and drawing from his pocket a neatly folded paper.

"Here," he said, "look dis."

I read it carefully. The typewritten document was an agreement between himself and an American missionary, conferring the ownership of one Polomo Mill for the nominal rent of an Ethiopian dollar a year, roughly fifteen English pence. It transpired that Laurienne had a wife who lived just downstream and this branch of his family were successfully farming the river bank with their mill. His was the only one that still worked, he told me smugly.

"Why did those missionaries leave?" I asked him. He did not know. I was about to question him further because I felt sure that he had known that he was taking us to a police post, when a smiling figure in red came up to greet Gregory. It was Tito, the mission cook. He had been waiting over four months for his employers to return, and now he was planning to leave Geleb and return to Kenya. He was therefore happy to change some Ethiopian dollars for Kenya shillings with me.

"Those missionaries left four months ago did you say?"

"Yes," he told me, "about four months, then the police just move their headquarters to here from Kalan because here better houses with radio, boat, airstrip and many things."

"So you knew the police were here?" I looked at Laurienne. He stroked his hair, rather nervously.

"Just this the only place to cross here Bawana Satibon, not bad you just wait." Hanging about is not my scene.

"Here's your money, Laurienne," I said. "We won't be feeding you after tonight." He looked hurt.

At mid-day our delicate ferrymen of the night before came hurrying past, their short ostrich plumes nodding at the trot. They both carried long frayed wands held high in the air and their names were Walkari and Yergulem. Lt Tafasa sent for me and in his office Walkari handed over both my compasses which surprised me as I had not missed the little one. George translated.

"These men they like have your things for you. See their sticks? Wow! They sure beat that thief." George's voice had the liquidity of a detergent ad. He "hung loose man", never lost his cool and looked beautiful beneath his tasselled head cloth. Lt Tafasa looked tired when I asked him about going on.

"Uh, he sent the message, but we have to wait you see," said George.

Walkari and Yergulem were happy with their small reward and I paid them for ferrying us the night before. They wanted posho but we could not spare any food at all. Even with Laurienne and Edekoi going we could only last another week, but they asked for torch batteries and I gave them a couple. They said that they would send their women to sell us milk in the morning and trotted off with their sticks. I was very surprised that the things had been recovered but the others said that they knew there would be no problem.

Strange days, I thought, drifting off to sleep. Timeless birds turned in the white sky to the distant applause of thunder and through the singing heat came the lazy swing and squeak of a wind pump trickling water between the shady paw paws. Vinaceous doves coo-cooed inside the green mango tree above me where sleeping bats twitched safe in the deep shade. Desultory conversation passed between the guards as the sun pivoted imperceptibly down to free the baking plains. Three black herons flapped north against an angry muddle of cloud caught like a tangled rose garden on the distant hills. And, eventually, the flag was lowered by a sergeant in reasonable uniform with a whistle in his mouth. A soldier whose boots were coming off presented arms, raising dust on the whistle blasts. We all stood up in silence as the orange, the yellow and the green was gathered in.

Greg had caught a liver-coloured mud fish with long whiskers which he skinned and boiled and a mormyrid which he fried in the last of our Cowboy cooking fat. The mormyrid was about two feet long and shaped like a pike, except that the snout was longer and more snout-like. Its eyes were mere pinheads, a mole of a fish, but its brain was of abnormal size which may be why the snout fishes were venerated by the ancient Egyptians. Our supper was correctly called *Mormyrops deliciosus* and it certainly was.

Laroi lay asleep in the firelight beside Edekoi who sat in curious silence watching me scribble up my diary. The donkeys stirred as the mosquitoes made their first runs of the evening and I rose to rig up our net between the spears and the mango tree. Huge wolf spiders sped like ghostly rafts of poison hither and thither, nocturnal horrors for the weak and crawling things of the evening. I turned back to the fire and saw, to my alarm, a hairy freak rush up Laroi's body. It stopped for a moment on his unprotected neck before pattering horribly across his face and off into the night. Laroi sat up slowly.

"Was that a spider?" he asked. "Allah! If it bite to me, very hurt. Not die but just running until you fall down. Only cure to catch that man and bury him in sand. He stay eight days to get out the poison. This bad wadudu."

Whenever afterwards Laroi came close to the spiders he repeated the cure for their bite. "Eight days in the sand" joined "Fookin' mousakeetos" as another handy phrase for most occasions, including tea with mother-in-law. Laroi and Laurienne decided to sleep in a nearby manyatta that night and left Edekoi crashed out by the fire.

"Just take her under the net with you and Gregory, Bawana Satibon?" asked Laurienne as he strolled away.

The guard was relieved and he came over to the dying fire. His name was Petros.

"So, my friend," he said shyly. "Let you come my ouze eat." I thanked him and followed into one of the big huts, first crossing a small courtyard. A mud wall partitioned off part of the room where Petros's wife moved in the gloom among black pots and smoke. An oil lamp hung on the central roof post and in the dim light I could see two beds under furled mosquito nets, a table and a couple of wooden trunks. Petros's clothes hung on a line across the far corner of the room and family photographs in glass frames dangled on nails pushed loosely into the flaking walls.

"Let you sit down," he said, "zis my wife. She was student in Addis." A girl of about twenty in a plain cotton frock brought tea on a round tray from the fire. We sipped it sweet and black from small glasses and then she brought in the food. "In zis it is wadj," said Petros taking off the lid of an enamel bowl full of steaming peas. He poured them over a tray of enormous pancakes on the table. "And here is injira. Let you eat." Tearing off a strip of floppy pancake he scooped up a little wadj and gently put it into his wife's mouth. "For ze cook

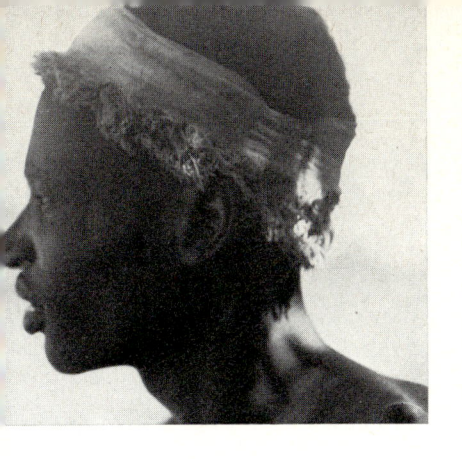

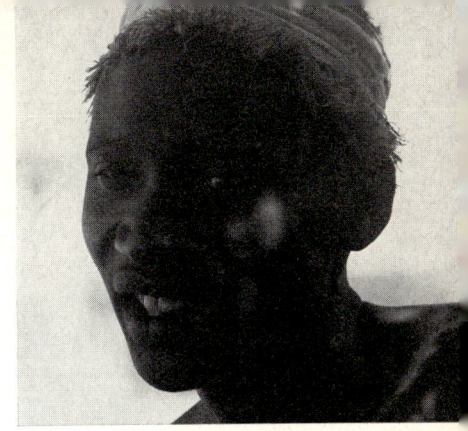

Yergulem

Walkari

Greg and Edekoi—our kitchen at Geleb

The great escape. Laroi and Esenyon pushing Komote into the river. Greg pulling from the police launch

Kaset fires an arrow into the cow's neck

Atol hangs on while blood pours into a bowl

Atol, Kaset and their father ferrying Komote and Lobrolei; arrival at the bank

Atol getting Komote out of the mud

Christmas dinner, Lowarangak

Esenyon's cousin, Nakutha

Karim, our guide in the Loriu. His hair has grown out and needs redoing. His head is resting on his wooden pillow

"...Hoo c'mon bois..." Laroi
crossing the Kerio river

A typical Turkana with blanket
and stool in the Lapurr Hills

"A hundred silent camels" p. 218

Me and the donkeys skirting the lava fields. Nabuyatom and Kulal in the background

of food. We do so like zis. Let eat now." The injira was cold but I really enjoyed it, and especially liked the slightly fermented taste of the peas. We drank more tea.

"All zis polis 'ere two maybe three years and no go back Addis," said Petros.

"No leave?" I asked.

"No. Just we stay. But I to going home at six months. Zis pless very bad for us. Too hot mek us sick. No food we like and no pless to go. I show you a somesing." He rummaged through a trunk and produced a Bible in English. "Let you read eet," he said, lifting another Bible from a shelf. I obliged him by reading the first few verses of *Genesis* whose majesty always grips me, and he followed with the Amharic version. Putting the books away he sank quietly to his knees.

"I am sick," he said, "I feel faint." He looked very ropey and felt weak as a kitten as his wife and I put him to bed. I noticed dark blotches on his cheeks but he smiled wanly and waved goodbye as I thanked him for the meal. Geleb, it seemed, was an unhealthy place.

Edekoi was decidedly unwilling to come under the net with Greg and I. The guards laughed their heads off as we struggled to keep her in but rather than have the net torn to shreds and our ear drums pierced with her wails we let her sleep by the fire with the mosquitoes. I tucked a sheet round her and let her be. She crawled in between us about two hours before dawn though. She smelt of sour milk and leather. Since the indolent Laurienne was to come no further with us, he took her away at mid-day to her mother in the delta and himself left that evening, more an unremarked departure than an escape. I rather missed Edekoi. She had lent the expedition the pleasant air of a family outing.

There was another prisoner in the compound with us, a mad-looking bloke with woolly hair, bare feet and drainpipe cotton trousers which were much too short for him. According to Dandel (our present guard), the "pisoner", as Laroi and Esenyon called him, had been a policeman once. He had been sent on a mission across to the Sudan, but overstayed his posting by a year before returning to Geleb to give himself up. He was remanded for trial charged with desertion and was waiting for transport to Jimma, the district capital. He spent most of his few waking hours begging cigarettes from the guards and posho from us. He had an irritating tic. Every time someone farted or coughed he would give a little shriek and shout something, even late into the night. We did not understand what it was but his penetrating cries kept us awake on the following nights.

We had eaten all our beans, and had had no luck fishing that day so we just ate posho and drank tea. Our sugar was nearly finished but like the others I would rather have enough sugar in tea or none at all and so we did not ration ourselves. I complained loudly (and not entirely accurately) to the lieutenant that I had no Ethiopian money and that since we were his prisoners he should feed us, but he refused. As luck would have it, it was a Friday and the camp store room had been opened. The women were going in for their weekly ration of peas, lentils and barley flour. There were lumps of cooking fat, bars of soap and bags of salt as well. I got a pot full of split peas by begging from the storeman and swapped a good Meps spinner for some sugar. We had plenty of milk and so our third day of incarceration was not too hungry. I was again invited to supper, this time with the guard Dandel. He was a bachelor but had a couple of Shangalla women working for him. They dished up injira with a mean brew of peppers. I had been surprised at how bland the food was in Kenya but the Ethiopians spiced things up nicely.

Lapurr peak stood out tantalizingly clear in the sharp dawn light. Greg and Laroi went fishing. The best time was between six and seven in the morning and they came back grinning with a good-sized snout fish each. There was still no reply from Jimma and so I got hold of George and we went to see the lieutenant. After a heated scene he finally agreed to open the mission store room. I asked why the missionaries had left so much behind. Besides the substantial buildings and the radio equipment there were heaps of unassembled windmills, piles of sheet steel and sawn timber stacked against the outhouses. Inside was an Aladdin's cave of a workshop with all the spare parts and tools imaginable and an area where some small machine tools and a generator were bolted down. Round the back was a tractor, parked among a confusion of pumps, pipes and fuel drums, including a sizable dump of aviation spirit. A Toyota and a Willy's jeep stood in the shady forecourt with a blue Suzuki 250 cc motorbike. It was as if the Americans had just gone to town for the day.

"Ah, yes," said George, "they left real quick. They went to a conference somewhere and, uh, well they didn't get the permission to come back. They only could take what they had with them."

He led me into what had been one of the houses, where the radio was installed. The other house was the place to which I had been taken on the first night. The contents had been stripped and neatly stacked in a couple of rooms. One was locked and inside, all sorted in tidy rows, was the food the missionaries had left, mostly baking powder, salt and peanut butter. I noticed a number of other people creeping in behind us.

"Why don't you give this stuff away, George? It really isn't worth the bother of accounting for."

"It all belongs to the government now," he explained. It was useless to discuss it further. I took some Swiss bouillon cubes, a few packets of dried soup and two cans of hot dogs. The peanut butter was rancid. George locked the room again, after I had paid.

"Did they leave any books?" I asked.

"Yeah, whole roomful. But they're all locked up. They belong to the government too. No one can touch them."

"A wise move," I said. "You don't want the local people getting hold of Mark Twain."

Earlier I had asked the lieutenant why, despite the American withdrawal, the windmills had been allowed to break down.

"It's temporary," he said. Notwithstanding the Somali and Eritrean wars it did seem sad that such a successful project was being allowed to fall into the river. George had a nice red motorbike which did not work.

"You know about bikes, man?" he asked.

I was short of sugar and would attempt anything.

"Yeah. I've had a few," I said, knowingly.

"Maybe we can fix mine together?" he asked. The bike had a fairly obvious electrical fault. "Like, er, great," said George when I had fixed it. "I was changing the oil you know but none came out."

"Have you put any in?" I asked.

"No," he said.

"How long have you had the bike?"

"Uh, nearly a year." He was rather shaky on two-stroke engine lubrication but got the general idea after some explanation. He was certainly no mechanic, but he was not a policeman either. We rode over to his house and he made tea.

"What actually do you do here, George?" I asked.

"Political department," he said, "like I explain all the revolution to the people. It's a department bike, I didn't buy it."

"Where did you learn English?"

"At a mission in Kenya, but I'm from Sudan. My tribe is related to Turkana, we speak about the same language. I was in jail a year you know but I'm OK now." He had plenty of sugar and books, mostly heavy political works, ill-bound and tightly printed on coarse paper. I took a Hemingway and some Marx just to show willing.

Petros, the Bible-reading guard, had recovered enough to take an English lesson that afternoon. His heart's desire was to leave the police and return to Addis, there to study medicine.

"Why d'you want to be a doctor?" I asked him.

"Because of money," he said.

I could not teach him much in one session but I hope that I cured him of his habit of prefacing all his remarks with "let you" this or that, and that I knocked some of the "zeds" off his accent. I walked back to the mango tree, my stomach happy with chai and injira, and my feet smelling of wet dung. We had played musical chairs during the lesson while Petros's wife worked her way over the floor and lower walls of the main room spreading a thin paste of cow dung and water, worked well into the cracks. She did this each week to seal off the dry mud walls and it made the place look spring cleaned.

Ernest Hemingway and a couple of pied kingfishers kept tedium at bay that afternoon. The birds were nesting in tunnels pecked out of the soft river bank and I spent hours trying to stalk them, for I did not have a telephoto lens with me. They looked like fluffy chess boards shooting up and down the river, rising acrobatically and plummeting down in a harlequin flurry on shoals of small fish. As I crept through the paw paw grove towards their perch, I kicked a pile of dry grass and inside were a dozen ripe fruits. They were slightly green and had been stored there to ripen. All four of us felt rather sick that night after I had dug up two more caches under the trees.

Five days passed. Excited men in leopard skins danced by one morning with women in mantles of Colobus monkey fur, their faces fierce and streaked with coloured clays. They shook their spears and shields at every compound door, waiting for a hand-out as was the custom at Shangalla weddings. Walkari and Yergulem came to talk with us and the guards became more familiar. I ate with one of them every day and George kept us going with his sugar. Every morning I spoke with Tafasa, but he had caught malaria and eventually became quite ill. One evening they searched us, quite politely but in the dark. I had to lend them our torch and I turned out everything, even undid the camera and opened the food bags. I took the pots from the fire to show that they were empty.

"Are you joking wiz us?" they said.

"No!" I said, "I just want to co-operate with you."

We laughed together when they had gone. I learnt a few words of Amharic and studied my Swahili book, but I was impatient. The hills and the border were so close.

"Don't worry," said George one afternoon. "Some French tourists came here in a car once from Kenya. They had to wait for one complete month for an answer to go on."

"Did they get permission?" I asked eagerly.

"No!"

I decided to wait for up to ten days, and, if by then permission had not come through, I would then drop everything and strike west to the Sudanese frontier. I could evade the small Ethiopian border post at Lopemukath by walking in the night. Once inside the Sudan I could swing south and enter Kenya. Even without water it would only be an uncomfortable 24 hours at worst. The only problem was that I would then have the trouble and expense of re-equipping myself, and I might have lost Greg and Laroi.

The guard Dandel came off duty early on the fifth morning. It was a Sunday but no church parade was held. Dandel invited me to breakfast, and Esenyon came along too. We had delicious spiced macaroni and calabashes of yoghurt with peppery tea. Esenyon rolled back to the tree and his donkey-minding and Dandel and I paid a social call on his neighbour, Girma.

Girma's wife was hardly more than a girl, but a big one. Tucking her generous breasts away in her frock she bent over the embers of her cooking fire and blew them into a sparking roar. She was making wide injira pancakes and Dandel wanted me to see how it was done. She took a solid iron pan about an inch deep and two feet across and plonked it on the flames to heat up, while she stirred a bucket full of frothy batter made from barley flour and water fermented overnight. She lightly greased the pan with sizzling grey butter before pouring on a gourd of the mixture with a deft and steady hand, corkscrewing from the edge to the middle. The batter spread thin and evenly across the hot iron, cooking beneath a heavy earthenware lid which she lowered over the pan, sealing the edge with damp rags. After a few minutes she removed the lid and rolled off the finished pancake onto a growing pile. She usually made enough for two or three days at a time she said, and asked if I would like to have a go. Dandel and Girma fell about at my puny effort. I greased the pan without burning myself too badly, but the batter-pouring was not a success. The result was an ugly yellow jelly fish, the sort of thing they throw away in hospitals. The wife smiled pityingly and put my effort to one side, not on her pile, I noticed.

The whole camp had been expecting an aeroplane from Jimma. It was already two days overdue, and was to bring some officials on a tour of inspection, which made George and the lieutenant nervous, but held out some hope for me that permission to continue would come too. Whether the "pisoner" was happy or frightened in his anticipation I did not know, because he was to be part of the return cargo. My Hemingway bored me to distraction with its powerboats and big fish and so I walked along the bank to join Greg and Laroi who were fishing near the usual horde of small boys. Laroi had caught enough for lunch but both he and Greg were becoming demoralized.

We lay on the bank smoking cigarettes. Greg had run out of snuff and was reduced to sniffing local tobacco ground crudely between two bricks. We ran over the escape plans, and were discussing what action to take if our flight was compromised when a soldier shambled over, his Czech-made sub-machine gun slung casually over one shoulder. The circular magazines hold 70 rounds which can be fired off rapidly, an inaccurate weapon over much distance but adequate for close-up stuff in the undergrowth. The soldier turned out to be an officious little corporal with bad teeth. Lt Tafasa wanted to see me.

'Thank God,' I thought, 'we can go on.' I was sure that the permission had come through. "OK chaps, let's go. Pack up the stuff. I'll go and see the man."

He had malaria and lay in his bed with weak eyes and a wan smile. George was in the room.

"We got the message," he said. Lt Tafasa spoke briefly. "He says to tell you that, uh, like you have to go back." George smiled.

I am ashamed to say that my legs trembled. Tafasa told George to give me a chair. I was thinking of having to plough through the swamp in Allia Bay again.

"Back?" I said. "Back where?"

"Back to Kenya," said George.

"Yes, but we are only twelve miles from Kenya now, it's quicker to go straight on. We'll be across the border before nightfall."

"They just say you go back," said George in his lovely voice.

"What the hell's the point of issuing visas then?" I asked. "We haven't got enough food to get back and anyway we don't know the way because Laurienne has gone." Arguing was useless. I put my case more for the sake of form than anything else. Then I stood up. My knees were better.

"Thank you very much, lieutenant. I hope you recover soon. We'll be going straight away. Goodbye."

In defence of the Ethiopian authorities it is only fair to say that there was a considerable flow of cash and baddies across this border after the revolution, and so movement in the area was tightly controlled, but I felt that Ethiopia's economic problems were pretty remote from my insignificant caravan and seethed inwardly with frustration. On my way back to the others I reviewed my options. I could comply with the order and return to Ileret but failure and hunger, for we had very little food left, and a natural reluctance to do what I am told, did not incline me to obey. The chances of getting caught going west into the Sudan were high now, because the police knew that we had to go and may have expected a move in that direction. Floating down the river in stolen canoes appealed to my imagination, but crocodiles might have detached useful bits of the donkeys on the way. I decided to return to the east bank, and so be seen to comply with Tafasa's demands, but then to walk south into the delta, and tiptoe back over the river at night. The chances of being actually caught by a patrol were small, but I was worried about the prospect of being ambushed or betrayed to the police by the local Shangalla, or, worse still, of simply getting lost.

Esenyon, Greg and Laroi listened to the bad news impassively.

"OK Steebon, let's go. Fookin' Etopia. We come with you."

Laroi spoke for all three. It was a far greater risk for them to enter the delta than for me because Shangalla and Turkana traditionally molest each other with often fatal results. I thanked them and was about to send Greg off to find someone with a canoe when the aeroplane arrived. The post buzzed with excitement and people rushed here and there in lorries, blowing horns and shouting. The whole camp turned out to watch the small green-and-yellow machine land in a swinging cloud of dust out on the airstrip, except us.

Working fast we got the kit down to the water's edge where the police outboard was moored. I had a struggle to remove the motor but left it on the bank with a good handful of mud in the air intake. As Greg and I rowed across with the kit he turned to me and laughed.

"You see how to cross with donkeys now, free example!" he said. I had been sorry to miss the first crossing in the dark. The donkeys, sleek and complacent after their long rest, were unenthusiastic about getting wet and muddy again, but by the time I returned, leaving Greg guarding the stuff, Laroi and Esenyon had got Lokarangan half submerged. They looked like a turn from a Hamburg nightclub, with mud and donkeys and half-naked men splashing about in a frenzy. When they were actually in the river the trick was to get the donkeys out of their depth and facing the right way. You then hung on to the nose rope to keep the snorting nostrils above water level while whoever was at the back paddled like mad until the donkeys' swimming helped you along. Once across it was a simple but dirty operation to heave the panting beasts out of the belly-deep mud to stand wet and miserable in the sun. Komote was the last to cross and as we heaved him out by ear and tail the plane took off with a roar. We quickly washed off the worst of the mud and loaded up. The boat we left in the slime for the gendarmerie to collect and we set off, picking our way through the millet fields until the river and the wind pumps had vanished.

II

SILLY INSECTS SANG invisibly up in the trees and a thin steam rose from the damp earth. The heat was oppressive but we decided to get well away from the river that day. I strode forth, outwardly confident, my men and pack animals behind me. Our progress was slow as we pursued our erratic zig-zagging course between the millet gardens, continually urged away by the owners in wide thorn-ridden arcs. Despite their gibbering and their wild gesticulations we had little to fear from the biological scrap in the gardens, but the Shangallas in the bush were a different and uncertain proposition.

By late afternoon I reckoned that we were far enough east of Geleb to change course south without fear of blundering back onto the open river banks. We had put four miles of dense and trackless scrub between us and the police post, and we all hoped that we would soon come to easier country where cattle might have opened up the bush. Cattle meant people and our nerves danced in pessimistic appreciation of our very weak position in unknown and possibly hostile territory.

We stopped for a rest in a tangled grove of tall acacias. Flocks of weaver birds twittered in the thin canopy above us, their domed nests hanging off the lower branches in dry clusters. I squatted down to change the compass and to study the over-familiar map. I wanted to walk south now, parallel with the river for about ten miles, and cross it, I hoped, well out of contact with the police. The bush was too thick to see Lapurr and the other landmarks and, despite my apparent confidence, I was worried that my dead reckoning in such thick scrub would be hopelessly wrong. The problem of how to recross the river when we reached it also worried me, but first we had to get there. I rechecked the bearing and lit a cigarette. Greg took a deep pinch of tobacco over my shoulder and Esenyon lay back, sweating in the shade. All was peaceful in the humming bird singing, prickling bush.

"We'll have ten minutes here and push on," I told the others.

"OK," said Greg, "quiet isn't it?"

"It is rather," I said. I was on the verge of having a funny feeling. "I'll just set the compass and we can——" CRASH!

I spun round. Laroi had leapt into cover, every muscle taught. His eyes were gleaming and his vibrating spear was poised for a throw.

"Shangalla!" he whispered hoarsely. Greg and Esenyon froze.

"Where?" I whispered back. "How many?"

Laroi mumbled something inaudible.

"What? I can't hear you. What d'he say, Greg?"

"He see one man," said Greg calmly, "he got a gun. It's pointing to us." Greg sank back to his knees.

'For Christ's sake,' I thought, 'that's all we need.' I deliberately completed the adjustment to the compass, cool as Drake on Plymouth Hoe.

"Let's go back to Geleb and tell the police that we can't get through," suggested Greg.

"OK, just wait a minute," I said testily. I looked over at Laroi. 'Guns beat spears,' I thought, 'we'd better make friends with these guys.'

With the bearing set I stood up very slowly and tossed the machete over to Esenyon. Armed with a silvo compass I stepped out from cover, expecting the massed Shangalla infantry to open up. I could see not a damn thing.

"I can't see a damn thing," I said, "hang on."

"Naa," I yelled. "Naa, Naa, Jambo. Pya." Silence. The birds continued to twitter. I began to feel a bloody fool but walked forward to where Laroi had seen the man. More naa's and pya's. Nothing.

"There's no one here, can't see a thing," I shouted, walking back. Laroi must be getting jumpy, I thought, he's seeing things in bushes. Can't take the strain. I'll have to watch him. I walked round a thick bush on my way back to our tree and leapt out of my skin.

"Naa," said the bush, rustling gently, "Naa!"

A lithe and naked Shangalla moran stepped out, a fighting stick and spear in his hand. There was no gun, but I made profuse mental apologies to Laroi, who rose from cover suspiciously, his spear at the ready. After a brief altercation in which I caught Laroi's repeated "Mimi Rendille, mimi Rendille," the moran suddenly grabbed Laroi's face and kissed him full on the mouth. It was peace.

Atol the moran was beautiful. He had a high, domed forehead and quizzical eyes. His cheek bones were aristocratically set either side of a neat nose, his ears were small, but his mouth was full and good humoured above a hard beardless chin. His body was splendid. He wore earrings the shape of young beech leaves and a band of leather to accentuate his biceps and calves. His height was increased by a cockade of frizzed-out hair running front to rear. He looked like a cross between the last of the Mohicans and Adam before the fall. 'This man,' I thought, 'is a cut above the other Shangalla we have met.'

Stubby Esenyon could be passed off as nothing other than Turkana, but Gregory became a sort of Samburu-Rendille who had fallen on his face, leaving a Turkana tribal scar on his forehead and Laroi, as he had explained many nights ago, was Rendille with the scars to prove it. Whether the conversation went on in bad Turkana or bastardized Shangalla I did not discover, but Greg held the floor for five or ten minutes and the moran followed with grunts and sighs and gasps as our journey unfolded. He wrung his hands and snapped his fingers as Greg described us paddling back over the Omo, away from the "white men" from Ethiopia. Greg's monologue closed and there was a short exchange.

"OK, Steevan, he agree to take us forward to Kenya. We give him one donkey and a little money because his father got three canoes." I thought the offer of a donkey a little hasty but immediately agreed. A good guide would be a godsend. Later Greg explained.

"These people, they want animal. Even more than womens they need animal. Then they like sheets to wear and posho and sugar. Also tobacco, but most import is an animal. Now you see this Atol, he walk like a man with sun in his eyes, he only think of donkey, and he not badding on us."

Three silent soft brown calves lay in the deep shade of Atol's bush. He spread goat skins for us and passed round a gourd of milk.

"Maziwa lala, this is sleeping milk in Swahili language just become to be yoghurt," said Greg. "This man," he continued, indicating Laroi, "this man say we just wait, drink tea while people come from bush then we go to their manyatta." Laroi was pretty pleased with himself.

"Told you someone was there," he said. "I was shifta you know. Good eyes. Yeah. Shifta!"

Esenyon stirred posho into boiling water. Finding a guide was one thing, keeping him and getting there were others. Atol still had to check with his family that he could go with us, for someone had to look after the cows. Cut-and-dried agreements are unusual in the bush where time passes in unrecorded days.

A gawky boy materialized but hung back out of spear range until Atol reassured him. The boy called back and two young women appeared, ripe, prime and smiling, followed by Atol's brother, Kaset. He was less good-looking than Atol but both morans and girls had a taut health and quick intelligence with none of the affected nonchalance of Samburu youth.

Kaset had an avaricious gleam in his eye when we discussed his fee but he agreed on 15/- and a sheet to be purchased on our arrival in Todenyang. During the negotiations he had been combing out Atol's hair with a twig. He teased a parting on either side of the crown and working backwards braided short plaits like a tonsure round his head, leaving a frizzy crest which he wove down into a mat tight on the skull. He drew each plait straight and stood up, folded his thin blanket and wrapped it around his middle like a broad cummerbund. The cows were coming.

Atol and Kaset examined the slowly moving herd, physically checking half a dozen cows as they passed by. I wondered why. Atol eventually seized a brindled cow by her horns and after a brief struggle managed to twist her head round and hold her still. The boy slipped a soft leather thong round the base of her neck and tightened it with a stick. Two yards off, Kaset squatted with a simple bow and an arrow of strong reed, tipped with a piece of broken razor blade. With the fluency of an accomplished vet he sent the arrow directly into a bulging vein, rose and withdrew it. The boy was there with a wooden bowl to catch the thick red jet released by the arrow which Kaset was wiping on the cow's backside. He broke off a small twig of toothbrush tree and peeled back the bark. The bowl held about half a gallon of blood when Kaset stepped forward and plugged the hole. He let go the tourniquet and the cow returned, a little dazed, to the herd.

"We are going far," said Atol, patting his stomach, "we need for our strength." He took a long swig and offered me the bowl. The thick warm liquid went down like castor oil.

"What do they usually eat?" I asked Greg.

"Just milk and meat. These people with the cows only have milk and meat. Sometimes like today they take blood but mostly only drinking milk once in morning and once in the evening."

Our boring old posho was a treat for them and they tucked in with abandon. Atol was the first (and only) man to ask me for injections for the cattle, which I could not give, but Kaset wanted something to make him strong. I had some flashy antibiotics in grey-and-red capsules and I gave him one with a pep talk on how strong they were, explaining that the grey end was food for the red bit which killed all enemies in the body. I overdid it and Laroi had to swallow one to demonstrate no ill effects. The women had Aspirins and a Danish hot dog each. I had opened a can in honour of the occasion and much to Laroi's disappointment there was no steaming mashed potato inside, only salty water. The mouth-watering picture on the can had fooled him.

We packed up and walked south for about two hours in the dust of a cattle trail, joined at intervals by other tracks much travelled and disturbed by herds converging for the night. I hung back at the edge of the trail to be as inconspicuous as possible, for betrayal, said Atol, was a likely possibility.

When finally we arrived at their manyatta we camped outside the perimeter fence, tucked in under the thorns like escaped POWs. Several thousand cattle were gathered here in an extended line of bomas each with its dung fire smoking in the crimson bud of evening, which opened black petals and flung out the stars one by one into a moonless sky. An old man who spoke Swahili came across and we went over the whole deal again in minute detail as Kaset had changed his mind and decided not to cross the river with us. The mosquitoes were very bad but the few people around us seemed heedless of them. Later, when the people had gone we strung up the net and all huddled in together. A black crowd gathered out in the night, murmuring and shuffling in the ivory white dust, and then a song began.

"They are happy," said Greg, "just pleased of the rains and now so many people together so they dance."

The song developed, ran its course and died but between the leaping shadows and woven through the grunts a haunting melody trailed, sustained by the women, but underscored with hard dry feet on the reverberating earth.

"They are singing about the cows and a black bull, how it is beautiful," said Greg, picking up the chant, "just moving among the cows his name is Asupaiteea like the man we saw." Esenyon was singing too, for the words were in Turkana. We fell into a lonely, insect ridden sleep.

Atol and Kaset emerged before the purple tints of dawn, whispering us away, delicate, and shrouded like bone china for a move. Esenyon's eyes were swollen with bites and Laroi looked as if he had gone the distance with a bruiser and lost. We left silently itching, and swung in a wide arc at first southeast into the dry bush and dust of the cattle roads, then south with a little west bringing us back to the river and the floodlands. The millet groves rustled gently but by nine o'clock, when we stopped, the breeze had gone and they hung flaccid and emotionless, like limp flags. We were in a clearing on the river bank, just off the footpath we had picked up earlier and round us the trees lay tangled and smouldering where they had been cut. The ash would later be kicked about a little before the millet planting. Lookout platforms had been erected and we could hear occasional shouts from the bird-scarers.

The river was supposed to divide into two sizable channels, but everyone I had asked had been emphatic that there was but one stream. I supposed that the other had dried up. That meant our position was only a couple of miles from the small Ethiopian outpost of Lopemukath, on the actual border, and I was nervous. I crept stealthily through the clearing to the green river and scanned the far bank with the binoculars. It reminded me of a scene from *The Bridge on the River Kwai*, but the heavy peace of the sliding river and sporadic plops of lazy fish brought "Grantchester Meadows" to mind. Humming the tune I returned for an ant-infested mug of tea. I had to admit that I really had no idea of where we were and tried to put my trust in our guides who were sat beside the fire telling stories about lion hunts. Kaset mimed the part of a lion his brother had killed, following the blow-by-blow account with great skill. He was shot three times in the spine and scrabbled furiously, biting the earth and coughing in his frantic pain. He arched his body tight as a snapping bow and with a convulsive heave, died. They played with the compass and binoculars for a while, long boned hands clapped in astonishment over their mouths as the needle followed the machete round the fire. Atol handed back the binos with a shy smile and bird-like expressions of surprise, the sort of fluttering "Ooh!" one's maiden aunts might give during a mildly indecent television programme.

The plan was for us to stay put until nightfall, when Atol would bring up his father's canoe. I wanted to move further south, to get away from the border post completely, despite their assurances that it was far, and so we walked downstream for a few miles until, apart from a thin fringe of trees on the banks, the bush had given way to open grassland and we could see clear across the delta to the hills behind Ileret and Lokobanya, but we could not see the lake.

We were now in the area where the brothers' family had their millet shamba and Kaset went off to search for his father. He returned with his mother and a few sisters as well. By and by I counted over 40 people under the trees with us and they all seemed to be suffering from malaria, stomach ache or headache. Some of the young children looked very sick indeed but I could do little more than issue broken Aspirin. I asked why they were so thin and the father, who was a handsome well-built man himself, said it was because they had not caught many fish recently.

"You don't feed babies on fish do you?" I asked, "what about milk? Maybe you can go to Kenya and buy sugar. You are rich in cattle. I have seen them."

"Yes," said the father, "we have cattle, but not always. Sometimes they die or raiders come, and now the cows are far away in the bush. We are here just looking after our farms, eating fish and crocodiles because the millet is not ready."

"What about goats and sheep?" I asked.

"We have no goats and sheep here, it's too wet and they eat the millet. They are far away."

The balance between life and death was fine and if the weak were hungry in a good year I wondered what happened when the rains failed or disease knocked down the herds. I was ignorant of the Shangalla economy and the conditions over a number of seasons, but I felt angry over the state of the children. The men were again discussing the journey to Todenyang. The whole deal was gone over with a fine-tooth comb as Kaset had again changed his mind and was going to come with us after all. I paid the brothers their money and agreed that Lokarangan should be the donkey to stay behind. The father got 10/- for the use of his canoe but Greg had to explain which were the ten-shilling notes and which the five-shilling ones. The money transaction seemed a bit futile as I had offered to buy them goods in Todenyang, but I think that they were rather taken with the idea of just having the notes to show to people.

My heart was like a yoyo trusting and doubting in turn and I was much relieved and greatly assured by the sight of Atol punting a canoe upstream in the afternoon light. The river bank dropped sheer to the water and we had to dig away a chute for the donkeys. Lokarangan stood on the bank fastidiously twitching at the flies with his tail, seemingly relieved that his journey was over. He watched disdainfully as Komote and Lobrolei were pushed rudely down the bank and into the water. They were immediately out of their depth but once across the river they sank to their shoulders in the soft mud of the shelving beach. It took quite an effort to pull them out. A cow came with us too. I hung on to its muzzle grimly as we paddled across.

Kaset took the cow away to a nearby manyatta and Atol returned the canoe. I was sick with worry when they both disappeared, for we had paid the bulk of their fee with the money and the donkey and were in a vulnerable position. I passed the burgeoning minutes by collecting the sweet fruits which lay scattered on the bare ground like beech mast from the enormous trees beneath which we stood.

"They make their canoes from this tree," said Greg.

"Do they?" I said. It was one of the few species I could recognize. "It's got very hard wood. There's a little statue carved of it in a museum in Cairo. It's about 5,000 years old.

They reckon it's one of the most ancient wood carving sin existence."

"What's it called?" asked Greg.

"Ficus Sycamoris," I said. "D'you know Zacchaeus from the Bible, Greg?" From his silence I assumed that he did and rambled on, picking up odd fruits here and there. "He was a short tax collector who climbed into a sycamore tree so he could see Jesus. Taste nice, don't they? It's called sycamore from two words in the Greek language, 'sykon' meaning fig and 'moron' meaning mulberry, that's a kind of fruit. You know I said those fish we ate used to be respected by the Egyptians? Well this tree was too. It was dedicated to Harrhor. She was the goddess of love and parties, things like that. Her head was shaped like a cow's head. Amazing really isn't it?" There was no reply.

"Well it's quite interesting anyway don't you think, Greg? Greg?" I looked up. The glade was deserted. Everyone had gone.

"Bugger!" I swore to myself and cast about for fresh hoof prints. By sheer good fortune a pile of steaming droppings got me onto the right path and I caught them up after a fifteen-minute run. Greg had assumed that I was in front and Laroi thought I was at the back. Esenyon had not thought at all. I was rather disturbed that we seemed to be going north again, back towards Geleb. Greg questioned Atol closely.

"Look," he said, "don't keep asking me questions. I am a moran and you will see how I am strong and I will take you to Kenya. Just not need to ask questions."

We were joined by a gang of small boys returning wet and naked from an afternoon's fishing. Their giggling warmth seemed to me a happy complement to the strings of cold dead fish they were carrying. Small boys and dead fish go together, I mused. I was watching my feet in an abstract way and realized that one of them was about to descend on a fat green snake, disturbed by the passing donkeys. On the rare occasions that I have seen snakes within striking distance I have usually retired gracefully as killing them is often less an act of self defence than of blind ignorance. On this occasion the boys were behind me and liable to be bitten in the failing light. I brought my stick down twice and we continued into the rising dark, our path swinging slowly west then south in a great arc. I had by now realized that the map was correct and that we were heading for the western branch of the river and, of course, the small patrol post. Atol explained that his father had another canoe, moored on the river some way below the post, and we were going to cross over in it that very night. Absolutely no need to worry, he assured us.

The moon was only three days old, and gave us just enough light to see by. Every so often one of us would fall into a swallow hole with a muted grunt. I assumed that these holes and trenches had been left in the soft-red earth by earlier flood waters. It was like crossing a glacier and I prayed that no one would break a leg. I felt close to God that night, faithless believer that I am, for supplication comes easily in adversity. Eventually Atol stopped us and we could see the sleeping river glistening in the moonlight.

"Unload the donkeys," he whispered. "We have to pass through many shambas and the people watch for raiders and damage. The loads will break down the millet."

With a sack each we carried on into the fields. It was pitch dark down between the rustling stalks and we followed each other by ear. Inland, away from the water, we began to see fires in the bush, a few at first but then long lines and groups where another great concentration of cattle was gathered. We could hear singing out in the night and the glow of the fires against the sky. Then suddenly we reached the river itself and we stopped. The bank had been cleared of trees, and lay indistinct, all blacks and greys with the moon gone down. Eighty yards over on the far side black undergrowth hung down over a steep bank. 'We've nearly made it,' I thought. Good old Atol. I began to hum "One more river" to myself as we unloaded the donkeys, and Atol went to fetch the canoe.

He returned five minutes later. "It isn't there," he announced. I stopped humming.

"What does he mean, not there?" I asked, stupidly. "Where is it?"

Atol did not know. Someone had probably borrowed it and hidden it for the night against robbers, as was the custom. He went off following the bank upstream to try and find it. We lent him the torch, but he dared not use it to search the far bank in case the police saw us. Despite the oppressive heat I had put on all my clothes and handed my sheet over to Esenyon. It was impossible to sit still in the whining, biting air. I could feel a drizzle of mosquitoes against my face and hands. Laroi had even stopped swearing at them and was miserably slapping himself. Komote broke free from his rope and ran off in torment towards the murmur of the distant manyattas. Finding him in the dark was a real bore as we staggered about whispering desperately without the torch. Atol was ages.

Jaws and tails smacked the water where crocodiles hunted the humid horrid night away. We could have made a raft, if there had been logs, rope and axes, but swimming the infested river was out of the question. Laroi and I shared a tactical cigarette down behind the sacks and at last Atol returned.

"No canoe," he told us.

"Not a complete surprise," I said. "OK. Let's get away from the river bank and make camp." It was nearly midnight. We slung the loads loosely over the donkeys' backs and shambled inland for about half a mile, towards the manyattas. The earth, trampled to sterile flour by countless hooves, became a white sea in the starlight, the eroded bushes breaking through in black, leafless gasps. We could hear singing and see the fires of the enormous camp ahead and so we moved aside into a maze of domed and twisted branches, wrenching what little firewood we could from the broken and half-buried roots around us. Atol thought it safe to have a fire if Kaset remained with us.

"These people here very bad," he said, "Kaset stay to protect you. I just go to see my sister is OK. She is married here. They steal many things and not like Turkana. Very bad."

Despite the continued carpet bombing from the mosquitoes Gregory prepared a pot of ugali which we devoured fast. Esenyon bravely made tea and I spread the net out as best I could. Laroi lay with his hands over his ears because, as he pointed out, if you could not hear them it was not so bad. We settled for a pretty miserable night. I hoped that a canoe could be arranged for the following evening and we would re-attempt to enter Kenya after laying up all day. My thoughts were suddenly interrupted by an almighty bellow from the manyattas, followed by screams and confused shouting. "Spare us," I pleaded silently.

"OK, lads," I said, "if there is trouble run south. Get across somehow and we'll meet up in Todenyang." Greg laughed.

"Ha. This just the bulls fighting. Not bad. Womens always screaming when they fight close to the manyatta."

"Idiot," I said to myself and tried to sleep. We had worked out a guard rota, but it was unnecessary as sleep was impossible. Even Kaset had borrowed the groundsheet to give some protection and you could hear the light "fizz-spat" of the myriad creatures throwing themselves onto the fire.

Atol returned, after nearly an hour's absence, with a wizened little gnome. The gnome skipped around the fire examining everything with the usual fluttering cries while Atol scraped the pot and spoke rapidly to Greg.

"This man got a canoe. He take us across tonight," he said, grinning.

'Good God! This trip is a series of bloody traumas,' I thought, 'first we're going, then we're not, now we are.' I had written off our chances of getting through that night anyway as apart from the canoe problem we had barely enough time to cross the border before daylight and that was assuming there were no hold ups, like getting lost. Being caught out on the open plain in daylight would be a disaster with the border post so near.

"OK, OK, great," I said, "let's get going."

"Wait," said Greg, "he want to eat first."

"Oh no! We're in a hurry and we haven't got enough food anyway, only a little bit of posho." There was a brief exchange and the gnome settled for the last of Laroi's tobacco and a little tea.

"Right. Super. Let's go," I said impatiently. I felt like a cat on hot bricks.

"He says what you pay him?" translated Greg.

"Tell him it's up to Atol to pay him. I've already paid Atol to get us to Todenyang."

"Atol says he won't go to Todenyang because this man say Turkanas very dangerous."

"Bloody hell, all right, I don't know . . ." I had the machete to hand and could have cheerfully used it. Violence was not the answer though.

"Leave it, I finish the thing quickly," said Greg, turning to Laroi. I had been trying to impress on the gnome the fact that our food was very low and that if we did not get to Todenyang that day it would be finished, when Kaset chipped in with a treacherous demand for a present too. Atol remained silent.

"Look, Steebon, just we give them what they want," said Laroi, "if we hungry, OK, not bad."

"All right let the twisted little bastard at the food," I muttered, "only for Christ's sake get a move on."

Eventually we parted with all our posho, shaking out the empty bags to show there was nothing left, our packets of soup and bouillon cubes, all but a handful of tea, torch batteries and a knife. The gnome was like a kid in a sweet shop, handling and asking for everything indiscriminately, giggling and cackling like something off the blasted heath. He bundled up his loot by which time we were ready to go. More talk.

"Kaset says he needs a clothes box," said Greg.

"What? A bloody clothes box? The stupid boy hasn't even got any clothes. Where the hell do I get a clothes box from? Tell him the shops don't open till nine around here."

"Never mind," said Greg. "I tell him you get it in Todenyang and send it to him."

"Tell him, anything, Greg, only we must go now." And, miraculously, we did, but not before the gnome had lifted Laroi's spear and trotted off into the darkness. I collared him and retrieved the spear with an oily smile, then followed close behind, compass in hand. By my reckoning we should have been going south but our initial course was a little north of east.

'The little bugger's trotting us off in the wrong direction. He's just going to leave us and run off,' I thought. We stopped and I explained this tactfully to Atol.

"It's OK," he said, "don't worry." I did worry but there was nothing to be done except carry on. Eventually we turned south and hit the river, and there, to my amazement, was a canoe pulled up on the beach. It was a twisted, leaking old thing like its owner but it was a boat and the far bank was in sight. I thanked God from the bottom of my heart. We quickly unloaded and hefted the kit down into the dug-out. The opening slit was too narrow for my hips and I had to kneel, which raised the centre of gravity to an interesting point of imbalance.

"OK, OK, let's get the kit over with one donkey. I'll go first then you three follow with the other donkey." I felt that a strong rearguard would be a good thing. The mosquitoes had abated slightly as I shoved off, naked, into the dark.

"Hang on," called Greg, "they're just talking." The gnome ran down the bank and pulled the canoe back in.

"He says this very dangerous work. Turkanas very bad people. He wants my shirt."

We were at the stage where we could have just taken the canoe and shoved off, but there were possibly hundreds of armed Shangalla in the manyattas close by who could have been summoned in the time it would take to get the donkeys across. I did not see why Greg should have to pay with his only shirt, and so I gave him my sheet.

"Take this you ... and ... off," I said and I think he caught my tone of voice because, stuffing the sheet into a bush, he dashed down to the canoe, gibbering like an idiot. At that moment Lobrolei broke his head rope again and cantered off. I nearly stood on my head with vexation and it took five heart-thumping minutes to get him back.

"Hold him tight and check the bloody rope," I told Esenyon, "sit on him if you have to."

Getting Komote into the water was frustratingly difficult as we had to push him out a fair way before he was out of his depth. He began to swim upstream but hit a sandbank. Crocodiles were the least of my worries. I jumped out and pushed and the gnome finally managed to get the canoe going. It rocked appallingly and I hung on tight to Komote's snorting head. I ceased to worry. My mind was like an empty fridge. 'Only a few yards to go,' I kept thinking, 'and we're there.' Luckily the far bank was quite firm and I soon had Komote tied to a bush, and I began to pack the kit into noiseless bundles for the final stage.

The canoe slopped back across the river and I could hear grunts and muted exhortations to the reluctant Lobrolei wafting across the black water. There was a sudden shout and a scuffle which I assumed was to do with the donkey, then the canoe was coming across. Kaset and Atol came too, but there was no sign of the gnome. Greg jumped out and ran up the bank.

"Someone try to kill this my huncle," he panted, "when he pushing Lobrolei down a man come from the bush and take his spear, bring it behind to kill, but Esenyon saw the man and hit him with your stick. The man just leave down the spear and run away. Better we leave soon." My own thoughts exactly. Kaset was agitated.

"He wants medicine," said Greg, "then they go back."

"Give him these," I said, handing over two Nivaquine pills. They taste nauseating. "Tell him to suck them very slowly."

When they were half way back in the canoe Kaset called out something.

"He says don't forget the clothes box," translated Greg. My reply was colourful, vehement and unprintable.

I set the compass and looked at the stars. Esenyon, Greg and Laroi had done their bit and now it was up to me to lead us safely into Kenya. Esenyon had taken the lesson about securing the donkeys to heart.

"Hang on," said Greg as I set off, "I can't untie this rope."

Komote, Lobrolei and a small bush were tangled together in a mariner's nightmare. 'Here we are,' I thought, 'we've walked for days, tired and hungry, the end is in sight and we can't untie the bloody donkeys.' It had its funny side, but we cut the ropes in the end. It was just after two o'clock, giving us about four hours of darkness left to cover what I guessed was about seven miles to see us well over the frontier.

We followed a track leading westwards towards the border post to get us clear of the frog-croaking, mosquito-whining river, but I turned south too soon and we blundered around in a thick belt of spindly bushes for over an hour. Despite our pantomime efforts to keep quiet, the snapping of branches and the occasional fart from a donkey sounded clear in the stillness and every few minutes I stopped to listen for danger. A vivid green flash in the western sky lit our faces and for a moment I thought a patrol had sent up a signal flare. It was only a meteor but bright as a firework.

At last we were clear of the bushes and, skirting a marshy

trough, saw our route fair across the plain, with Lapurr inky black on the horizon. One hundred and fifty thousand light years away in the southern sky hung the Magellanic clouds like signs of welcome seen through a dark mist. Jupiter and Mars had followed the young moon over the firmament and Orion had begun to fall like the slowly moving hand of an immense time piece, a colossal insect pinned out and turning with Cirius and bright Procyon loyal beads of light strung out and drawn behind. The Southern Cross and the Great Bear were there in opposition and between them, but behind us now, shone Aldebaran in the Hyades. Years before on a star-struck granite hill a man from dry lake Chad had told me about walking by night.

"Go into the night humble like a child," he had said, "leave your deeds and your pride by the fire, for under the stars you are less than sand."

I remembered his advice and we moved on across the rolling plain like small creatures of the deep. Eventually the blackthorn fence of a sleeping manyatta rose stark against the inkling grey and a cock crowed as we padded by. Laroi touched me on the shoulder.

"Steebon, Steebon," he was smiling, "I think we made it." He turned and looked back. "Fookin' Etopia!" he said.

12

"OK," I said, "stop."

"Kenya!" said Esenyon, and he actually took off his hat.

We sank happily to the ground with the donkeys, certain now that pursuit was impossible, and I made an incongruous little speech of thanks to my three friends. Laroi and I shared a cigarette on the bare open plain, laughing because it was our last one. The vault of open night was dissolving into a magnificent dawn, eastern trumpets of light announcing our safe arrival. Translucent grass covered the plain down to the steel-grey lake and over the water clouds sped low from the red of an open throat through rose and vermilion to harsh blue. The bare ground picked up the glow and blushed strong, each rock and stone burnished in the rich light. Lapurr became closer and more distinct, capped by thick layers of basalt broken off sheer in lordly cliffs over the crumpled foothills, like trampled cellophane, each fold and crease picked distinctly by the sun. The early clarity anointed our eyes and tired heads but tediously deceived our feet. The Kenyan police post at Namuruputh appeared from a fold ahead, like a scale model precise in every detail, but it was ages before we reached it. As we did so a single man in white vest and shorts crossed by ahead. Esenyon sang out a greeting and the man waved.

"The pump-house man been to start the motor," Esenyon said. "Here Kenya now, with Turkana people. No troubles any more." He was happy because he was nearly home.

The last four miles were a sandy drag and seemed much further, but we eventually reached Todenyang at eight-thirty, so eager for chai and a fag that it hurt. About 30 shelters were scattered like chicks round four or five breeze-block buildings, a fish store, a dispensary and the school. There was not a single tree in sight. A few wattle-and-daub dukas stood apart, for which Laroi and I made a bee line.

"Ah, chai, chai," he hummed to himself as we entered the first duka. "Wapi chai?" he asked.

"Hakuna chai, hakuna hoteli," was the reply. Laroi turned to me with pathetic disappointment in his eyes.

"No hoteli, Steebon," he said, in the voice of a plaintive waif. "No chai."

"There must be some, we'll try another duka," I said and we walked over to the next one. The dickensian counter was the only substantial thing in the shop and sitting behind it was a thin Somali with a self-effacing smile. He stood up and flapped away the dust with an exercise book as we crossed the threshold. Stacked against one wall was a pile of maize meal in 2-cwt sacks which dusted my brown arms white as I leaned against them. Jars of boiled sweets and toffees, candles, small packets of detergent and very old-fashioned razor blades stood on the rickety shelves, loosely nailed to the flaking mud walls. It was very hot. A neat pile of coarse sheets was folded on the bottom shelf beside a jumble of tyre sandals and a pungent sack of dried tobacco. A pair of scales cast long ago stood at ease upon the counter, the scoop reflected dimly golden in the scarred old school-desk surface of the wood. Laroi began to speak but was cut short by the Somali whose name, we learnt, was Abdi.

"OK, OK. Make you sit down," he said hospitably. He set two folding chairs out in the courtyard and went back to a solid drawer in the counter from which he took an open packet of cigarettes. The shop had run out and these were his last. Before the baggage train had caught us up Laroi and I had drunk a mug of sweet gruel in the shade. I got up wearily to help unload.

"Sit down," said Laroi. "This my nephew with the other boy they will do it. We elders just rest."

There was a dark hut in the courtyard and another mud-walled room in which the Somalis lived. There were three of them, all brothers, and some of their relatives from Isiolo and Marsabit staying with them over the Christmas holidays. There were no women. The cook and his mate were Turkana and a couple of local boys helped with chores around the shop. A tall bird-like man emerged from the living quarters.

"Yis, welcome?" he said. "My name it is Mohammed Said Guled and this my brother's shop. You stay here, put down the loads, and resting." A heavier, bearded man in a long robe came out and was introduced by Guled.

"This Abdul Bareza, my brother who is owning shop." Abdul Bareza smiled openly but spoke no English. In his hand were a string of beads and a book. It was the Koran. He was not a rich man, a stranger himself to Turkana land but, like Abdi, he had immediately accepted four hungry strangers and their chattels into his house, asked no questions and locked nothing. I felt immediately grateful, more for the immediacy of his trust than for the physical refreshment his household had brought us. The past two weeks had frayed my nerves a little and it was good to be resting easy.

I began to pull on my ragged and smelly plimsolls but a fourth brother, Fara, stopped me.

"Take it this," he said, slipping off his flip-flops. "Yes this is the better for sand condition. Just take it."

I walked down to the lake with Abas, a bright young cousin of Bareza's and in his last year at Marsabit Secondary School. He tried to cover his unease in the company of the Turkana girls bathing naked in the lake by overt speculation on their virtue, the sort of immature and aggressive self-titillation one might associate with young men of sexually repressive cultures and a world away from the lowly freedoms of the bush folk. I found one of the household's two sprung beds prepared for me on our return and, after a gutful of chicken, chappatis and omelettes, I slept deep into the soft mattress. The police from Namuruputh had been when I woke up but seeing me asleep they had only given our loads a cursory inspection and kindly let me snooze on.

In the few days I had spent in Nairobi I had been introduced to a Danish nurse working in Lowarangak, a Catholic mission station twelve miles south of Todenyang. She had smiled and asked me to drop in on the way round the lake. By coincidence she was due in Todenyang that day to inoculate the children and in the late afternoon she rattled in at the wheel of her Toyota. I went over to greet her and after her initial surprise got an invitation to dinner the following evening.

Mohammed Said Guled spoke fairly good English and we had a long conversation that night. He had a habit of giving precise figures for everything, which were mostly wrong.

"Yis," he said, "eighteen miles to Lowarangak, two hours walking exactly, ah, but with pundas three, yis, three hours then four days to Kalokol. There you will take vehicle, much better for you." He did not really grasp how it was that we preferred to walk when we could drive. He had read Islamic studies at a university in Pakistan and wanted to go on to study geology at Birmingham University, but as he tactfully put it, "the money is not sufficient".

After evening prayers Laroi entertained them all with a lively account of the journey, which ended in general agreement that Shangallas were fisi, hyenas all, and also that their colonial experience had been bad, unlike the just British rule enjoyed by the good folk of Kenya. I could see that Laroi would dine out on Ethiopian stories for some time to come.

Laroi and the others set off early the following morning but I stayed for the light to increase and took everyone's photograph. Since there were three different addresses to send them to Mohammed Guled said that he would dish them out if I sent them all to him.

"So you need the addressing, yis, write it here," he brought a piece of paper. "Write 'Prospector'. You see, I am prospector interested in rock stones and crystal. Yis that is my address, Prospector Mohammed. P.O. Box Isiolo."

Catching the others up over the plain took a couple of hours and on the way I rejoiced in the generosity of the Somalis.

"You see, we are not like they," Prospector had said, talking of the Shangallas. "We call them fallen Somalis, people who have gone to the bush. They used to be with us but now we are people of the book. We are their old relations but they have fallen."

Between our footpath and the lake was a high belt of palm-studded dunes and beyond them on the shore rude huts cobbled the beach in isolated clusters. Strings of split fish were hung on lines to dry in the sun like washing, and thin, tongue-hanging dogs ground rib on weary flesh among the broken sea-washed vegetation, the crumbling polystyrene floats, frayed bright-orange cord, and all that wrack of the lake. The dunes had been a promontory years ago separating Sanderson's Gulf from the lake. We were now moving off the dried bed of the gulf onto rockier ground where thorn trees grew and increased as we went south. We stopped for water beside a shallow pool called Angurupus. It would soon be dry but now verdant grass grew down to the water's edge grazed to a uniform lawn by goats. A herd of maidenly pelicans stood off in the muddy water when we dashed in for a swim. As we were leaving, a group of fifteen men appeared, in ragged black jackets and shorts. I felt uneasy about groups of strangers on the road but Greg reassured me.

"This is Kenya now. No problems here. These men're going to collect a cow. They all relatives of this man." He pointed out a short but hard-looking chap with scars all over his belly. "They all raiders. You can tell because they got jackets like this with pockets they can put bullets in. They all got guns but they leave them in the manyatta." He explained that vertical scars on the chest and belly stand for a kill. This group could have supplied a municipal cemetery.

Lowarangak arrived surprisingly quickly. Apart from the mission buildings, the settlement was not a lot bigger than Todenyang. We camped in the dry Lowarangak river bed, a torrent of dusty stone and sand swept from the Lapurr range behind us. I sent Greg off with some money to buy what supplies he could and gave the others enough to sample whatever delights they might, then I went up to the bungalows to greet the Danish nurses. Helen and Elizabeth fed me beef and bread and tea, and took me down to the lake in the afternoon. A few bright-red fibreglass canoes were pulled up on the sand, each with a boy guarding it. The canoes came from Norway as part of an aid programme.

Elizabeth had been in Lowarangak for over two years. She was big, blonde and one of the warmest-hearted women I have ever met. She swam every afternoon and ignored crocodiles.

"Just here I see logs floading," she said sweetly, "but odder peeble see dem swimming away!"

Back at camp Laroi looked sick. He lurched over to me as I approached and tripped over a root. I helped him up.

"Ah, Steebon, I hope everything OK. I buy 2/- of meat. Ver' naice."

"That's OK, Laroi. No sweat. Here's the money."

"And I buy 20/- of pombe," he added, waving two dark green bottles dangerously. Inside them had been an oily brew made directly from sugar, very powerful but nasty.

The hospital dispenser, whose name was Julius, was related

to Esenyon and looked astonished to see him. While they caught up with each other's news Greg and I went to a duka and bought Esenyon a goodbye present. We got him the largest sheet we could find. It was maroon coloured and he was like an emperor at the games as we sat by our tree and watched Laroi performing. Gleeful boys dropped like giggling flies from the lower branches as Laroi went through a few preliminary drill movements. He was saluting with his empty bottle at the shoulder but fell over twice on the about turn. He became verbose.

"Mungu, Mary and Jesus," he bellowed, blasphemously close to the church. "Gonna kill Laurienne if I ever see him. Swat I'm gonna do. Fookin' Shangalla. Wasn't worried by Atol. No. Mimi shifta." He flexed his biceps and with a series of drunken roars drove the audience behind the tree.

"Laroi," I said, "I don't like to be drunk often, but I know that half drunk is no good. You call that woman over and we'll get some more for you." He staggered off across the sand with the women who made the liquor, his words of command punctuating the sizzlingly hot air. He would soon fall asleep.

Elizabeth and Helen had a refrigerator stacked with brown bottles of beer so cold that the dew ran down the necks and made round puddles on the table. That night they wore long dresses and we had a fabulous supper of roast goat out on the verandah. Two priests came over from their house for coffee and later came a beautiful American nun. We heard a cattle song and laughter from the fires across the river and the waxing moon shone a thick white slice over the lake, but, best of all and much later, when the ash trays were full, a night bird began to sing, a pop gun firing rubies in the dark, just simple notes but the price of sunlit dew on grass.

Prostitutes and smelly bars are very much a part of township Africa, but I had forgotten about such things since I had left Nairobi. I felt quite virginally embarrassed when an ugly girl in a blue woollen jumper stopped Greg and I outside a shop. We had walked up the gorge to Lokitaung, the district capital, as we had found very little to eat in Lowarangak except posho. To our chagrin there was neither sugar nor salt nor cooking fat in Lokitaung, "because of the rains" but we got some rice and beans and dried milk with a few goodies like sweets,

Aspirins and toothpaste to make up a reasonable load. We could not get chappatis anywhere and so we sat in a Somali tea shop guzzling tea as fast as the sweet glasses cooled down. As we were leaving five mean-looking Shangallas came in noisily demanding tea. One of them looked at me, let out a great whoop and leapt across the table. He grabbed my hand and pumped it up and down, doing a little dance with his feet on the floor.

"It's Yergulem," said Greg, "the guy that got the compasses back."

"So it is. What's he doing here?"

"He says he just come with his brothers to make journey to the town."

Yergulem had acquired a jacket and some sandals and even a pair of shorts but he retained his slim beauty withal. He was genuinely pleased to see us and happy that we had reached Kenya. We left him smiling at the duka door, one hand in his ripped jacket to keep it on and the other waving us off on our way back through the hills down the dozen rocky miles to the mission. At the bottom of the gorge the vehicle track twisted along the river bed, but a footpath cut out the major bends. On a rocky bluff high above the blue-grey gravels of the road we passed a heap of stones with leaves and bits of grass stuck in the spaces.

"Take a stone, or leaves if the season good, and put it on," said Greg, "this we do in Turkana at some places high like this for travel man's luck." I put on another stone. We saw baboon and camel in the rocky scrub and heard the metallic red cliffs of broken lava echo to the cries of occasional young goat minders. An hour from home we met a man with a bag of sugar.

"Ah! Persist!" I said to Greg. He did and when we got back he managed to persuade a reluctant shopkeeper to part with a few kilos. My canvas rucksack was sodden with sweat and cold on my sore back and my feet were blistered from their beating on the rocks. We had done the return trip of 25 miles in just under six hours. I went up to see Elizabeth and Helen and knocked back a most welcome beer. We had a quiet supper and discussed money, for I had only £25 left. They had some good music on tape, including a few old melodies which went round my head for several days afterwards. One particular tune stayed with me right until the journey's end. It was called "Pennies from Heaven".

Sixty miles south of Lowarangak lies the town and fishing station of Kalokol. It took us four days to reach it, a partly monotonous plod down plains of lava and sand with little sugar and no salt. One noontide beside a muddy hole the boy Nakutha joined us, a slender lad with eyes as soft as does'. He was a cousin of Esenyon and ate with us for two days. Supine in the shade I watched a bull moving through the herd in the marshy ground beside us drowsily nudging the cows with his soft nose and swinging dewlap. He took my mind off the plague of squashy caterpillars invading our kit. A large cluster dropped from the acacias into Greg's hair.

"Little buggers," he said. His English was improving. He took the machete to hack a log from the green mswaki bush behind us. He made a new posho paddle, a symbol of the passing days for the old one had lasted since the day we had seen the Grant's gazelles fighting nearly a month before. Esenyon was on home ground and walked ahead in his hat and blood-red toga with an enormous grin, greeting amazed friends with a wave of a wooden stool he had acquired in Lowarangak. Laroi had on my sky-blue tee shirt and walked between the donkeys with a stoop, and Greg still carried the rod in its calico sleeve. Nakutha sometimes showed me things, like the river where you had to touch your chest and forehead with dust for luck. Camels came from the west to drink and Turkanas walked the windy beach in leather togas, bold silhouettes with nodding plumes, and spears in their graceful hands. Choro the white island shone in the east out of the deep, blue lake.

We passed by Esenyon's manyatta at noon on the second day. His mother had gone to search for him in Kitale where he was rumoured to be, and his father was dead. His elder brother insisted that he remain at home and so we did not tarry, but continued when the heat had left the sand, walking on in tired silence and missing Esenyon. We camped beside a brackish pool, fouled by birds and circled round with soft wet mud pressed delicately by the pit-a-pat and criss-cross of birds' feet.

That evening a natty man strode down the track and shared our meal, a black Dick Whittington with his bundle slung from a stick over one shoulder. He wore a denim cap and the trousers of his safari suit were rolled up to his calves. Beneath the matching jacket was a yellow tee shirt with a picture of two chimpanzees doing the bump. It was Tito, the Geleb mission cook. He was on his way to join his family south of Kalokol and had just come from Lokitaung. Yergulem, he told us, had been arrested and was now in Lokitaung jail. He had been caught smuggling radios from Geleb police who got them cheaply in Addis. A couple of dark men in jackets came into camp behind Tito and ate with us too.

"Where are your guns?" I asked.

"Mine is hidden," said the smallest man, "trouble with the Kenya police last year."

"What happened?"

"There was a big raid," said Greg. "Mzee said to stop it so police do the crack down. Even this man he make the raid at that time."

"Tell him I would like to know about raiding."

"OK, he say he tell you of the last year. He don't know the day but his family decide to doing a raid. They go to the bush just so far away and each man he bring a goat, some sheeps even a cattle, whatever they can afford. They stay for three weeks killing the meat and hunting, just all the raiders together and they make a plan. Some go out very carefully to check the place where they go. This man he say last year eight enter forward to Sudan checking out where the cattle, where the villages. He was one. Then they were 300 guns, many people, and they attack. Sixty people of Sudan killed but only three Turkanas. They take 600 cattles and run back to Kenya just fast in the night, cattle dividing small so no one see they stolen. They kill everything in that area where they raid so no one coming chasing. Also this man he kill two. He says he take his gun through the bush until close like me by the fire and shoot fast. Two dead. He got sixteen cattles with his brother. Now he is just resting."

I had heard similar accounts of raids, with a concentration of forces and feasting out in the bush while the reconnaissance and planning went on. The execution seemed to be a swift and bloody shoot out followed by rapid flight to a place of division where previously agreed shares would be taken and the flight continued.

At mid-morning on the third day we reached the mission station of Kataboi and flopped out in the inadequate shade of a small acacia. Elizabeth had passed us earlier on her way to Kitale for Lowarangak's monthly supplies, and with a telegram to my bank for more money. Moving south it had become steadily hotter with progressively little shade and only a light breeze at dawn. Greg stood under the tree in a daze.

"There's no firewood," he said. I took hold of the machete and cut some dead branches out of the river bed. We were becoming weary. Laroi had a niggling, persistent cold and the donkeys were thin and knackered. I returned with an armful of wood as Laroi turned the last of our Lowarangak goat from a sack. It was crawling but still dry and so we ate it anyway. Laroi lost his temper with a bunch of gawking youths and I got mildly ripped off over some sour milk. I slumped apathetically in the singing heat and watched a grasshopper with pea-green thighs and a red-brown body swaying through Gregory's hair, stopping occasionally in the curly forest to suck its back feet. A balled spider swung like a pendulum in the thin breeze, looking for a fresh anchor above the deadly ant lions spitting dust from their cones of death. A tiny itch began in my throat and developed through the tedious afternoon, building up with the humidity. Snatches of song, mostly sad, passed through my mind, but I could not tell if I was humming or just thinking. When we stopped in the dunes I could not eat, but got down some penicillin and lots of Aspirin. I felt muzzy and suddenly I did not feel anything and Laroi was wrapping me in my sleeping bag. I had fainted briefly and lay by the fire, shivering. 'The moon, it's like a buttercup in ink,' I thought, slipping back, 'I mustn't fall in with it. At least there aren't any mosquitoes.'

Greg ended a rotten night by bringing tea at four-thirty. It was a painful swallow and I thought about resting for a day but decided to try to reach Kalokol and the dispensary. I had a lonely walk as the others soon left me behind, limping along on blistered feet and feeling sorry for myself. Especially in adverse conditions there are destinations one feels ought to have been reached long before they ever are and the temptation is to believe they never will be. I crossed endless belts of palm and river bed always thinking that I had left the last one behind, and expecting to see the town ahead. It was only supposed to be twelve miles away. At last a clump of trees spoke to me.

"Ah, Steevan, it is you. We are close now," said Greg from the shade.

"Great," I croaked, "but there's no need to humour me." But Greg was right and soon we had skirted the corrugated-iron roofs and were looking for a base. I stayed with the donkeys but before long Greg and Laroi came back and led us to an empty hut which Laroi swept out with gusto. He had never struck me as being a houseproud man but when I saw the fleshy green scorpions in the sweepings I understood his zeal. Greg chose a tall young man from the audience to direct me to the hospital which was a fair step from our house. I sat on the low wall surrounding the porch with a gaggle of women and vomiting children, and wallowed in self pity. Patients were shown into the surgery in batches of about half-a-dozen and eventually it was my turn. A child widdled on my foot as kaolin was stuffed down its throat by an accustomed nurse who was translating for the doctor at the same time. I have been treated for a variety of diseases in bush hospitals and I very much like the informality of them. The doctor was a largish American lady, short-sighted and the wrong side of 40 with a well-scrubbed face and pink hands.

"Well young man, what is it?" she asked.

"Bit of a sore throat, doctor," I said, opening my mouth. She looked down.

"My word, yes," she said, "you've got acute tonsilitis. That's awful bad but don't worry because we're going to fix you up."

I was fixed up with a jab of penicillin in the backside by a very pretty Kikuyu nurse, who issued me with a handful of pain relievers and Aspirin. I thanked the doctor who was wearing the sort of light blouse that ladies with large arms wear, and noticed her cotton-print skirt, stretched tight over an ample rear. It was dark-green in colour and printed all over it in different styles of lettering were words like wow, HA HA HA, CRUNCH and SPLASH. What really cheered me up was an onomatopoeic PSST in bold capitals running across each buttock. 'Good on you Uncle Sam,' I thought, walking slowly back to the hut.

Laroi and I walked up dusty Main Street in the late afternoon and hit the Chopper Hotel. I have ever remarked the extraordinary ability Africans have of working in and tolerating chaos. Crowding the counter were beggars and country boys, prostitutes and kitchen hands and covies of table-high urchins who dashed from place to place fighting over the scrapings with lightning curs. Above the din, orders were shouted through the serving hatch into the inferno of a kitchen by waiters with pencils in their hair.

"One tea two tea three give me fourteen teas and one I said ONE TEA!"

"Give me rice and beans two ten twenty seven times no TWO!" The eyes of the screeching waiters would roll while unhurried cooks stirred cauldrons on the mud-brick oven, cuffing boys for firewood and water. A girl of about thirteen came in with a ragged belt of cotton waste and rags trailing from her waist. There was a sad vacancy in her beautiful face but nothing in the twisted club of a hand she held out between the tables, shuffling through on deformed feet.

Greg arranged the donkeys' Christmas holidays with a woman called Ekadeli. She agreed to look after them for ten days in exchange for three kilos of sugar. I thought that very cheap and offered her five. She promised to keep an eye open for another donkey to replace Lokarangan. Across the dusty square from our hut was a strident bar of wriggly tin called Mojong Edukon and Laroi was rubber-kneed by mid-afternoon. I gave him more money in the vain hope that he would knock himself out. He turned up the following morning like some kid having lost all his money, with a scratched face and torn shirt to boot. He was ashamed and did all our washing, but by noon he was stoked up enough to do a spot of drill. I got a second jab at the hospital and with Greg bought our stores for after Christmas and left them in a duka for safe-keeping.

A good fight was in progress outside the hut and we watched through the sparse walls. A furious woman in a cotton skirt and bleeding from the nose stood screaming loudly at a maiden greased and beaded, dressed in silent leather. The screamer's heavy blows were mostly wides, but the silent girl scored suddenly with a slashing left hander that opened the other's blouse and spilled out her breasts like melons. Laroi bestirred himself to stop the action, but we advised him to leave it. A swinging mammary got bitten hard but with that the young one over-reached herself and tripped, screeching beneath a painful and dusty drubbing. Laroi moved again.

"Leave it, huncle," said Greg, "people are outside if it gets bad. Just mind your own business."

"Yeah. You'll end up getting done over yourself," I added. And of course he did. Lurching outside he made straight for the struggling women, entangled like waltzing spiders.

"Stop, stop," he shouted. "No fighting!" Quite suddenly it did stop. The Turkana girl was dragged off by her friends leaving Laroi and the woman with sore breasts looking at each other. She smacked him smartly in the mouth. He looked surprised, then remonstrated. Boiling invective and raking slaps fell about his face and she drove him back inside. Greg barred the door and she satisfied herself by screaming insults through the thatch.

"Hivyo better we go to Lodwar now," said Greg wisely, "we don't wait for tomorrow." They were going to spend Christmas with Greg's elder brother John who had a job in Lodwar. We agreed to meet up again roughly three days after Christmas and they left Kalokol on a swaying stinking lorryload of dried fish.

I visited the fish store, the town's only industry and its entire *raison d'être*. Queues of women were waiting patiently in the compound with their loads in baskets for weighing. Behind the scales, inside the warehouse, the husky fish were stacked in heaps from floor to ceiling. Great presses were being charged between the gloomy piles to squeeze down the bales of dried or salted fillet, prettily arranged and sown into sack cloth, then bound round by protecting withies for the long journey south. Cool Luos watched their purchases bundled, flicking out the small fish and the thin. Agents scuttled from weighbridge to office with white papers of commerce and beyond were the tills where the fishermen waited for their money. Nets and cordage and hooks could be bought at the co-operative store and Esenyon had told us that he planned to spend his money there on fishing gear.

The afternoon wore on and passed me by. I sat outside the Chopper drinking tea with only 15/- and a bag of sweet mandazis left. Like a shoal in the broad street a long thin group of Turks were gathered sitting in the shade of four gnarled trees against which were tethered their snuffling goats and a couple of puppies. The women with their gourds and babies formed a warm, butter-brown and gossiping group, but the men, all sticks and mud and stools, sat apart. Spears were not allowed in town. Confident youths but short began to taunt a lame boy who stood crookedly above them, laughing despite it all.

People came to stare at me and went away ignored. I drank more tea in the cocky vroom of a festooned lorry swaying dust back south to Luo land. Land-Rovers swirled in squarely beyond the central knot in the street, a few whites like hidden marrow somewhere inside. The sun acquired red beauty but cooled slowly away in the west and the hotel door was closed, hiccupped open to let a couple out but sternly ignored a latecomer trying to get in. The boys went away and loads were taken from the sidewalk. The trees in the middle of the street were deserted but for a lonely puppy, thin and already dog-faced. The lame boy was alone and watched me as I curled in the tree above the puppy and sat waiting. Elizabeth's lights were already on when at last she bowled in from Kitale, raising dust to the evening moon. I jumped into the cab beside her and we drove back up the last four days in three hours twenty minutes.

Lapurr still beckoned and I wanted to go up there. I retained the services of a guide through the local councillor, a cherubic-looking man, short and fat but sly. He wore long trousers and pointed plastic shoes and he had a twirly moustache. His name was Chief William and he introduced me to his protégé like a seedy manager with a bright new boy.

"This boy is good," he said, "he knows the way up to Lapurr. He speaks sharp Swahili and cooks fast. A definite prospect."

"What's his name?"

"Norman."

"You're kidding! OK. Tell him to bring his stuff here at six tomorrow."

Norman Lochinchu Longolia was not so much a guide as an

asker of the way. Having walked with our backs to the objective for a day it became obvious that Norman had no idea of the route. He had a nice smile though and a sore shoulder which had been trampled by a camel. Stopping at an isolated camp Norman caused excessive mirth when he told the people where we were going. They all stood up except one old man who had fallen off his rock laughing. He pointed back the way we had come. A little tobacco induced him to lead us for a few miles and he gave Norman's shoulder a massage, churning up and down his back with heel and toe. We slept among thick cacti on the first night with a hill wind that cut through our shivering blankets and blew out the fire. Norman saved the night with a dry ball of donkey dung in which he kept an ember smouldering. By noon on the second day we had returned to the spot where we had entered the hills and we sat, rather tired, beneath a tree.

There was little to say for Norman's swahili was a very small and withered shoot, but sharing our tree were two old boys from whom we asked directions. They were discussing something in a series of competing monologues, yelling their heads off at close range. The listener distracted himself with a scratch, a yawn or a spit while the other wound himself up in a five- or ten-minute speech of some force and gesticulation. Emphasis was achieved by repetition and time expressed in long drawn-out consonants with clicks of the tongue and snapping fingers bringing each point home in vivid colour. Asking the way in Turkana land could bring anything from a short "it is near" to a complete description of the country for miles around with an energetic tarantella to emphasize the tricky sections.

We filled the plastic water bottles and walked off in hope, approaching Lapurr peak from the west. The sugar-loaf tip is the eroded remains of an old volcanic core, steep sided but grazed right over the top by strong white cattle and the view when eventually we reached the summit filled my soul to the brim. Pencil-thin swifts sliced the muzzy blue in evening hunt around our vantage, three quarters of a mile above the lake. We could see the Omo river, a convoluted steel ribbon winding through the indistinct green down to the oozing delta. On a bend where the yellowing plain touched the river I could just make out the solid black of police huts in Geleb, but the Kenyan post at Namuruputh was invisible, lost in the deep shadow of Lapurr itself. On the blind side of the lake the hills fell away into a shattered bowl, with coinciding layers of basalt broken over the valleys and dipping far west into the Lotikipi plains. At sunset we heard a growing hum around us and prepared for instant flight. I have known men stung to death on hill tops such as this.

"Nyuki?" I asked Norman. "Bees?"

But it was only a hatch of beetles, scattered on the wind and colliding with the hillside. Norman and I made a fire each, tucked down out of the wind, but the night was exceedingly cold. Below the pitiless moon, pin-prick fires dotted the plains and the lake was a silver sea.

The dawn was not spectacular, but good enough, for it was Christmas Eve. Crows flew in the coming light, their wings and tails constantly changing shape to accommodate the wind which roared in our ears, bringing the thick clonk of wooden cow bells up from the herd stirring in the bowl below. "Fookin' Etopia" and the delta were spread out to the north, Geleb, Namuruputh, Todenyang and the mission were all there, lacking only the dotted line of our route to join them up. Choro and the Turkwell delta lay away to the south, and I thought that I could make out Moite in the haze, nearly 100 miles away.

The valley behind us fell out of the hills through a cavernous ravine, gouged through the hard lava beds and deep into the underlying sandstones. Grey boulders bigger than elephants choked the valley floor down through peppered lines of trees studding the crumpled foreland which smoothed and lost itself out on the plain. To the west but now in shadow lay a hazy alternation of mountain and plain away to the Ugandan marches and north the dry Lomogol river swept the eye into the marsh and desert of the southern Sudan. A fish eagle soared out below into the singing wind, turning for us like a marionette on rigid wings.

Norman excelled himself that morning and by ten o'clock we found ourselves walking up a blind valley with little prospect of being back at the mission for Christmas. A passing youth revealed that we were on the back route to Lokitaung and so we returned to our last water hole where the humbled guide cooked posho and washed up. He went off on a recce and returned to say that the path was "mzuri kidogo" or "rather good" which, apart from an early precipice into which he nearly fell, it was. Within eyesight of the mission Norman asked me the time and predicted that we would arrive in 30 minutes which barring an act of God was a very safe bet. When we put down our loads to a cheer from the Danes he became loudly boastful and Chief William waddled over to ask how things had gone.

"A good boy?" asked William.

"Brilliant," I said, "highly recommended. Here's some tobacco and the money. Happy Christmas."

"Ah good. We merry Christmas now all singing. I tell you Norman very good man."

Five easy days passed in eating, sleeping, drinking and washing up. We had picnics in the gorge and beside the lake with tilapia cooked into battered twists like scampi, bowls of fresh pineapple and cans of olives with Martini and ice on starched white table cloths. I became sluggish to a degree. Von Höhnel was right when he wrote that "Inaction after a long period of strenuous exertion always has pernicious results. Body and spirit become enervated, attacks of indigestion occur, and the traveller is far more liable to be unfavourably affected by the climate than when on the march." On the morning that we left the house we had a final breakfast of omelette, lovely bread and home-made jam, pâté, pineapples, coffee and tea, and stilton cheese and sherry. Elizabeth and Helen drove me down to Kalokol with gusto and I emerged from the rear of the Land-Rover like a dusty zombie to say goodbye.

13

"Problems? You got problems? Ha Ha Ha! Look—I got a problem too. Problem of no cold beer. Yours didn't happen yet so forget it till it does." I was rapping about the trip to a happy Dane on Boxing Day, worried about two rivers ahead, both flooded and reported impassable. He laughed when I told him that Greg and Laroi were in Lodwar for Christmas.

"That's problem number one," he said. "You got to get them back, and the donkeys too."

I was confident that they would all be back on time but anxious about Laroi who might have overdone the festivities and rendered himself unfit for duty. With no horses or lariats, springing him from Kalokol jail, if he had drunk himself inside it, would be tricky, 'Tea and mandazis,' I thought, in Kalokol once again, 'fortify yourself against probable hassles.'

The Chopper Hotel was leaping. I squeezed my way to the water butt for a sluice and got generous shouts of recognition from the scuttling waiters. Shaking my wet head I reached for the grimy rag of a towel.

"Here Mr Steevan. Yis indeed it is you. I know exactly now, um, two o'clock precise." I knew the voice immediately.

"Prospector! Good Lord! Happy Christmas. What brings you here?" He was on his way home to Isiolo. "Let's have some tea together." I turned from the basin and got two enormous grins in my face, one bright, the other bleary.

"Hello!" they said.

"Ha!" Fresh greetings of old friends are brimful moments. "Superb! How are you? Oh bloody great. You both OK?" I was really pleased to see them.

"Yes. We OK. My brother not in Lodwar but we stay with my people from my father's brother. I got malaria very bad for three days, and this my huncle have a little trouble here but all OK now."

"Look dis ver' naice," said Laroi, miming his bush hat. "Sasa hapana. It is gone. I sleep and my hat gone. Also my spear stolen. This people here just mkora—bad people. Also my tee shirt that is yours, taken away." I commiserated with him. It didn't strike me as odd that he had not reported the thefts to the police until a couple of days later.

"He sold them didn't he?" I asked Greg.

"Yes," he said, and I knew why Laroi had had no spear when I met him.

In addition to the stores I had got before Christmas we bought sugar, posho, tobacco, plenty of cigarettes and a razor for Laroi, and a new donkey. Our donkey-minders had produced a young male of Lokarangan's age for us to buy.

"I try, I try but they don't take less than 200/-," moaned Greg. "They been here two days to wait for you coming."

We strolled out through the rustling palms to a shady grove where the little beast was tied. His owners lurked in the shade, two handsome brothers with fine hair-dos. I asked them why they wanted to sell.

"For money to get stuff as present at a wedding," translated Greg.

"Tell them thank you for waiting two days but this handsome little donkey has never carried anything before." The light grey flanks were unmarked by harness rope. I imagined breaking in a new donkey to be a trainer's nightmare.

"Doesn't matter," said Laroi, "two or three days pass and everything OK."

"Really?" I said, disbelieving.

"Yes just ver' naice and all OK."

I thought about the price. Waiting around in Kalokol for another donkey would be expensive, and Laroi's constant wheedling for drinking money was wearing. We needed the donkey, but since they had been waiting so long the brothers were obviously keen to sell.

"Tell them it's too small, but I feel I have to buy since they have been waiting. 120/-."

Silence.

"What do they say, Greg?"

"They say they can't sell."

More silence.

"They say 198/- last price."

I sat on a log waiting. Donkeys were more expensive on this

side of the lake, I knew. Sporadic haggling dragged on for an hour and a half before we got to within five shillings of each other. Another half hour and we had whittled it down to three shillings and I called it a day.

"OK, 160/-. Done." We all shook hands and Laroi led off the new donkey to tie him up with the seniors beside the Chopper. His name was Kalokol.

While we ate a school mate of Gregory's came in. His home was in Loyangalani but he had a job with the Fishing Co-operative in Kalokol. A long and intense exchange took place during which Laroi groaned several times and frowned. Gregory turned to me.

"Steevon. Look this my friend from our home. You saw his brother there. Anyway this my friend Lowan got a house here. In the house is a woman but he just helping who is his sister from Loyangalani. Not completely sister but just the same. She want to go back from Kalokol now with us to greet her families."

"Hmm. It's a long way for a woman to walk," I said, "and maybe our food won't be enough. What about her husband and children?"

"Husband gone away to near Lokitaung. She got two children and he take them too. He was a policeman in Loyangalani but he is Turkana from this side and he just beat her too much at any time. So now he leave and she want to go."

"Well. OK. Why not? Let me talk to her first and I will tell you." I was prevaricating.

They jumped up. "She just outside. Come."

Squatting on the sidewalk against our sacks was a young woman. She had the same aggressive quality of expression that I had seen on the face of Lopuran, the woman who owned Komote, but she looked sad and hopeless withal. All she had was a milk gourd and a pair of worn leather sandals. Her body cloth was a simple green sheet that she tucked over as we approached. She was nervous but moved heavily, and then I saw why. She was very pregnant.

"My God, she's pregnant," I said and sat on the sacks.

"Yes," said Lowan. "She says about 30 days left."

"Karibu," muttered Laroi. "Karibu. Very near."

"Look, tell her I'm sorry but the road is far and very hard.

We aren't going to take the usual way but we just follow the lake. Tell her there are big rivers and many hills, even mountains. Also by the time we get back she will only be two weeks off. What if she has it on the way?"

"She says not bad," said Greg, "just she stop in a manyatta. But she don't think it will come on the travel."

"There won't be any manyattas a lot of the way," I said, "and no more towns or missions. Good God, she must be round the bend. She definitely can't come. She might die."

Much later that night we set off.

"What's her name, Greg?" I whispered.

"Erdund."

"OK, tell her to walk at the front not the back. We don't want to lose her in the dark."

I had decided not to spend another night in Kalokol but to leave directly, partly because I was exceedingly restless and wanted to be moving again, but mostly because Laroi was unlikely to retain his sobriety for long. I refused his last request for a bottle of pop despite his protestations that it would make him strong for the journey, and we set to loading our new chum. Kalokol was a small donkey and no great problem to load, once we had enlisted five or six helpers. He stood beneath his light burden shivering and uncertain. The other two looked resigned but were in good condition with glossy coats and rounded flanks. There was an ugly scene at the end for the donkey-minder turned up suddenly and demanded 200/- in addition to the sugar I had given to his wife. He was quite insistent and a crowd gathered. I was prepared to pay him something extra as I had thought the deal had been cheap, and offered him 20/- which he refused. His shouting attracted more people and I felt uneasy, for our kit was scattered about being sorted for loading and we were heavily outnumbered.

"Tell him to take the 20/- and fuck off, Greg," I said, forcefully.

Greg offered the note but the man dashed it to the ground. I snatched Greg's spear and stabbed the note through with the steel shaft.

"OK, you bastard," I said, in English, waving the spear under his nose, "I'm going to call the police. Take this and fuck off."

At that moment the waiters came spilling out of the Chopper, adding noise and muscle to our case. The man took the money and shuffled off.

"Let's get going, we don't want any more trouble," I said. "Farewell Kalokol."

We padded into the cool dome of night and the sounds of the town diminished until we were out of earshot. The land and the lake were one in the moonless dark but the shoreline was beaded with fire. Only the glow of the town lights behind us remained, shielded by low sand hills through which we had passed, but the coloured lights of the Angling Lodge were clear out on the black spit enclosing Ferguson's Gulf. Elizabeth and Helen had gone there for the new year and I was sorely tempted to swing round the southern end of the gulf and on up to a beer and a bath.

The moon was with us by midnight when we spent a painful hour floundering through acres of prickly straw. *Sporobolus spicatus* is a wicked little grass which produces a liberal supply of grimly tenacious burrs. Over on the other side the spicatus burrs had been green and easy to brush off but here in the driest part of the lake shore each one became a brittle demon burying tiny thorns like slivers of glass into one's fumbling hands. My plimsolls looked like small bales of hay leap-frogging themselves in the moonlight and poor Gregory, who was wearing a pair of long trousers, appeared to be striding along on a couple of bird's nests. Erdund exclaimed loudly and giggled.

"Roi-to-roi," she muttered, "rrroi-to-rroi." I never found out what that meant but the Turkana women used it continually. We reached the Kalorukongole river, at the south end of Ferguson's Gulf, with a fair sample of the countryside attached to us and stopped for a short sleep. Because of the increasing heat we had decided to try walking at night and apart from the obvious disadvantage of not being able to see, it was far more comfortable. Greg surpassed himself by producing a deliciously sweet and creamy brew up at four o'clock and we were moving again by four-thirty. It was the last day of the year and almost cold. Walking was sheer delight until about eight o'clock when the furnace doors opened. At dawn the sun caught clouds unfolding like pink flamingoes across half the sky. Palm trees were silhouetted up on the dune belt before the lake, which we followed round inland in deference to the shifting sand.

After a six-hour march we found ourselves on a low bluff. Below us the old lake bed stretched down to the shore which turned east forming a shallow bay called Eliye. A lagoon, cut off from the main water by the sand, had become a lake of twittering water birds, fringed with doum palms. The clear lake water dropped steeply away from the white beach like a bath of blue-green mint. Central Island glowed with fresh colour just off shore and across on the other side, smoking in the hazy clouds, Moite stood like a shrugged shoulder rippling the hills up the shoreline to Allia Bay. I stood up on the bluff watching the others pick their way down and took a deep breath. 'Great,' I thought and pelted past them straight into the lake. We made camp in the shade and ate. All three of us were fatter and Laroi had the shakes quite badly. A small group of Europeans had driven up in a Land-Rover, and he could hardly keep the binoculars on them.

There was another tourist lodge down the coast, exactly where I was not sure, and these people must have driven across the bush from there. They did not see us but later, when we left and walked beside the lake, a German came up with more holiday-makers to see the birds, a mixture of flaming pink and blue on the still water. The white sand and green grass were reflected under the flamingoes' legs and they rustled like pink triffids as a photographer crept up with his tripod. As we passed I shook the driver's hand.

"Hello," he said, as Erdund filled his windscreen. "Iss dat your wife? Ha! Ha! Ha!"

"No," I said. "We're just good friends. How far is it to the lodge?"

He reckoned that we had about ten miles to go and the quickest route was to follow the vehicle tracks. I thanked him and we went on as best we could for it was New Year's Eve and I wanted to celebrate with a beer at the lodge bar.

Komote, Lobrolei, Erdund and I drew ahead of the writhing cursing knot that eventually merged with the bush in the failing light. Greg and Laroi were having trouble with Kalokol. Leaving them to sort things out we pressed on and we arrived at Eliye Springs Lodge just before nine, led the last two miles by the throbbing diesel of the lodge generator. I unloaded the donkeys outside the gates, made a fire and brewed a little posho for Erdund and myself. Later in the lake I reflected on the wearying unpleasantness of walking on soft sand in the dark. Rummaging down into a sack I found a clean tee shirt and my long trousers, wrinkled as old apple skins but the best I could do, and then I walked over to the bar. The subdued atmosphere was disappointing as I had assumed that I was in for a riotous New Year's Eve. The guests were arranged in rows at two long tables, coolly turned out men and women in long dresses with glowing tans. They were mostly French and German. I ordered a beer and felt uncomfortable. A middle-aged man came up and offered me a cigar.

"Have one of these," he said, "you must be tired walking from London."

"London?" I said.

"Yes, you're the chap who has walked from London."

"No, it's not me. I've come from Loyangalani."

"Where's that?"

I explained my route as well as I could, but he was obviously disappointed.

"Well, have a beer anyway," he said kindly.

We chatted for an hour and I danced with his wife, then Greg and Laroi came in. They looked vexed. Kalokol had been giving considerable trouble. We had a beer together and I bought more for them to drink out by the fire. Just before midnight I went out to collect the empties and sat down for five minutes while they finished. I woke up at seven the following morning with the sun on my head. Greg chuckled.

"Steevan, happy year. You miss the old land sign." I had told him about the performance that we go through on New Year's Eve. "You just fall asleep so we leave you. Erdund said maybe you can dream old land in your head."

I sat up and thought about breakfast. As if to a telepathic summons a girl came over the dunes with a string of freshly caught tilapia. I bought the lot and soon our tree was festooned with split carcasses. Greg stirred the fire and dusted off a couple of the big ones with salt. They roasted quickly in the ashes and the mixture of tangy burnt crust and powdery white meat in the mouth was a fit first taste of the year.

A French couple came over from the trinket stall by the gate. She would have liked some of the fish we offered, but he, with sunburnt thighs and pale eye shades, patted his rubber belly and declined. I walked down the beach to where an English couple were camping. We had discovered last evening a mutual friend from university days and I thought that they might like some fish. The husband was visibly hung over but I offered the food anyway.

"Thanks, but no," he said. "I'd offer you some coffee but my wife is half naked." Since I was standing right beside her I could see that for myself.

'What an extraordinary excuse,' I thought as I wandered away, 'so is every woman for miles around.'

Greg had got a local woman to grind some snuff for him in exchange for the rancid fat we had left over from the goat before Christmas. She and her daughter came with the snuff in mid-afternoon and led us out on to the path through Eliye village. She pointed south.

"There is Turkwell river, far by the black trees," she said. Being only mortal I couldn't see over the horizon, but she meant that the river was not far below it.

The bush was sparse with very little greenery left apart from occasional mswaki trees. Acacias and palms relieved the monotony but everywhere the signs of heavy grazing were manifest. Tall women with silver bracelets and golden rings passed by with a sporadic traffic of goats and children. We saw few cattle or donkeys but several groups of camels were draped round the taller trees, browsing in their unhurried way.

Laroi walked ahead with the torch for the last hour as the path was indistinct, dividing and winding through the thickening bushes. The final quarter mile before the river was pitch dark and we stumbled along beneath a canopy of enormous acacias and writhing creepers. A shrill chorus of frogs' song urged us on, telling us that the river was near. Apart from the perennial Omo river, the Turkwell and the Kerio beyond it are the only rivers worthy of the name that flow into the lake, and then for only a few weeks each year. They rise in the high plateau over 100 miles south of the lake and commonly flood the wide plains as they flow north. This year with the rains so unusually prolonged and intense the flooding had been particularly bad, and although we had heard that the rivers had subsided recently, we were worried that we would have to make long detours round what waters might remain. It was with great relief therefore that we found the Turkwell almost dry when we finally burst out of the trees, scrambled down a low bank and stood on the open river bed. I could just make out a dark line of trees on the other side and a silver glint of water in between. We started gingerly over the sand until the water lapped our feet. Greg began to wade across. Suddenly he dropped to his knees.

"Quick," he shouted, "get this my hand!"

I was right behind him and grabbed the outstretched arm. Laroi hung on to me and together we heaved Greg from the sinking mud.

"Better we wait till morning," said Laroi, "we could lose a donkey."

We returned to the bank for the night. Things could have been a lot worse for us, as they were for starving Major Austin and his party when they reached the Turkwell in the May of 1901. The corporal in charge of his grazing guard was stabbed by a Turkana who had crept up to him in the grass, plunged his spear into him "in several places" and decamped with his rifle. "Our position," wrote Austin, "was fraught with the gravest anxiety; the men in an exhausted state from want of nourishing food exhibited traces of indifference and apathy regarding their ultimate fate: whether death came by the slow process of starvation or by the swift sure plunge of a hostile spear they seemed to care little."

Far away across the stars lightning flickered and thunder like the sound of distant battle came faintly on the air.

"This wet season funny," said Greg. "That rain is distant, maybe as far as Cherangani hills or Loriu. It miss us now but we still have to cross it in the rivers in front of us. Maybe tomorrow this Turkwell will be full," he added cheerfully. The Turkwell in spate must be quite a sight as the bed was over half a mile wide and could fill up inside a couple of hours.

Our sleep was plagued by sand flies and mosquitoes but at last a rich dawn silhouetted Mount Kulal above the black palms like a far distant cloud. We could hardly believe our eyes at this first reminder of Loyangalani and home, and the intervening 100 miles of lake shore seemed as nothing. The river water lay still, a stiff metallic ribbon on the sand, which we crossed with no difficulty despite Kalokol's friskiness.

Kulal soon vanished in the haze and the rising sun. Shambas of green millet grew on the southern bank of the river in cleared patches among the well-grazed acacia woodland. This ran into a belt of sand and grass and another area of millet and then there was nothing but a wind-blown plain of mud with desolation on the air. Dead bushes stood through the baked earth like coarse wigs powdered by the sand which blew snaking over the bone-dry sea-white wood. Over to our left the dunes were stuck with palms, some burnt and others dead, leaning at amazing angles, like the broken rampart of a long-abandoned stockade. The effect was that of a far-off *plage* seen in winter, deserted and cold, once overused but now an abandoned wreck.

Dust blew off the ground like spindrift and the wind roared in our ears, at least cooling our mosquito bites. A maze of drying trenches and muddy channels crossed our path and soon we were making tedious detours round stagnant pools of water and clumps of young palm trees. The going got worse as the water channels became longer and the palms more extensive and densely packed, but after several hours of shoving through the rattling leaves the trees became taller and more open. I assumed that we were crossing the Kerio river delta, and as Greg stewed our lunch-time beans I congratulated myself that our last obstacle was conquered. "Should be well away from this in a couple of hours and out in the desert," I wrote in my diary.

The beans always took a long time to cook and although she didn't eat them Erdund usually ended up looking after the fire. Being so pregnant I had assumed that Erdund would eat vast quantities of food at my expense, but I later became ashamed of my initial parsimonious feelings because she hardly ate a thing. She drank our sweet tea but only took solid food every day or so and then in microscopic quantities. How she managed on such a diet will forever remain a mystery. The donkeys were released into the trees to graze and doze away the heat. Greg stood up and peered through the grass.

"You see," he said pointing to the south-west, "the usual road to Loyangalani goes the west side of the Kerio river, two days with no donkeys, then just across over to Loriu following the path and only three more days to home. Loriu very dangerous place. This your tea."

"Thanks," I said and took a sip. "God! Why don't you just take the sugar neat?" The amount of sugar in the tea had been getting ridiculous. A crackdown was required so that I could at least drink the tea without needing a glass of water afterwards. "Why is Loriu so dangerous?"

"Because of Ngorokoi."

Laroi woke up. "Ngorokoi?" he echoed. "Ngorokoi wa Loriu, watu mbaya sana. Fisi tu." He reckoned the Ngorokoi of Loriu to be a bad lot, just hyenas.

Erdund put in her two-bits' worth. "Ngorokoi? Roi-to-roi!" she giggled, clucked her tongue and spat.

"What is it though, what does it mean?" I asked.

"Ngorokoi mean 'old team' in Turkana language. It is morans and some old men who just go up to Loriu and do raiding. Loriu is bad country because just not belong to any people. Samburu, Pokot and Turkana all meeting at this place, so no one know who should be there. Also many hills to hide in. Last year they kill a woman and three mens walking on our road, but usually they only taking things from small travellers such as we and not killing. Mostly they like sheets and tobacco and also they got guns. Last year 1976 the army general was just ready to take soldiers there to stop them but Mzee say 'no' we don't need war in Turkana so just police deal with them."

The missionary with whom I had spoken in South Horr had warned me off going through the Suguta valley to the lake because of raiders. According to him over 30 people had been shot or speared during the most recent bout between Turkana Ngorokoi and local Samburu. Erdund, triggered by the talk of raiding, launched into a long speech over the seething beans.

"She say her husband also Ngorokoi. He go away a lot and he is like many of them being ex-police or army. They all got guns too. She says these people too bad."

I lay on my back, anchored by a gut-busting dollop of rice and beans and watched the hover flies hunting over my head. Greg had gathered intelligence from a local boy with goats that we were close to the fish store of Nakwanga, sitting, overfed, in the delta of a minor stream called Orengaloup. The boy told us that the Kerio river delta which lay just ahead, was flooded and the channels were swollen with recent rains. I lay torpid and uncaring.

'Bugger it,' I thought drifting into a sweaty doze, 'what's the hurry?'

Despite my abandon we pushed on south with a certain resignation, for only a mile away the dry plains stretched easy and inviting way down the west bank of the Kerio. In the places where trees were sparse we could see the tin roofs of the store. Providence in the hairy shape of the Nakwanga duka man strode through the grass in an orange wrap and a floppy hat. In an entertaining mixture of Turkana, English and semaphore he explained that he was buying a cow, and that we should head for the inevitable black trees ahead.

"This Kerio river is too big before," he said, "but you luck and you pass."

We followed his directions precisely and swung far from the lake and onto the open plain, until we struck a footpath running south-eastwards across a shallow river. As we reached the far bank a tall man strode past us with his cloak and woman struggling behind him in the wind. Some way beyond the first river was another, narrower channel, waist deep and flowing strongly. We gave Erdund the shoes and a stick. She brought up the rear, filling the donkeys' ears with a screeching tirade and encouraging them with hefty thwacks as Greg and I struggled on the flanks to hold the loads above water and Laroi pulled like a Trojan on the head-ropes. The striding man reappeared singing lustily with his woman still behind him, but swerved suddenly into a bush. He fell over in abrupt silence and was helped to his feet with some difficulty, he being large and she small.

The next stream was only fifteen yards across, but brimful and moving. A section of the soft bank collapsed and fell like a demolition job, whisked away instantly as it hit the water. I waded in up to my navel.

"Unload!" I shouted back to the others.

"Wait!" yelled Greg. "This man say he know the road. Just we follow him."

The fallen strider had caught us up. I turned to watch him

stagger down the bank and enter the water. 'There's something odd about that guy,' I thought, as he splashed across. He got half-way, but lost his footing with a shriek and was swept with great good fortune onto a beach on the other side. He crawled away from the water and was sick. His woman crossed behind me and sat patiently waiting for him to recover which he soon did and off they went again, his arm over her shoulders weaving flamboyantly across the plain. 'I wonder what it is with him?' I mused.

"Hivyo my huncle see that man," said Greg, "say he is drunk."

"Well Laroi ought to know!" I replied.

Greg and Laroi reloaded and I returned for Erdund who was extremely heavy but a good floater. We followed the path which continued in roughly the right direction through sparse bush. Great towers of yellow dust rose on the wind from somewhere below the horizon rendering the whole country bleak and colourless in the evening light. Just before sunset we crossed an extensive clearing where a scattered fleet of browsing camels stood like moored boats on a lake. I made for the nearest of several groups of huts and greeted the women inside loudly. They sold me my first taste of camel's milk, thin with an almond tang, and they pointed to the east. I had told them in my few words of Turkana that I was going in that direction. The others caught me up and drank before I had to say any more. Greg translated.

"She says one big river here, maybe we not cross."

The Kerio was doing unmapped things and I had become confused. I did not really understand how many branches we had to cross, but I could see that the whole delta area was bigger and wetter than usual. We walked slowly towards the belt of palms through which the river ran, then saw it sliding past, wide, fast and deep.

"OK chaps, wait here, I'm going to find a way across," I said, dramatically removing my smelly plimsolls. "Hold these, Erdund," I ordered, and strode out, head high. I fell over twice and was up to my thighs in glutinous black mud before I reached the water. The chosen place had not looked too bad from the bank. I struggled out like a kinky wrestler and saw Laroi in conference with two women who had been shouting at us from a millet patch. 'Warning us off their bloody corn,' I supposed.

"Steebon, the women say this bad place to cross but the river become smaller to yesterday. It get big this three days because of rain we saw from Kalokol. Also one place up she say may be OK to cross if river fall more. But here not. Look dis tree." Laroi pointed downstream to where a fair-sized tree had been swept down by the flood, its branches sticking out of the channel. "You see a thing in the tree?" I could see a dark mass in the branches, and we walked closer.

"What's that smell?" I asked Laroi.

"The man," he said, unhelpfully.

"What man?"

"The man in the tree!"

A poor chap had tried to cross the stream and been caught by the flood a few days before. He had been left rotting by the receding waters. I thanked the women for their help and we set off upstream to the place they had described. It was becoming dark and we stopped shortly outside a manyatta called Nawoo. The family turned out to sit with us in the gloaming and took tea. A son agreed to guide us over the river the following morning and we bedded down. Greg was talkative.

"Do you know a Wazungu called Siger?" he asked.

"No," I said.

"Yes, he like you in the bush Siger or Sesiger like that."

"Never heard of him."

"This man speak Arabic completely and circumcise boys. Even my brother John."

"Not Wilfred Thesiger?" I asked incredulously.

"Yes. We call him Mzee Juu. He knows me. John my brother work for him on many safaris. He gave John that tent I sold to those boys in Sandy Bay. His vehicle is in Maralal with the Somalis and maybe he's coming to Loyangalani for another safari soon. His food is better than yours. He takes lemons." Greg smiled in recollection and said gently, " 'Limau, bring limau John.' He say this all the time, very good man." I went to sleep amazed that a traveller I so much admired had been that close without my knowing it.

We sat round the fire in the darkness shivering off the pre-dawn cold. A woman rose to kindle a long twist of grass from our embers. She walked back towards her hearth to the rhythmic swish of a shaken calabash churning butter in a hut. At each step a drop of burning grass fell from her torch, leaving a molten trail on the cold black dust. But the lingering night had dispersed with the arrival of Looio, our guide, and his friend Ekase. They conversed for half an hour in violent gesture, discussing the road ahead in minute detail like two tipsy generals describing a battle.

Greg's great-uncle, Epetet, lived in the district lying just across the river and according to Looio was even now preparing for his annual visit to Loyangalani. We all agreed that for him to show us the way would be a tremendous advantage and having crossed over the water at an easy ford, we made straight for the uncle's settlement. Unfortunately he had already gone, and so we faced the path across the desert ahead on our own. Laroi was on good form leading the donkeys over the last water, urging them on with happy whoops and cries of "Ho! Keerio River finis now. Comon Bois naice! Kerio finis!" He was undismayed at the rumour that three tourists had been murdered the previous month by Ngorokoi down at the south end of the lake. Looio the guide said that the populace had been issued with new rifles for self-protection, which I discounted as a bit of wishful thinking.

14

We walked beside the river awhile past plots of ripening millet then crossed a dry meander, stopping to knock down a bagful of doum fruits which Laroi and Erdund adored. The trees disappeared abruptly and Looio stopped us, pointing into the hazy distance with a grin. There was nothing but the odd bush and spiky tussock out on the shimmering desert.

"Nachurugwai," he said turning homewards, "better you don't stop."

Soon we were ploughing through the sand, sometimes climbing isolated dunes to fix the route ahead. Stinging clouds of grit and dust were blown by the wind off the lake, obscuring the mountains in a menacing yellow fog. A hundred silent camels stalked along beside us for a while but ghosted away to the lake shore as we pressed south. Skeletal reminders that the Nachurugwai had not always been dry stuck out of the sand and incredibly, right in the middle of the desert, grew a patch of millet. Each stalk was lapped by fine white heaps, but the heads and leaves rustled bravely green in the wind. Just beneath the sand lay a hard pan of clay which had been broken by the farmers and which, I presumed, retained moisture in the ground below.

After a broiling four-hour plod I climbed a prominent dune and gave the others a shout. I could see the turbulent surf on the lake shore and white horses dancing far across the water. The thin green strip of grass along the beach was parched and ragged compared to the lush grazing over on the eastern side but the donkeys tucked in gratefully and were relieved to reach the firmer ground where their hooves no longer sank in to the fetlock. Erdund had had a struggle in the soft going and cheered herself up with a wash. Across the waste she had fallen back in silence, and fearing we might become separated I had walked along beside her. She carried her milk gourd full of water which gained a creamy taste from the murky bowl, much better than our kerosene cans which still gave the water an unacceptably high octane rating.

Patches of bare rock and stones became more frequent as we proceeded south along the shore dusted by gossamer-light seedheads of the feathery grasses. We were heading for the water hole of Loelilia and rounding a low bluff we saw the dry wadi in which it lay running down to the lake between grassed folds of lava. Beyond the palms of Loelilia the first hillocks of the great Loriu massif rose brown out of the lake, squeezing the narrow coastal plain into a strip of beach round the embayments and to a mere tangle of wet rocks on the headlands. The whole plateau, which rises to over 5,000 feet, was once a ribbon lake of basalt, poured out from fissures in the earth's crust, flowing down and eventually filling an ancient valley. Frozen, and resisting the forces of erosion which ground down the surrounding land, Loriu has been left upstanding, much faulted and dissected, to become a refuge for the Ngorokoi and a barrier we had to cross.

A black-and-white flock of fat-tailed sheep tinkled down over the exposed rocks of what is known as the basement complex, already ancient when the lava drowned them. The sheep were nibbling their way to water across rocky ground far older than the rising hills behind them, unaware that I was contemplating not geology, but the dispatch and consumption of one of their number. We had all decided that it was time to rest and we stopped in the deep shade of a palm grove. Greg went off to buy a sheep while I swam in the turbulent blue waters, losing my soap in the swell. Drowned trees stood well out into the water and here and there wet grass appeared in the troughs between the waves.

After a bath I lay on my back, my head propped up against the kit. I looked out from our bower and across the windy lake which here was less than ten miles wide. The almost perfect cone of Porr stood clear and familiar on the far shore and beyond I could just make out El Molo Bay. I decided not to continue that day but to rest and gather strength for the last stage of our journey across the hills and down the rugged coastline to the southern end of the lake where, as Greg had warned, the heat was terrific and people walked only by night. We had slipped back into our day-time routine because although the night was cooler it disturbed our rhythms and made us very tired.

We got a good-sized sheep for 25/- and a cupful of tobacco. Small brown autochthones sprang to help Laroi butcher it and they pegged the skin out in the sun, abandoning their strings of fish for the greater feast of meat. They diced and barbecued the stomach and a length of entrail, some of which Erdund squeezed out and roasted for herself on our sizzling ashes. One small child was given a kidney by Laroi and held it dangling by some tissue for a cursory glance at the fire before wolfing it down in a gulp. I spiked crisp chunks of liver on flexible sticks which bent under the weight into the heat and crunched through them slowly as they were done. Erdund beat off the flaky husks of a few doum palm fruits with a log and a rock and boiled the result with water, milk and sugar, a quite delicious concoction with which to wash down the spitting, salted offal.

A pair of cormorants sat on a dead tree above the water. Every time I woke up that afternoon I expected to see them leaping about catching fish, but they just sat tight. Miles behind them over the lake was the place where Esenyon had joined us.

"Poor Esenyon," said Laroi, "dis brothers stupid boy not allow Esenyon continuing with us."

"Yeah," I said, remembering something that I wanted to know. "Maybe he was fed up with walking. Laroi, why do people on this side have their front teeth out?" Everyone I met seemed to have lost their lower incisors. Greg smiled, exposing the gap in his teeth.

"This is how we do, just our custom, when about seven years old. Not bad because the family have a small party and maybe you get a goat. One special man who know the work take out the teeth, then no one call you a donkey."

I slept with the rattle and roar of the wind and the smell of roasting mutton, and dreamt that I was an antique dealer in Hong Kong. Laroi woke me gently with a call to drink tea before first light. The sheep had roasted slowly in strips during the night and was almost dry. We hung it to air over the donkeys' backs and set off with Kulal brooding deep blue until the sun rose over the northern flank. Rocks with surfaces like cauliflowers and warts appeared regularly between bands of lava and hundreds of spherical geodes lay scattered on the surface. Some of the geodes could be broken revealing a hollow core, sometimes lined with delicate crystals of many colours. A plane swooped over us and waggled its wings, heading for the landing strip on South Island with tourists from Kalokol. One or two people stalked the plain with feathers in their hair and blankets on the wind and we passed several deserted manyattas, but by mid-morning we could see the gently sloping coast land disappearing.

We stopped to dig out water from a dry river bed, where all was bare rock and drying scrub, silent and still but for the wind on the shore and a dancing flock of whiskered terns above. They spun together like a swirl of driven snow, white bellies and grey backs flicking together precisely as they tumbled in the sun. I could almost hear them laughing as they swept up the river bed, flick-flacking white and grey out across the rocks oblivious of the senile cripple who sat chanting on the sand below. Seeing us she crawled over on tattered knee pads with sandals on her hands. Her white hair was bound round with a dirty head-band which gave her a desperate, freaky look, but she was only an old woman, fixing to die. She came from an isolated manyatta way up in the hills. We gave her a bit of tobacco and left her to her day.

We halted at mid-day where the hills ran steeply down direct into the lake and made our camp under an ancient acacia all running brown with sticky tar. It stood on a rise in a shattered river bed choked with boulders swept in tempestuous storms from the Emuruabwin hills behind us. Greg and I cooked rice, then lay back hot and tired. Laroi was sick and ate nothing and Erdund as usual just drank tea. The far shore looked very yellow and dried up and I doubted if the meadows we had crossed in pollinated shoes nearly two months before were still standing.

When the waves broke on the beach the sky appeared to become darker for an instant. I thought that the water may reach a critical depth and then have a polarizing effect on the light it reflected. Waves were rolling in quite strongly and the boulders underfoot were shiny with a soft brown growth but beyond the swiftly evaporated spray moisture was a hidden thing, held deep in shade and preserved from the hunting tongues of the sun. A long green snake slid its delicate body round the tree and shifted into top gear across the rocks at Laroi's shout. It moved as mysteriously as a wave into a jumble of stones and disappeared before exposing its head like a slender periscope to observe. A pair of glossy crows nuzzled each other in a dead tree and flew down to drink together on the shore where a flock of goats was bleating uselessly in the heat.

I took a last look at the dozing lion of rock that was Moite hill, over the water and far to the north, before we climbed a high divide and dropped steeply down to Kopoi, the open end of a deep embayment in the hills down which the Nakwoakten river ran in its season. A path led back up the valley from the shore at Kopoi, through the hills to the Kerio river and the main Loyangalani track, but I had decided to press on as close to the lake as possible. An old man from a manyatta on the hill above us reckoned that the local donkeys would get over the cliffs and I was confident that my well-travelled mokes could do so too. We made camp down on the stones by the water and took palm leaves for fuel. Erdund ate a can of baked beans and Laroi recovered his appetite later at the sight of headlights twinkling faintly from Loyangalani, about twenty miles away across the lake.

"You going to get married, Greg?" I asked after supper.

"Well, sometime, not just now. I buy some nets and go fishing before."

"When you do get married, who chooses the woman?"

"Maybe I just see a girl. I speak with her. But sometimes the parents cannot agree. You saw that girl in Loyangalani?" He had pointed out his latest heart-throb to me before we left. "My father don't like her."

"Why not?"

"All this area we are now is the family of Lokok. Very rich people in this district here and also here there is a famous laibon. But he is absent at this time. Well, they are rich but still people don't like to marry these girls because we say if you marry to Lokok girl the man immediately become poor or die very early. Also weddings expensive and we're poor." He stared into the fire. "You want to see a wedding? We have it every night. Look," Greg pointed to the Milky Way, "that is what we call the Camel's road. It have a river going on both sides. Follow." His finger traced out the Pleiades, a tight little diadem hanging over the black lake. "That we say is a wedding. First star is husband, then wife following, then the best man and woman, then a porter with a sheep, then a dog. All these people coming to home from a wedding."

A sheer headland forced us into the lake early on the following day. The noise of the wind and the waves among the rocks made the donkeys nervous and they exhibited considerable reluctance to cross the slippery and irregular jumble of submerged stones. For me it was like a day at the seaside, scrambling over headlands bleached white against the lake by salts evaporated out of the spindrift. There was no path to follow and I walked ahead to find the easiest routes through. Round the first obstacle I found some scattered bones among the rocks near the surf, a lower jaw first then odd ribs and bits of knee, and then with a whoop Laroi got the skull. The socket of the one tooth left, an upper incisor, was worn right back to the root. I concluded that the owner had been a fair-sized old man with bad but goofy teeth, and propped up the skull on a rock looking out over the water. Laroi and I scouted ahead and sat waiting for the others on an intervening divide. The lake sparkled Aegean blue in the sunlight, but became jade green down among the rocks where hungry cormorants and darters speared fish down oily necks. Headland succeeded weary headland like giant toothmarks in a sandwich. Behind the Kalomongin promontory the hills rose higher and became more steeply dissected. It all looked a little forbidding.

"Mbaya sana," said Laroi. "No fit to pass. How we get round that?"

"Christ knows," I replied.

Greg and Erdund caught us up, clattering up over the boulders with the donkeys and two strange men. The younger one was tall with a little beard and a green woolly blanket. His name was Lowoi. The other had a worried expression and a red sheet and was called Karim. They were cousins, belonging to the Ngupusho section of the Turkana tribe, and lived locally. Mooching along with little idea of the way except to follow the lake was all right when the land sloped with decent civility into the water, but a different matter over the Loriu Plateau. Mistakes were expensive in time and effort and we would have made a three-day blunder by attempting to pass round Kalomongin. The risen lake had all but obliterated any beach there was and although an unladen man could scramble round, the road for pregnant women and donkeys was blocked.

"We too lucky to received these men," said Greg. "Karim say he will guide us. He's going to Lokilio there just in the hills with his brother to their home and our road passes that way."

Turning our backs to the lake we wound up a narrow gorge, bone dry and brittle with cacti and strange euphorbias. Cobalt-blue flowers of the spiky plant *Blepharis persica* grew out of the river bed below silent crows roosting in the thorn trees. Occasional barks from hidden baboons echoed fittingly in the harsh landscape. After a climb of two hours the gradient eased and we came out onto a hilly plateau where burning white river sand wound back between scrubby acacias to another fortress wall of hills before the high plateau itself.

Karim called out the way to me as I was some little distance in advance. I found myself in a short, blind ravine with undercut banks of friable white rock on both sides. I chose a good stone to lean against and settled down for a quiet crap while the others caught up. The view was restricted somewhat by boulder-strewn flanks but good enough to absorb one for a while. I then realized that the silence about me was not due to my being ahead of the crowd so much as to the crowd not being behind me. I went down my little gully looking for tracks in the main river bed. There were thousands of them as Turkana donkeys find the hills congenial and wax plentiful among them. I milled around for twenty minutes or so, shouting lustily but despite my echoed yodelling which would have roused a canton, answer came there none. I scrambled around for five or ten minutes more and my heart went pit-a-pat.

'Spudsville,' I thought, 'you'd better get a grip because they've got the water. He said go up the gully, so go up it.' I did and there was only one possible place that the donkeys could have crossed out and down into the next water course. The trouble was that one could not tell which way the winding stream would eventually go when it broke off the old land surface and tumbled down its steep gorge.

"Have faith kid," I told myself. "It's only thirst. At least you'll know what Beau Geste would have been like." I carried on in serene panic, wondering if I could live off lizards. It struck me that I had not seen many and I began to look about with more attention and saw, with vast relief, a little heap of fresh dung. That was the second fortuitous offering of the journey. They were digging a hole in the sand when I caught them up.

"Estevan," said Erdund, "it's is you."

"There you are," said Greg. "We thought you were ahead so we pass round a bit different."

"Super," I said. "Next time you do that make like a Boy Scout and leave bits of paper along the way will you? Give me a drink." The water was fresh, a delight after the lake water we had been drinking since the Kerio river.

It turned out that Karim was related to the skull on the beach. 'Thank God I didn't take it,' I thought. The owner's name was Epurr and he had indeed been old and tall with goofy teeth. He had keeled over and died on a fishing expedition in 1973, or the year of the eclipse as Karim put it. Loyangalani had then been invaded by astronomers observing an eclipse of the sun which had lasted for seven minutes. All the stars had come out and, according to the local women, the fishing had been ruined. Greg knew the dead man's children back in Loyangalani. I asked him why they had not come to bury him.

"Long way just to dig a hole," he replied, "not bad for him to stay on the beach."

We stopped at the towering entrance to a side valley and a young girl came stepping daintily down the sand. She was Lowoi's daughter and presented him with milk. I could not believe that it was possible for his family to live in the hills all year, when now, at the end of an exceptionally good wet season, the grass was already dried up. The herds were taken down to the lake every few days to drink and according to Greg the family knew the hidden places in the hills where the water never dried completely. We passed on with Karim who draped his sheet on Kalokol and walked naked in the heat.

By evening we had descended again to the lake and camped,

refreshed, just north of the Mugurr river. The valley follows a great southward crack in the plateau, an ancient fault line from upper pliocene times which divides off the plateau proper from the younger highlands which block the rift valley at the southern end of the lake. Six men tramped towards us across the beach to joyful croaks of recognition from Laroi. He knew a couple of them from home. They all had spears and wrist knives, for, as they said, Loriu can be a dangerous place. The news from home was good, except that in Loyangalani everyone thought that we were dead. The police had received a report to that effect from Ileret. We could only think that the feckless Laurienne had started the rumour. One of the men stayed to eat with us but the others crunched off into the darkness. Laroi had recovered his appetite and as we ate he asked me about the lake.

"Why is it called Rudols?" he asked. I told him and asked what the name was in Turkana.

"Anam Narukwo, means long lake," he explained, "I tell you the story about it, but in Samburu. Greg help you to hear me." Laroi stopped every few minutes to allow Greg to translate.

"Long time ago there was no lake. The country was dry all around, hanimals in every place. A woman called Akai went to the river for water. Her name it means a house in Turkana language and she was pregnanted just as Erdund. The area was so dry no water any place except small water hole. She dig it for water but nothing. Then she dig more but even nothing. So she pray God and dig all the day, just digging and praying God to give her water. Then God say, 'Hokay Akai you my daughter, I give you water.' Then Akai dig a stone, maybe two kilos, and she take it from the well. Water start to come, little bit then more and more until she have to run from that place to climb a hill near the village. Everybody there run to the hill and the lake started to flow everywhere and spreaded. Then they went up the mountain with their hanimals. And Akai was having four children, two boys, two girls and her husband. They stayed in the hills for so long time and started to marry each other, sisters and brothers because there was no anybody on the island. Then they all died and just the goats remain. They still there." Greg pointed over to the volcanic turrets of

South Island. "That is why just goats and no people over there."

Laroi was on good form that evening and had us all in stitches. He was a first-class story teller and got all the sounds of the animals and the mime so right that I hardly needed a translation. He became rather involved in another Akai story about a woman whose earring turned green when her brother was killed on a raid and I missed the point of his final effort, a half-hour-long monologue about a giant who left his poor mother and went off raiding cattle. He eventually returned to find her living off donkey milk and his girlfriend taken by another man. Needless to say the rival was dispatched and mother returned to a civilized diet of cow's milk and blood.

The rocks in the dawn light had a strange luminosity and shone the colour of tawny rum. Steep cliffs again drove us into the hills, first up the Mugurr valley then over a pass into the next river bed which we climbed until the land flattened out at about 2,500 feet. Laroi had been vomiting over the last steep stretch and we stopped where we found sparse shade at the top. I dosed him up with tea and nivaquine. Greg thought that he had a relapse of the malaria he had caught in Lodwar at Christmas time. We rested for four hours with Laroi shrouded and shivering in his sheet. Erdund whined softly, rocking herself on the sand where Greg lay hunched in sleep. Karim was also asleep, flat out in the sun, his head cocked up on a wooden pillow and his arms outstretched. I passed the time beating off the ants and flies which searched out every bite and scratch on my badly itching body.

Fat rock hyraxes whistled as we penetrated the next rocky gorge. Pink rock rose blossomed from bottle-shaped *Adenium* trees which looked as if they had been poured molten on to the rocks. A sweet and heavy scent came from the small green flowers in a tree which Greg was showing me, *Boscia coriacea*.

"This one called Erdund," he said, "like this woman." He pointed out other trees, including several species of Commiphora, some used for making gourds and others for stools and pillows. "Many trees in the hills, but no many cows," he remarked.

Laroi staggered on in a trance. We were making for the

manyatta of a relative who, so he assured us, would be delighted, even honoured by a visit and would assuredly slaughter a goat for us. We had climbed another step upwards and now the valley opened out into a broad flat enclosed by low hills and bluffs. The whole country was dry as a bone but flocks of goats grazed up among the rocks and the sand was impressed by the pads of many camels. Four young eagles were tumbling through the air in play as we entered a shallow bowl of the river, and I thought that we must be close to the summit. We passed a couple of women who pointed to a large and shady acacia. Beneath it, taking his ease, was a substantial man in a red blanket, sitting fat and pretty, his biceps encircled by ivory bracelets, a neat black ostrich feather in his newly arranged hair and a cabur of a chewing stick hanging casually from his mouth. He looked prosperous, intelligent and glowingly healthy and if any man in Turkana could be called established, this was he. I could not imagine how he was related to Laroi. I asked Greg.

"Yes, just we greet them first, then I tell you. The man my huncle's relative called Ekale." I shook the great man's hand. Sitting around him were three other men. One, an imp-like old chap with a disarming smile and a lithe young son I took to immediately, but the other was a tall and scrawny old oaf with four ridiculously long white feathers nodding from his head in the breeze. He looked like a scraggy chicken. Ekale shifted his chewing stick as Laroi sank down in front of him, scant recognition for a sick kinsman and not the rapturous welcome one had been led to expect. I doubted that we would have a chicken slaughtered for us, let alone a goat.

"Who is this guy?" I asked Greg.

"Well the father of my huncle was kidnapped from Rendille long ago and brought up in the house of Ekale's father. My huncle father and Ekale's father together as brother in that house, so now Ekale and Laroi also relatives, but Ekale very rich man, too clever. Also he got four wives. You see the huts as we pass, that is two and other wives got huts up there." He pointed beyond the tree to a boma nestling against the bluff. I still did not understand how all these animals and people could live up here in the rocky desert of hills.

"Ask him where they get water, Greg."

"He say no need of much water because they don't grow any crop. Just taking milk morning and evening."

"Yes, but what about the animals?"

"They go to the lake. Camels each four or five days, donkeys maybe three days, cattles two or three days, sheep and goat every day. The people here they get water from the river."

"How far away?"

"Too close."

I was curious to see the water supply and so Ekale called a son to take me there. Before we set off his mother came flapping over from her hut.

"If you are going for water take these." She hung a couple of gourds on the boy's shoulder and I carried our jerry can. We scrambled up a few hundred feet to the rim of the bowl and looked down. I caught my breath. Facing us was a chaotic jumble of hills sliced deep by sunless clefts and directionless gorges, and behind them lay the lake. I felt like a bird, soaring above and beyond South Island and over the little dropping that was Porr, sweeping down off the plateau into the aquamarine ribbon below. Before we dropped off the rim and lost a horizon I saw the wall of the high plateau faulted and sheer as a rampart hiding high peaks in the far west.

There had been a certain bravado in my water expedition because Ekale had expressed surprise that I should fetch it for myself. I could understand why because we leapt downhill for the next two miles like klipspringers and, as I kept reminding myself, what goes down, goes back up. We had descended the boulder-choked section of a high canyon which tumbled in a series of near-vertical drops, jinking blindly left and right down to the Mugurr river. As the gradient slackened patches of dry sand appeared with old water holes dug in them. Eventually a little damp patch survived under the larger boulders and then, round a bend, a rocky tank of cool, clear water lay etched in the river bed. Below that was another cleft as big as a bath, then the water vanished. We filled our containers and I had a splash about to cool off. Carrying the water back was a strenuous job and took nearly three hours. I recalled Greg's words. "These people no need of much water, just taking milk in morning and evening."

Back at the tree a patient circle of women and children were waiting. I gave them whatever medicine seemed appropriate, laughed with the children and complimented Ekale on the beauty of his wives. He grunted and went off to watch the goats coming in of which there were two main streams pouring down the hill. He stood where the torrents merged, watching.

"This man, he does not count," said Greg.

"What's he doing then?" I asked.

"Just checking everyone is OK. He knows all the animals that he has, no need of counting. Even the far-away herds with his relatives and friends he know what he has. He got some of camels belonging to Laroi."

"Why?"

"I told you Loyangalani was raided it was in 1963. Laroi's relative take ten camels to prevent them getting stealed to this side and give to Ekale to look after and now they still here."

"Some must have died, it was fifteen years ago."

"Yes but the children of those camels still here. They increase to even more than the first ones."

It struck me that the repayment of livestock lent over a period of time could be a very complicated business and must involve some minutely detailed bargaining when an accurate and well-stocked memory would be at a premium. Natural hazard and increase affect the animals in obvious ways, but how to account for negligence or raiding or plain fraud? For various reasons a man's herds tend to become divided and farmed out to friends and relatives and his increasingly complex account must be kept without the infallibility of stock record books or the rapidity of the telephone. As well as recording, a man like Ekale is also managing, constantly assessing pasture and likely grazing, and calculating the needs of his sons for herd nuclei of their own and for women. The fortunes of the herds and the family are inextricably bound up, and not just in simple terms of blood and meat. For in the maintenance and continuity of the herds lies the continuity of pastoral society. The beasts are living statements of relations between the people and are the social currency of ritual and ceremony and the usual means by which obligation and status are expressed.

Night fell and we squatted round the football of ugali that

Greg had turned out of the pot. Laroi's fever had abated and he felt hungry. So did the scrawny chicken man who begged tobacco and food loudly. I disliked him on sight as he had a cadging manner and an unbearably self-important expression. He kept up a running wheedle as we ate. Through Greg I asked why a man of his age and apparent standing behaved like a beggar. Greg laughed.

"We know this man from Loyangalani. His name is Aletia Emese Aitaak, means the son of a sheep, because he is always disturbing people like this. He can eat too much at any time. You know the Somali duka where we bought the tyres? That Somali said, 'OK I just see what this man who is always crying to me can eat.' And he called Aitaak and he say, 'Aitaak, here is posho just eat.' And he gave him a big pot, not as ours but a very big one. It was full of ugali with mafuta and salt. Aitaak just eat it all. Then the Somali very angry and say this man never in my house at any time more again. But the people there at home like this man because he tell very funny stories." The comedian stood up and stalked away, his feathers had been ruffled.

A scorpion stung me in the backside just after midnight. I rose with a torch and my stick to avenge myself but it had disappeared. I had killed two or three small scorpions under logs on the beach the morning before and so there was a certain poetic justice in my position that night lying on my stomach with my backside cooling off in the air. Our sleep was further disturbed by a party of shepherds returning to their hill fastness from a journey of procurement to the Loyangalani area. They had been collecting debts, dues and obligations in the form of goats, hundreds of which shuffled through our sleeping place. The tired beasts seemed to lose control of their bowels as they passed by, considerably reducing the amenity value of our campsite. Two of the shepherds stopped for water, which they did not carry. They got a shock when they saw Greg and Laroi as they too had heard that we were all dead. One of them said that Greg's mother had even started looking for a suitable white goat with which to perform the funeral ceremony.

Much to my surprise our ascent continued for a further six hours the next morning. We followed up the Nardid river valley which wound gently back between low bluffs, then we crossed a rough divide into another dry tributary of the Mugurr. We were now well above 3,000 feet with only very occasional trees growing on the windy slopes. We entered a silent amphitheatre scooped from the hills. A lark rose flirting with the wind and dropped over the back stalls. We followed up to where the bird had gone and stopped, breathless.

"Jesus Kerrist!" I said, and felt like his father.

"Ver' naice," said Laroi, recovered from his fevers.

We sat up there for a long time, spellbound. The lake had become a little pond laid out like a blue jelly at a kid's party. In the middle sat South Island, a spiky lump of stiff cream, and Kulal was a mounting heap of icing running down the edge into the longer but lower ridge of Longipi. Dwarfing even Kulal stood the brooding massif of Ol Doinyo Nyiru, the crystalline summits lost in the clouds 9,000 feet above the adolescent geology around them. That was Samburu country where jungle grew beneath the clouds, hidden behind precipitous walls of winking granite and gneiss, where quartz and mica, feldspar and hornblend shone in the sun to deceive the hunters of precious stones. The rocks of Ol Doinyo Nyiru were old before the earth split and the great rift opened up, and they looked down like benevolent guardians on the volcanic tantrums below. Under the western wall of Ol Doinyo and hidden from us by a great volcanic barrier raised across the rift valley lay Suguta, said to be one of the hottest places on earth. The valley bottom is a burning desolation of alkaline flats and stinking mud, 400 feet below the level of the lake.

"No one goes there," said Gregg. "Only dead things in Suguta."

The barrier dividing Suguta from the lake rose to nearly 4,000 feet and formed the crosspiece of an H-shaped layout of hill and mountain with Loriu to the west and Ol Doinyo Nyiru to the east. The western side of the barrier was in dead ground but to our south and west the highest parts of the plateau appeared, windswept and bleak in the clear air. It was difficult to appreciate the distance over which one could see. The higher hills were all over 25 miles away and some features over 50 miles away. The lake seemed hardly more than a stone's throw down the hill but was in fact four miles east of our lookout. On a Himalayan scale this of course is nothing, but having walked only through low hills and across dreary plains for so many days it was stunning to see the juxtaposition of mountain, lake and volcano so close, and the clear view of where our path was to take us.

15

Karim's name for the hill on which we stood was Nakou Etom, meaning the Elephant's Head in Turkana. Picking our way off the summit Greg pointed out the volcanoes and the lava fields lying at the south end of the lake. Teleki's volcano was the most well-known feature but it could have been any one of the many pimples dotting the barren slopes.

"We'll have a look at a few of those when we get there," I said to Greg.

"Very hot," he replied. "Maybe too hot."

I could not imagine the heat increasing that drastically over a matter of a few miles but said nothing. Erdund and I found ourselves on the wrong side of a steep valley which developed alarmingly as we descended and we scrambled back to join the others who had found a cattle trail. Below us we could hear the cows' bells and the bleat of goats being taken down from the high grazing to drink. The cries and whistles of the young herdboys echoed round the valley. They carried only spears and blankets, and a gourd each for milk and water. Some wore tyres but most of them were barefoot or like Erdund had flimsy leather soles tied to their feet by thongs. I noticed that it was the smaller boys who were sent off to bring in the strays, a tiring job on the steep and thorny slopes.

"You see," said Greg, "these people are strong. No need of fires. Only wooden pillows and a blanket, drinking milk and blood. They don't take posho or tea, just water and sometimes medicine they get from plants. They stay with animals completely until their father call them back to his manyatta."

We were exceedingly joyful to reach the lake shore. Erdund gave a maniac cackle and walked straight into the water with her eyes gleaming, followed in short order by Greg and a much-recovered Laroi. The donkeys sucked in water like small fire engines from a hydrant, a troupe of thirsty peasants in dirty grey beside the local herd of chinless camels which stood cooling its knees in the surf, where suspended clouds of mica danced a slow roll under succeeding troughs, winkling and twinkling like sequins in the waves.

The passage over the last headland produced a spectacular display from the donkeys whose acrobatic talents were tested to the full. They twisted and leapt down the pathless rocks to the sound of ripping sacks and banging pots until their loads were in tatters. Strips of torn hessian trailed from the sacks, frayed by rock and thorn and despite our running repairs things kept falling out. At one point Kalokol got abruptly stuck. He misjudged a gap in the rocks and after a struggle became so firmly wedged in by his loads that his hoofs scrabbled furiously a few inches clear of the ground. We unloaded him and pushed him from below until he popped out like a dazed cork. Luckily he was undamaged, but the sharp rocks had cut the other donkeys' legs in several places, none seriously, and had reduced my plimsolls to rubber-soled string vests.

At last the headland was behind us and our day's march ended as darkness fell on the soughing beach. Nine days out from Kalokol we had reached the southern end of the lake and the following day we would turn towards the eastern shore. Karim and I had picked up odd bits of drift wood for the fire as we came down to the beach and we had a monumental brew of posho and baked beans with a relish of goat in curry powder. Even Erdund ate a little. Karim broke the silence with a contented belch.

"This place called Nangol," he informed us. "Many people sleep here because the road goes over Loriu from here and across the Kerio river, then easy up to Kalokol." Greg was translating slowly. "Even Ngorokoi sleep here. In 1975 they stole 30 camels from the other side of Suguta and the Samburu people run to the police in Loyangalani. Police came as near to here as they can by vehicle, then they just walking very fast in the night until they see the fires here where Ngorokoi eating one camel. Then the police go very quiet and wait an ambush in the rocks." Karim pointed to the rocky cliffs behind us. "Very early in the morning the police are ready but one Ngorokoi, his name Nafikiri, see a policeman move behind his rock and he shout very loud and they all just run. The police shoot one man in the ankle so they catched him and all the camels. Then they take that man away but no one catch that bad man Nafikiri, but now is OK because Nafikiri is dead."

"What happened?"

"The administration police caught him near to Kerio with his girl friend. The APs tell him just to stop but he refuse completely and try to get his gun. He was shot while he try to escape and they took his head to Lodwar. He was a bad man, beating all the people here."

Laroi's name had surprised me when we first met. Gregory had been given a Christian name at school but I could not imagine where his uncle had picked up his transatlantic horror. Perhaps it had been from a tourist. That evening I asked about it.

"Greg," I said, "why is Leroy called Leroy?"

"Just a Samburu name," he replied.

"That's funny, it's an American name too," I said.

"Ah!" said Greg, "you don't hear correctly. American is Leroy. Samburu is Laroi. Even I myself have my proper Turkana name. I am called Nawoi, meaning a place with many acacia trees. It was the name of my father's relative and he gave it to me."

"So—I'm as bad at saying your names as you are at mine!" I said with a grin. My voice was hoarse from shouting encouragement to the donkeys all day but I joined in the general laughter as Laroi told us a story about Karim.

"It was in the long famine," Greg explained, giggling on his back. "I think 1965. Karim and a friend were very hungry and they came to the village of an old man. Karim and his friend just think, Yes this old man very rich with all his animals still alive. He give us food. So they go to his manyatta and sit with him. In Turkana people it is the custom for a man who brings milk or blood to taste it first for the guests. The old man too clever. He bring a big calabash of milk and blood. Karim very hungry with his friend. The old man took the calabash and he tasted a big taste. 'Hmm,' he says, and he laugh, 'Ho! Ho! Ho! This calabash very sweet,' and he taste again and again and Karim just waiting for the calabash but the old man finish it. Then they left but they find him again in a place called Nalembo, north of Suguta. There was a shop of Somalis where this mzee was working. The man arrive and say they want to buy food from the shop but there was just a little posho for the workers only. Karim and his friend were very hungry because they have spend three days without food walking on the way. They wait until mzee given his evening ration, then they told him to find them some food but that old mzee pretended to be sick. He said, 'I'm sick,' and he brought the juice of Emuss cactus and he cook that plant and he get water and mix with the posho for medicine. And he say again, 'I'm sick,' and he eat that posho with the very strong plant and only he could eat because it was too strong. Yes that mzee too clever. He is the man you didn't like with feathers known as Aletia Emese Aitaak, the one who eat all the Somali's food."

We slept and in the morning Karim left us, his red cloak quickly vanishing among the rocks. He had tied his money and a present of tobacco in a twist of cloth for the journey home and set off happily back into the hills. The little hillock by our camp was called "The rock of young goats" and we soon left it behind us, but just after setting off that morning a man came running down the beach. He thought that we were dealing in goat skins and had some for sale but he returned empty handed the way Karim had gone. Three miles ahead a solitary clump of palms marked the extreme southern tip of the lake. The clear blue waters were teeming with fish, but we struck inland beyond the palms, slowly climbing above the lava and the shoreline of Von Höhnel Bay. What we saw on that second Sunday of 1978 was more or less what von Höhnel describes in his diary entry of Tuesday 6 March 1888.

"To our surprise," he wrote, "we saw a district covered with black streams of lava, and dotted with craters of perfectly preserved form, with one conical mountain from which clouds of smoke rose ceaselessly . . . we were, therefore, evidently amongst still active volcanoes." Having been on the march all the way from Zanzibar this must have been quite a day for them. "Although utterly exhausted after seven hours' march in the intense and parching heat, we felt our spirits rise once more as we stood upon the beach at last and saw the beautiful water clear as crystal stretching away before us." Von Höhnel records their disappointment at finding the water brackish but on the next page he and Teleki have a bath in it and "later we actually managed to quench our burning thirst with its water".

The discovery that the lake was brackish produced the following melodramatic drivel from von Höhnel's pen.

> This fresh defeat of all our expectations was like a relevation to us; and like some threatening spectre rose up before our minds the full significance of the utterly barren dreary nature of the lake district. Into what desert had we been betrayed! A few scattered tufts of fine stiff grass rising up in melancholy fashion near the shore, from the wide stretches of sand, were the only bits of green, the only signs of life of any kind. Here and there, some partly in the water, some on the beach, rose up isolated skeleton trees, stretching up their bare, sun-bleached branches to the pitiless sky. No living creature shared the gloomy solitude with us: and as far as our glass could reach there was nothing to be seen but desert—desert everywhere.

Good stuff. They lost three more men that day.

After an hour or so's confusion up a dry but thorny stream bed we were climbing over a small field of pumice, dumped like a truckload of stones on the ground. Across that we met the main footpath which skirted the worst and most recent lava. Scattered acacias grew on the higher slopes and I was lucky enough to find them green. All three of my companions were astonished at the amount of greenery about, for usually, so they said, absolutely nothing grew.

We stopped at mid-morning for it was exceedingly hot. I had planned to climb one or two of the volcanoes (they were only the size of slag heaps), but unfortunately Laroi had cut things a little fine when filling the jerry cans and we had barely enough water for tea. I should have checked it myself because he had miscalculated before. For some reason he did not like the donkeys being overburdened by excess water and tended to take too little. He did not mind them carrying plenty of everything else, though. It was one of his little foibles. We lay under a spindly tree, panting. I had a headache. Greg was humming the advertising jingle of a well-known brand of fizzy orange. He stood up, swaying in the heat.

"FANTA," he shouted at the blackened rocks, "tastes so good it's fun to be thirsty!"

He sat down to mild applause from myself and blank stares from the other two. I now regret not having stayed longer in the south, perhaps to explore the barrier region and the Suguta valley but besides not being rationed for a longer trip we had Erdund with us, and we were very close to home after a fair walk.

We passed between two heaps of soft volcanic ash and the path took us on over the flank of Likayiu then dropped to lake level again. I caught my breath. A black swathe had been cut over the rocks from a vent on the knoll ahead. The boiling rock had poured out and obliterated everything in its path to the lake. Below us were five or six square miles of pristine basalt with nothing, not even a blade of grass or a brave shoot, growing on it. Patches of older lava oxidized from black to rich red stood above the charcoal sea like rocky islets. Our path skirted the newest flow, heaped up like a frozen bank of snow some five to eight feet above us. Stretches of the path crossed the sharp rock which in places was just a vast pile of cinders and clinker. Lone trees stood half buried and roasted to death in the toffee-coloured rock which had solidified around them. Others had their lower branches frozen in but still grew merrily on. It was an instant landscape, of Hollywood or a holocaust, with no mellowing history on its burnt-up baby face. We did not see any eruptions or puffs of smoke but to judge from the complete lack of vegetation the last outflow could not have been very long ago. The vents and cones of the volcanoes themselves were covered with a black scoriaceous ash from which successive flows could be distinguished by their freshness of colour. The Turkanas called the area Lopean, the place of the devils.

The donkeys clattered on over the iron foundry floor and although she must have suffered a good deal from thirst and the weight she was carrying Erdund swayed stoically on. We met a woman going back up the hill with water, a tough leathery old squaw whose harsh world had left its mark in her squinting eyes and puckered face. Down on the shore two pink ash cones jutted out from the deeply embayed coast. We had already passed Warges, the eastern cone, and were rounding Naboiyotom, which sat circular and squat, a perfectly hollowed mound of ash spewed from the deep vent inside. Off the most recent lava odd clumps of grass reappeared; and a couple of small boys threw stones at their browsing goats from the rocky cliffs running down to the lake. Laroi said that it was rare to find people down in this area.

"They usually live up there," he said, pointing south-west over the barrier. It didn't look much less barren than where we were.

Three little girls and a strong-looking man were sitting at a rock pool just above the water into which I threw myself with great relief. The man stood up and shouted.

"He says be careful. A crocodile took a camel there this morning."

The water in the rock pool was less contaminated by the goats than that of the stony inlet and I sat back while the girls refilled our gourds. Erdund got some milk from them, but we pressed on for a couple more miles to reach Nakujabon, meaning sweet well in Turkana. After a little digging down into the deep river bed we found fresh water, but gathering enough firewood took a lot longer. Laroi disappeared with the machete and a determined look and returned with a few acacia roots, and I found odd bits and pieces on the beach. Looking back across the lake to where the evening sun was dying behind Loriu I felt that I could almost lick the sweet colour off the landscape. The mountains on the far side dropped steep and dark into the lake but the lava fields were fluorescent, glowing in copper and orange, and around me soft feathers of yellow-white grasses nearly concealed the black stones on the river banks. I breathed in the azure lake and the distant mountains and my eyes followed back the grey stone of the path along which we had come. It seemed incredible that our journey was so nearly over and scudding there along the beach with little bits of wood in my hands I felt a lump rising in my throat. 'You must be tired,' I thought, and I was, but beneath that was the sad knowledge that the friends I had made over the past months would soon be gone. I felt like a slowly filling jar, balanced over a well. A few drops more and the jar would tip forward to empty all the precious water that was our walk round the lake. What would come along to swing me under the drops of experience again? I had no idea. I returned to the fire and the stars were out.

"Estevan, chai." Erdund handed me my mug. She had begun to call me by my name a few days before, but we had not really felt at ease together until Laroi had made us all laugh with his stories. She only knew one word of English, a strong but mispronounced blasphemy she had picked up from Laroi. We had the last of our ugali number 1 that night, a superior grade of flour to the coarser ground posho. When cooked it came out like semolina. As he was stirring it Laroi spilt a small amount and burnt his fingers.

"Fookin'," he said, automatically.

"Fookin'," mimicked Erdund from the fireside. She flared her nostrils and laughed like a child. "Ndyio, fookin' numma one," she said and rolled the new words round her mouth like chocolates.

After our number 1 Greg asked me if I would like to hear a story, and Laroi launched into the saga of the fox and the lion, a sort of Aesop's fable which had Erdund and I wetting ourselves, not so much at the story but at Laroi's extraordinary performance of it.

"I should say that boya is Samburu word for fox," said Greg by way of introduction, "and my huncle tell the story in Samburu so I tell you in English. One day," he began, "the fox was very sad. He meet a lion on the way and the lion call him, 'fox!' and he answer 'Hivyo?' and the lion ask him, 'What are you finding?' And he answer the lion, 'I am finding you because all the animals are disturbing me and I come to find my huncle because I know he will not disturb me.' And the lion told him, 'OK, come with me.'" Laroi had already eased himself out of the story from his place beyond the fire. The voices from the velvet darkness had four legs not two and together the straight man and the comic were hunting in the bush. There was a crash on the stones and the lion had killed an enormous bull near a huge and mysterious rock.

"Lion and boya eat meat, lion first then boya until they become enough and then lion send boya to find some water. Boya went there to the river and he drink clean water, but then he dirtify the rest of the water. He shits inside and he put urine and he bring some to the lion. And the lion ask him, 'Why is this water dirty?' and the fox answer him, 'The water is dirtified because my big huncle (the elephant) come to the river.' And the lion become angry and he tell boya, 'Look after the camp, I go to find clean water.' But he find that the water is really clean at the river and he get very angry to the fox. Before lion come back fox told the big stone near their camp, 'Stone of my God, will you open yourself like a door?' And the stone opened itself like a door and the fox collected all the meat inside that rock. After he cleared everything he get inside and say again to the stone, 'Stone of my God, close yourself as before.' "

The stone creaked shut in approved Ali Baba style and the lion returned.

"And then the lion arrive and said, 'Fox!' and the fox didn't answer him. He just remain quiet. And the second time the lion call him again and boya just say 'Yap!' in a proud voice. And then the lion ask him, 'Where are you?' and he answered, 'I am behind the stone.' And the lion went round the stone but he miss him and he ask, 'Where are you again?' and the fox answered, 'I'm inside the stone.' The lion asked him, 'How do you get inside the stone?' And he told the lion, 'I hit the stone with my head and get inside.' And he instruction that lion again, 'Go reverse and hit the stone with your head and you will get inside.' The lion hit the stone the first time and the fox say, 'Yes! Try hard again it is nearly broken.' And the lion tried to hit the stone more and more and the fox say, 'Yes! Yes! Nearly broken,' and he hitting more again until he just fell down and died dead."

Laroi was smacking his head against a sack in frustration, imitating the stupid lion.

"And after he died the fox sent a fly to check him if he is dead. The fly went and he saw the lion's ear being blown by the wind and he came back and he told the fox, 'He is not completely dead.' The fox stay for a long time and then send two ants, the kind that like meat and fat. They get inside the lion's eyes and bring a piece of meat to the fox. From there he recognize the lion was dead and he said, 'Stone of my God open yourself as before.' The stone open and fox see the lion's ear blowing by the wind. Boya frighted and he said in a high voice, 'Stone of my God! Will you close yourself, please.' And the stone close itself again. He stayed there for a long time again and he said to the stone, 'Stone of my God, will you open yourself again,' and he found that the lion was really dead. Then he come out and he stay out.

"And all the animals come to worry fox for the meat. And the fox chase them away and said, 'Do not distrub this my huncle because he is sleeping.' When after he chase the other animals away the hyena came and he told the hyena, 'I will give you some bones, but you must eat them slowly because my huncle is asleep and if he wake up he will kill you.' Then he told the hyena, 'If anything catches your tail don't move, just keep quiet and eat your bones very slowly.' Then fox brought a very strong rope. He tied the tail of the hyena and the lion together. After he finish tighting he told the hyena, 'Quick! Run away! My huncle is wake up!' He beat the hyena and tell him, 'Run away!' And the hyena jump and run away, pulling the lion behind him. The hyena run and run falling on the rocks and passing inside the trees until he reach to his house. He get inside his house and turn his head to the door. He stayed there for four days thinking the lion is alive and he said, 'Ho! you are thinking you are too clever. You are pretending. You are just sleeping there I know. You are still alive.' He stay there for so long time again and then he tried to make another hole, somewhere again to pass. He finish the hole and he pass through because the tail of the lion is rotten. Then he run away to the bush. He hunts for a whole day and he kill one goat. And then he stayed hunting for seven days and every day he eats a goat until he becomes strong.

"He went back to catch the fox and he brought a very strong rope again. He tied the fox under a tree and then he went to the bush to cut some sticks to whip him. And a striped hyena found fox tied under that tree and he said, 'What's wrong with you?' He answered to that hyena, 'My huncle is forcing me to drink cups of mafuta but I'm hunable to drink.' And then the hyena said, 'Cups of mafuta? How kind is he? Why don't you tie me and then I replace you?' And the fox told him, 'OK. Untie me then and I will tie you.' The striped hyena untied the fox and the fox tied the hyena again. And then the big hyena arrived with whips and the striped hyena called to that big one with a sweet name known as Chaiai, means 'My Sugar,' but the other just angry and ask him, 'What has happened? Why are you here now?' And the small hyena told him, 'I am here because the fox told me that you force him to drink cups of mafuta and I told him, let me help you to drink instead.' And then big hyena say, 'Because you have did bad I will teach you a lesson and I will give you the cups of mafuta he told you. Ho! Ho!' And he start to whip the small hyena. He whip him until he died. And that is why we say boya the fox is a very clever animal, fit to pass all the animals in the bush."

We left our camp of stories well after the sun had risen, heading north on the final stretch with about 25 miles to go. It was a lovely morning with a good strong wind blowing across our path and over the choppy blue water. The donkeys seemed to know the way and put their heads down determinedly for home. The path was clear enough but once off it the small boulders and rocks were painful on our ankles, swollen with continual twisting and bashing from the passage over the mountains and across the lava. The open foreland of Longipi had a windswept, barren grandeur which reduced our little caravan to insignificance. Scattered here and there were groups of tumuli, piled up like giant molehills about six to ten feet high and perhaps fifteen or twenty feet across. These piles of rock were the graves of Samburu warriors slain in battle with Turkana long ago. According to Laroi only the best fighters had been buried in this monumental style and if that was the case we had passed the tombs of over 60 heroes that morning. Arthur Neumann had first reached the lake at this spot in 1894. His account is subdued beside von Höhnel's exaggerated babbling. "At last," wrote Neumann, "early on the morning of 6 December, we came down the last step and reached the shore and I had the satisfaction of drinking and bathing in the bitter water of Lake Rudolph. It is a desolate and forbidding land but with a wild grandeur of its own which had a great charm for me." Still in the area two days later he came upon a mystery.

"Alongside a rocky gully, right on the lakeside, a patch of black lava débris was covered thickly with bleached bones. From a distance it looked like snow . . . but on getting close I found it to consist of the whitened bones of camels. Hundreds must have perished here, all huddled in a little corner. What could be the history of the catastrophe?" The answer had been published by Von Höhnel that year. In his diary for Friday 9 March 1888 he wrote, "Today also the path was strewn with the skeletons of camels, goats and sheep ... there must have been the remains of some two hundred animals in one pile and though the bones were already bleaching in the sun there was still an odour of putrid flesh about them." Later they questioned Turkana who had taken part in the raid which led to this slaughter. " 'It was night,' they said, 'and the Rendille whom they had robbed were following them, and as they could not get away with their booty, they had killed the animals with their spears.' " Savage dogs in stony mangers.

Beyond the Laisamis river the rocks were heaped up into a steep escarpment below which the rocky path ran in the echoing shade. It cut through in a high steep-sided valley at the far end of which was a Turkana shrine and we all added a stone or a piece of grass. The Laisamis area was all a treacly red-brown colour, like a melting scrapheap with the oxidized and disintegrating flotsam of bygone geologic wars piled massively against us in the blistering wind.

I took my mind off my swollen ankles to think about the division of the kit. Everything was threadbare and worn. My plimsolls stank and were only waiting for a decent burial and my new rucksack was well broken in, its blue canvas faded and stained with donkey sweat. The green piece of tent cloth I had bought as a groundsheet was bleached almost white and dotted with bloodstains from the donkeys' sores, for we had used it to pad the loads. The donkeys themselves were tired and travel weary and no longer frolicked off the march. Our spun sisal ropes had long since disintegrated but the woven ones were still good. The limp food bags were filthy and the shining new pots we had started with were now like dented black hub caps. My own enamel mug was chipped and ingrained with unhealthy grime and the handle of our faithful spoon had broken off.

Laroi not only slept in his sheet but wore it all day long because his shorts were one enormous patch and he had literally lost his shirt in Kalokol. I was little better dressed, my underpants just tattered wrecks hanging loosely round my skinny waist. The dried milk tins had been bashed flat by the rocks

and the maps were torn and falling to bits in my hands. I was
surprised that the plastic jerry cans were still waterproof
because we had sworn over lost screw tops on many occasions
in various sandy camps, but we had always managed to find
them after a frenzied scrabble.

The bare ribs of long-abandoned huts stuck up between the
boulders of a bone-dry rocky forest surrounded by a bleached
filigree of leafless thorn on brittle twigs. The old manyatta
was an appropriate last luncheon spot for my travel-stained
crew.

"Ah! We are nearly home," Laroi gasped, flopping down in
the thin shade. "No more women work."

"What women work?" I asked.

"Women work? We Turkana men we never get firewood or
bringing water and we don't building houses. Except in bush
no milking cattles and goats and never cooking food. Ver'
naice."

Greg was looking forward to a bit of men's work, too. "You
see that Ekale in the hills last week? He has children even so he
just rests. He gets up and checks every animals and directs
where they will graze for about half an hour then he will be back.
From that time if there are no guests at home he drinks his
milk in the shade. So he rests and when it get to about four
o'clock he checks his animals again and just talking with his
sons. Then he drink milk and tell the women where he sleep
and he just go to that manyatta of his woman for the night
sleep."

We laid out the kit and I told them who was to have what.
Greg got the fishing rod which he still faithfully carried and I
gave Laroi the jerry cans and other smaller things. We gave
Erdund the pots. Using up the last of the Daz we had a grand
washing session in the lake, which was bubbling with tilapia.
They came right in close to the shore attracted by the soap and,
unable to resist the flashing bellies any longer, Greg ran back
to get his spear. He looked heroic standing stock still in the
water with the blade poised, but he got nothing.

Rather than become involved with handing out money and
goods in Loyangalani I had decided to pay off in the quiet of
the bush. I gave Greg and Laroi double the agreed daily wage
with a bonus each of 50 days' pay, as well as their expenses at

Christmas and in the settlements through which we had passed. Greg was well set up to buy nets and hooks to start a fishing venture and I was glad that the journey had been useful to him in that respect, but I knew that Laroi's money would soon be sliding down his throat. Greg and I both agreed that there was little to be done, but we held back a third of his money for his wife.

We left at four o'clock and walked north over the stones until the southern tip of South Island lay directly west, then we stopped to sleep, only twelve miles short of Loyangalani. Several of the herdsmen and travellers we had met that day had told us that we were dead. After about the fourth person had passed us the news, Greg who had been walking in trance-like silence looked up. "Oh!" he said, "I've heard I'm dead so often that I thought I was an angel as I was walking along!"

His mother, we were reliably informed, had actually got a white goat for Akulur, the funeral ceremony. "Maybe we will arrive for the feast." Greg sighed. Our meat was finished. "We Turkana just call all the relatives and slaughter eight goats outside the village. Leave any food remaining at that place, then we put on fat and charcoal and shave our heads. The wives leave off beads for three months except just one white one."

A mess of flattened food cans lay near our campsite, abandoned by tourists too thoughtless to leave them undamaged for the local Turkanas to use. Good tin cans are not rubbish in Africa. We had reached the limit of the Land-Rover trail winding along the lake from Loyangalani, before it turned away over Longipi towards the Serema flood plain, from which I had first glimpsed the lake through grey drizzle and a mouthful of fruit cake.

"Hey," I said, "what if a vehicle comes along and offers us a lift. D'you want to go up to tell your ma everything is OK, and Laroi maybe you want to tell your wife?"

"Huh, no!" said Laroi. Greg was appalled. "Oh! We want to completely round by footing." "Yes, dis ver' naice. Ugali numma 1 kabisa!" Laroi added, emphatically.

Our milk, sugar and tea were finished, but we had a little coffee which Greg stewed up at two-thirty. By three we were on the road again, in the moonless night, stumbling over the stones to find the track. My own body was reluctant to move at this hour but as Laroi explained, "Better to arrive somewhere with a day, for what use to get home only to sleep?" He walked just ahead with the torch and finding the road gave a little whoop. Erdund and I walked together behind the donkeys like zombies until the first thread of light banished the Southern Cross and the Great Bear from the sky. Kulal gradually appeared as the sky turned white behind Longipi and the mysteriously horned and slumbering beast in the lake became South Island again, close in on our left.

Before the light was certain we passed the sleeping crews of two Land-Rovers from Marsabit, bound for Loyangalani to do a bit of canvassing for the local elections. They overtook us as we left the road to take a short cut along the footpath to the town. As usual the road seemed to go on for ever in the corrugated-iron rattling wind but then far away down on the shore we could see the fishing store and the jetty, and the pylons of the police radio mast were now visible beyond the palms ahead. At last we climbed a low rise which the donkeys crossed happily but which stopped us dead. Erdund waddled on down with the animals but Laroi, Greg and I just leant back on our sticks and smiled at each other. There it was.

"Loyangalani!" we said. Greg looked at me and laughed.

"Here, Steebon," he said, "take this your watch again. Maybe I forget to give you later."

Picking the way down over the fish bones and the rocks towards Greg's family huts I could think of nothing but an intense desire to eat chappatis until I burst. There were no hysterics or crying when Greg met his mother and brothers, just broad smiles and reserved hallos. I felt pretty restrained myself—a man whose winding road had abruptly ended. I would soon have to cast around for a new direction.

Unloading went according to plan and within ten minutes the kit had vanished, the donkeys had been led away, and all I had left was my rucksack, and the Rendille walking stick Laroi had given to me at the start. It was the only souvenir I took home.

Martin and his Luo fishermen had left town in their lorry the day before to go to Kalokol where the fishing was better. The Amani Hotel was padlocked and deserted, a timely reminder that the world does not stand still. Laroi, Erdund and I walked down Main Street towards another lodging, leaving Greg to his family. A tall man in a blue boiler suit stepped out from the shade of a palm tree ahead. He waved madly and ran full pelt towards us, stopping just short of Erdund. She fell into his arms, sobbing hysterically as he led her away to her mother's manyatta. She was with her brother at last and her journey was over.

16

MUCH LATER THAT night Greg and I had a goodbye drink at the bar of the lodge. Komote and Lobrolei had been taken back by Ekai Lour's daughter and little Kalokol was grazing outside Laroi's hut. He and Greg were going to swop him for goats. We left Laroi outside Mrs Paulina's hotel with a mixed audience of Samburu, Turkana, Luo and Kikuyu all clapping his rubber-kneed recitation of the Kenya police drill book, punctuated with slurred invective against Shangalla, Ethiopians, mosquitoes and lions. He was too far gone to say goodbye.

Greg had fixed me up with a lift to Maralal in a fish lorry leaving early the next morning. Strolling up to the lodge we had heard the booming reverberation of a twisted kudu horn blown by a Rendille shepherd against the evening sky to announce the new moon. He had seen it rise above Kulal, a slender crack of silver which vanished as we crossed the flood-lit gates of the lodge. I had finished writing Greg's testimonial when Erdund's brother came up to our table. He spilt himself into a chair with a happy sigh and a smile, quite overcome with gratitude.

"This thing too good, Mr Steebon," he said. His name was William. "Sometimes I don't eat, just taking chai and lying for three days, and people ask, 'What the matter?' and I say no matter. But when she my sister here I return to OK, no argue at any time, because you know, if one is fighting the other cries, so you make me too happy. Here this for you I buy all the beers." William and Greg had been to primary school together in North Horr and Greg had told me how close William was to his sister. He was a gifted mechanic and much in demand in Loyangalani where garages were tied to the church. "When I make a garage everything just free for you at any time you come to Loyangalani—so you not worry about vehicle you bring, just getting spare part and mending free. Tank you."

He and Greg lost themselves in a tangle of Turkana law

and custom. They were discussing the retribution due to the family for the behaviour of Erdund's husband and for the loss of the two children. I was following the conversation with interest but my concentration was spoilt by a group of French tourists who had entered the bar after their dinner. They had heard about the trip from one of the waiters. A woman of about 40 sidled over and stood listening as William unfolded his plans for returning over the lake with the 60 goats he reckoned Erdund's husband should pay him. She eventually butted in and asked me which part of the lake was "le plus joli".

"The north, madame," I said, picking up William's plan again.

"I'll get a permit for steering a boat because I know the engines," he continued, "and go from here to Kalokol then straight on to the administration police in Lokitaung."

"Ah! Le Lokitaung?" said the French woman, knowingly.

"They will help me, just call that man forward to the chief, then he have to pay."

"How much?" I asked.

"He says he wants 60 goats," said Greg, "but I think the man should pay William 30 goats and return him the children."

The French woman's husband approached. He was about five feet four inches tall with thighs of wobbling lard and a stomach to match. He wore the legend "Mon Cat Diesel" in fluorescent orange on his black baseball cap and, of course, he had a camera.

"Did you 'ave any of problem?" he asked. Greg had taken a deep pinch of snuff and sneezed all over the man's legs. I mumbled something noncommittal as I was trying to listen to Greg's continued analysis.

"Just Erdund's husband come here to Loyangalani, slaughter a cow and marry her properly," he suggested. "That's not bad, then he can do what he wants. But now he is not correctly married he should pay according to our custom."

"Un mariage? Où est votre femme?" The man was on to something spicy but was ignored.

"Yes, but how do you get him to pay if he is in Lokitaung?" I asked.

"Ah! Le Lokitaung."

"No trouble," said William ignoring the interruption, "I just go there with APs and call him. They will see he is a bad man beating my sister. Now he pay for that."

"Serpents?" the woman asked insistently. "Serpents? Vous avez vu beaucoup des serpents?"

"No, madame. We saw very few snakes," I replied, coldly. I turned to Greg. "Maybe if he comes here she won't want to marry him properly," I said.

"Incroyable," the Frenchman butted in, "c'était très dangereux?" His question remained unanswered, and the couple turned unsatisfied to the bar.

"Yes, but Erdund won't get another husband now, even for many animals," said Greg. William agreed. "If he come to slaughter a cow and pays properly for her and the children then OK he can take her again. We just remain to see what happens. Anyway Steebon, you know I am good mechanic. When anything break, the people in Loyangalani call me straightway. Even tourists they call me. So when I make my garage and I'll charge the percentage because they got nowhere else, but you come and get it free. Tank you. I just too happy with my sister. Tank you too much."

"Well, goodbye," I said. I felt thoroughly awkward. "It was a good trip, Greg."

"Yes," he said. "I see you later at the lorry just I speak with William."

"Where you go to next?" the Mon Cat man asked as I walked past the bar, and at last he got an answer.

"Au lit," I replied and went off to sleep in the lorry. It left at dawn.

GLOSSARY

s – Swahili   t – Turkana   a – Amharic   ar – Arabic   e – English

At the time of the trip 20/- Kenyan was worth £1.25 sterling. All sums referred to are in Kenyan shillings.

acaci	A family of trees and shrubs of the genus *Leguminosae*. Over 700 species recorded throughout the world, half of which occur in Australia. Widespread throughout Africa and the Americas.
akili (s)	Intelligence, cleverness.
akulur (t)	A Turkana funeral ceremony.
Amharic	The official language of Ethiopia.
Anam Narukwo (t)	The Turkana name for Lake Rudolph, meaning long or great water.
assault rifle	Czech-made 7.62 mm model 58 assault rifle. Wooden stock. 30 round staggered column detachable box magazine. Cyclic rate 700–800 rpm. Muzzle velocity 2,300 fps.
boma (s)	Fence, usually of thorn bushes.
Boran	Pastoral tribe of the eastern Northern Frontier District and southern Ethiopia.
chai	Tea, usually with milk and sugar.
chakula (s)	Food.
dawa (s)	Medicine, a powder, a chemical.
dik dik	Tiny antelopes of the genus *Madoquinae*.
doum palm	*Hyphaene thebaica,,* sweet fruits.
duka (s)	A shop.
duma (s)	Leopard.
fisi (s)	Spotted hyena *Crocuta crocuta*.
hakuna (s)	Verb form often used as a simple negative, no, not so, it is not.

hapana (s)	Verb form there is not there, there is none.
hoteli (s)	Anything from the Hilton to the Amani, usually an establishment at least serving tea.
injira (a)	A wide pancake of barley flour. Ethiopian staple.
jambo (s)	Universal greeting.
kabisa (s)	Completely, utterly, absolutely.
kama (s)	Like (of comparison).
karibu (s)	Near, close.
kidogo (s)	Small, little.
Kikuyu	The most powerful tribe in Kenya, basically agriculturalists by tradition.
kuja (s)	Form of verb ja, to come.
kumi (s)	Ten.
kuni (s)	Firewood.
Laibon	A spiritual leader in certain pastoral tribes of East Africa with powers that vary and depend largely on his personality.
(ku)lala	To sleep.
lugga	Dry river or stream bed (see wadi).
mafuta (s)	Oil, fat, grease.
maji (s)	Water, liquid, fluid.
mamba (s)	Crocodile.
mandazi (s)	A kind of small cake.
manyatta	A hut or group of huts, usually temporary, surrounded by a boma.
mashing (e)	Brewing.
maziwa (s)	Milk.
mbaya (s)	Bad.
mbuzi (s)	Goat.
Merille	See Shangalla.
mingi (s)	Form of adjective meaning many.
mirar	Succulent chewed as a mild stimulant especially by Somalis and related people, Rendille, Borana, Merille, etc. Looks like thin asparagus.
mkora (s)	Worthless person.

moja (s)	One.
moran	Man between boyhood and full seniority, usually a warrior.
mzee (s)	An old man or elder, a term of respect.
Mzee	The President of Kenya.
Mungu (s)	God.
mvua (s)	Rain.
na (s)	And.
Na (t)	A greeting meaning, roughly, peace.
ndiyo (s)	Indeed, yes.
N.F.D.	Northern Frontier District of Kenya.
Ngorokoi (t)	Baddies in Loriu.
nyuki (s)	Bees.
Pokot	A tribe allied to Turkana but generally ill disposed towards them.
pombe (s)	Alcoholic drink made from palm sap and sugar.
posho (s)	Flour derived from maize.
punda (s)	Donkey.
Rendille	A pastoral tribe of north-eastern Kenya.
safari (s)	A journey.
salam (ar)	A greeting meaning peace.
Samburu	A pastoral people closely related to the Masai.
sasa (s)	Now.
shamba (s)	A garden, a cultivated plot, a farm.
Shangalla (a)	Ethiopian term for negroid peoples of the southern borderlands. Tribes of the Omo delta area otherwise called Reshiat or Merille.
shifta	Bandits, mostly of Somali origin.
shitoose (e)	W.C.
simba (s)	Lion.
sojas (s)	Soldiers.
Swahili	Strictly speaking Waswahili, a coastal tribe and Kiswahili, their language, now the lingua franca of much of East Africa.
tatu (s)	Three.
tayari (s)	Ready.

Tigre	Part of Ethiopia, also applies to bandits from that area.
tilapia	A fish, *Tilapia melanopleura* and other species.
topi	Large antelope *Damaliscus korrigum*, allied to Hartebeestes and Wildebeestes.
toto (s)	Child.
tu (s)	Only, just.
ugali (s)	Stiff porridge made of maize, millet or cassava flour.
wa (s)	Several meanings, in this sense meaning "of".
wadi (ar)	Water course, ravine, bed of a torrent.
wadj (a)	A stew of peas and lentils.
wana (s)	Verb form they have.
wapi (s)	Where? or sometimes how?
watu (s)	People.
Wazungu (s)	Europeans.